SEEKERS AND THE SOUGHT

Alaknanda Bagchi

Dedicated to my Gurudeva

Sri Sri Mohanananda Brahmachari

Table of Contents

List of Photos

Acknowledgments

I wish to acknowledge my deepest gratitude to my Gurudeva, Sri Sri Mohanananda Brahmachari, for his immense compassion and kindness in being willing to initiate me and make me his disciple. Without his guidance and love, I would have been a rudderless boat adrift on the vast ocean of worldly life.

I am grateful to God for giving me a wonderful family and a home which provided a suitable environment for my spiritual growth. Later in life, I met my husband, Ralph Pyle, who continued to encourage me in my spiritual quest.

Throughout my life I have been supported by many sages, monks, nuns, and lay people in my spiritual practice and I am indebted to them for their invaluable help.

While writing this book, I was assisted by my friends who were kind enough to read drafts of the manuscript and provide necessary feedback. Anna Fisher's enthusiastic comments, Zeynep Altinsel's noteworthy reflections, and Lynda Group's meticulous editing have inspired me to take on the daunting task of publishing this book. Needless to add, no book of mine would see the light of day without the endless patience and hard work of Ralph, who not only proofreads my books but also formats them for publication.

Finally, this book would not have been possible without all seekers, through the ages, who have sought something beyond and better than transitory worldly pleasures. My heartfelt gratitude and bows to these role models for blessing us with their teachings and for assuring us that we too can seek what they have sought.

Members of My Family

Grandmother (Dida): Prativa Chakrabarti (Maharaj called her Ma)

Aunt Dolly (Mashi): Amita Chakrabarti (Maharaj called her Dolly)

Uncle Sankar (Mama): Sankar Chakrabarti (Maharaj called him Sankar)

Father (Baba): Lt. Col. Amarendra Kumar Bagchi (Maharaj called him Gour)

Mother (Ma): Namita (Lily) Bagchi (Maharaj called her Lily)

Bonie: Nivedita (Bonie) Bagchi Williamson (Maharaj called her Bonie)

Author: Alaknanda (Bubu) Bagchi (Maharaj called me Bobby)

Jim: James Williamson (Bonie's husband)

Ralph: Ralph Pyle (Maharaj called him Rameshwar)

Introduction

Through the ages people have sought peace and happiness, and India has had a long tradition of seekers who left their homes in search of the Unknown, the Truth, the Ultimate Reality. There were seekers who roamed from place to place and sheltered under trees and in forests, there were seekers who were monks and lived in ashrams or monasteries, and there were seekers who were householders who lived in the world but were not of the world. Some looked for God with form and attributes while others looked for God without form and attributes; some sought the Divine within while others sought the Divine without; some believed in nondualism while others believed in dualism; some spoke of God while others never mentioned God; some emphasized a permanent self while others emphasized the concept of no-self. In this way, many philosophers gave rise to many schools of thought. Great religions that have flourished for centuries were born in India, such as Hinduism, Buddhism, Jainism, and Sikhism. Other religions such as Christianity, Islam, Judaism, and Zoroastrianism have come to India and found a secure home among her people. The passion for philosophy shown by Indians and their open-mindedness in embracing religions other than their own is evidence of the spiritual nature of this country and her people.

In ancient India, Hindus lived life in four stages: student life, the life of a householder, the retired life, and the life of renunciation. The student went to live in his teacher's ashram and learned about both the worldly and spiritual ways of life. When he became a householder, he carried out his duties by earning money, supporting his family as well as spiritual establishments and spiritual seekers, and fulfilling the needs of the community. After retiring from the life of a householder, he and his wife gradually began to detach from their worldly ties and bonds and turn towards their spiritual practice. Finally, as renunciates, they withdrew completely from worldly life, moved to a forest, and focused solely on being liberated from *samsara*, which is the cycle of birth, death, and rebirth that human beings are trapped in according to Hindu and Buddhist philosophy.

Even though the life of the people of modern India may seem far removed from that of the people of ancient India, today one still witnesses a deep respect for all religions and a strong desire for liberation from suffering. Going on pilgrimage, visiting temples, participating in daily rituals in front of household shrines, following the scriptural instructions while performing ceremonies, and going to the sages to listen to their teachings on how to be liberated from suffering are common occurrences even in a world of smartphones and laptops.

It was in such a world that I was born to a family of spiritual seekers in Calcutta. I grew up in an environment where the focus was primarily on the quest for God. My mother and aunt had seen their little brother die of typhoid at an early age, and this had a lasting impact on our family. Their father immersed himself in books of philosophy and encouraged his teenage daughters to do the same. Their study of various schools of philosophy made them seek sages who had put theory into practice and had attained a certain level of realization. One sage they met in the 1950s was the loving sage, Swami Premananda, and it was with his blessings that I was born.

As I was growing up, I noticed that my family was different from other families I knew. Both my mother and my aunt were deeply spiritual. They meditated for hours, read books on spiritual matters, and sought the company of sages. What impressed me most was the fact that they embraced all religions with an open mind. I noticed that most followers of a particular sage or religious institution hesitated to visit sages and institutions other than their own. However, that was not true of my mother who felt equally at home visiting the tomb of a Muslim saint, the shrine of a Buddhist monastery, the altar of a Christian church, or the ashram of a Hindu sage. Mother's approach was influenced by our guru, Mohanananda Brahmachari (whom we called Maharaj), who told her to visit other sages when she could not visit him. Even though some may have disapproved of my mother's eclectic ways, she was a free spirit. I am grateful that this was a gift I inherited from her, and it has enhanced my spiritual life.

As a child, I studied in schools where the principals and most of the teachers were Christians. The day started with all the students gathering for what was known as "Assembly." After singing a few hymns, and reciting the Lord's Prayer, the principal usually led us in a prayer that contained a long list of names of people who were sick or in need of help. We repeated after her without giving this daily ritual much thought. Later in life while reflecting on my habit of praying for people, I realized that the method of prayer I had learned at school had become a part of my spiritual practice.

After I was initiated in 1971, Maharaj became my primary spiritual guide and this has never changed. From 1971 to 1990, I was lucky to spend a lot of time with Maharaj and his devotees. I was very young and knew that I felt a sense of joy whenever I was with my guru, but I may have been too young to understand the full significance of his teachings, which were conveyed through the songs he sang during kirtan.

Even though Maharaj has remained at the center of my life, I have had the blessings of many great saints, monks, nuns, and lay people who have helped me stay on the path. I have heard my elders speak of the *diksha* guru and the *shiksha* guru. The first is a guru who initiates a disciple; Maharaj is my *diksha* guru because he initiated me. The word *shiksha* means "education," and in that sense almost everyone and everything from which we learn can be considered a teacher. But here we will focus only on those from whom one can receive spiritual advice. I have been blessed by many *shiksha* gurus, both in person and through books and talks, and they have taught me much to continue my spiritual journey.

In 1990 I left India to pursue higher studies in the United States. At Purdue University, Indiana, I met my future husband, Ralph Pyle. In 1996, after we had both completed our doctoral degrees, with the blessings of Maharaj, Ralph and I were married. In 1997, after moving to Michigan, Ralph and I began reading books on Hinduism, and in 1998 Ralph was initiated by Maharaj. In 1999, much to our sorrow, Maharaj left his body at the age of ninety-five.

Strangely enough, the same year in which our guru left this world, Ralph and I met Ajahn Khemasanto, a Buddhist monk belonging to the Thai Forest tradition. He played an important role in kindling in us an interest in the Buddha's teachings. For almost two decades now, we have been associated with various Buddhist groups in our area. However, we still meditate according to our guru's instructions.

Unbeknown to us, Lorne Dekun had started the Ananda Michigan group, which followed the teachings of Paramhansa Yogananda, in our town of Lansing in 1999. However, it was not until 2003 that I met Lorne Dekun and was drawn to his kirtans. Ever since my guru had left the body in 1999, I had longed for kirtan. In 2003, after meeting Lorne, I attended kirtan every month.

Sometimes the Buddhists that I associated with would ask how I, as a practicing Hindu, could know so much about Buddhism. At other times, members of the Yogananda group would ask if I found it strange to see a picture of Jesus amidst several Hindu sages on the Ananda Michigan altar. I could not explain to them that I had no qualms about visiting the sanghas of various religions as long as I could listen to the Dharma. I had seen my mother attend services of different religious traditions and had followed in her footsteps. When she came to visit me in Michigan, she attended Lorne's

Ananda group and also went to see the Buddhist monk Ajahn Khemasanto. She loved listening to Lorne's kirtan and Ajahn Khemasanto's talks, and they were very fond of her. One day, we heard some local Sufis were going to get together. Ralph and I took Mother to the gathering and very soon we were all in a circle chanting along and dancing. Later the Sufis surrounded my mother and asked her many questions about her spiritual life. They were thrilled to have her. Having such a role model in my life helped me feel comfortable in various Dharma settings.

This memoir focuses not only on the great sages I have met but also on their followers because there is much to be learned from the devotees and disciples of spiritual teachers. Since I entered this field at an early age, I benefitted immensely from the company of my guru's devotees. Their approach to Maharaj was based on the *Bhakti* or devotional tradition of Hinduism, and growing up under the influence of members of our sangha I was deeply influenced by this tradition. Later in the U.S., I witnessed this strong love for one's guru among the devotees of Yogananda who befriended me in Lorne's group.

My study and practice of Buddhism taught me the path of knowledge, which is another approach to liberation emphasized in Hinduism and the Gita. I was not very familiar with this approach. Listening to Dharma talks by Buddhist monks and reading Dharma books gave me some insight into this world. The practical tools I learned from my Buddhist friends helped me negotiate my daily activities in a world of stress. I did not experience any clash between the paths of devotion and knowledge. In fact, Buddhism only enhanced and enriched my spiritual practice.

A third approach to liberation expounded in the Gita is the path of Karma or Action. I had heard about it in my youth when our elders would tell us to study for our exams, do our best but not cling to the results. At a young age, this did not make any sense. But in the U.S., I saw this approach in my husband. Most Americans work hard and their world centers around work. My husband Ralph works very hard. But what made him special to me was the fact that he did what had to be done and did not cling to the results. This reminded me of what I had heard while growing up. Gradually I learned to leave the results of work to God and to not have any expectations or desires for specific results and returns. Next, I tried to do everything for God and offer it to Him. This helped me realize a sense of freedom that I had not experienced earlier and I began to understand the significance of this approach.

When I look back on my sixty plus years of life, I am amazed at how the Universe has provided me with so much support on my spiritual journey. Maharaj planted a seed in me by initiating me when I was twelve. Every day I meditated and have done so for more than fifty years now. From 1971 to 1997, I meditated and trusted in Maharaj for everything. Being busy with my studies and teaching, I did not have much time to explore the spiritual world and learn what the sages had taught. However, after 1997, in the U.S., I had the opportunity to focus more seriously on my spiritual practice. While living in the small town of East Lansing, Michigan, I had the good fortune to listen to Dharma talks and kirtans, I had the support of spiritual friends and sanghas, I had the time to read Dharma books and meditate, and I had the chance to apply what I learned to all that came my way each day.

In this book, I have written about my memories of being with spiritual teachers and their followers. The intention was not to provide biographies of sages or share their teachings. Instead, I wished to share what I had witnessed both in India and in the U.S. of how devotees spend time with spiritual teachers. In some cases the teachers are a living presence and in other cases the teachers may have passed away long ago but their teachings have become the "teacher." Whatever be the circumstances or approach, the goal of the spiritual seekers is the same: to be liberated from suffering.

Part I: Sri Sri Mohanananda Brahmachari

Chapter 1: The Initiation

It is November of 1971, and my mother's guru, Sri Sri Mohanananda Brahmachari, whom we all call Maharaj, is visiting us in our home in a military cantonment in Dehradun. My father is away on a secret mission. An officer in the Indian Army, he is in what will soon be known as Bangladesh, where he is secretly training members of the Mukti Bahini so they can fight for their country's freedom. We live in Birpur Estate, which houses the 39 Gorkha Training Center and is situated at the foothills of the Sivalik range. From our front lawn one can see the lights of Mussoorie twinkling on clear nights. Set amidst spacious lawns, populated with flowering gardens and rare trees, is our bungalow where, at present, Maharaj is visiting us for a week.

It is a bright sunny morning and even though November can be chilly in Dehradun, I am playing hopscotch with my friends on the wide graveled driveway between the house and the front lawn. We should all be at school not only because it is a weekday but also because the annual exams are scarcely a month away. However, since Maharaj is visiting, my sister and I have been excused from school. My friends live in bungalows located within the cantonment, and each morning a military truck takes them to school. But ever since they met Maharaj after he arrived, they have been having so much fun in our home that my friends have refused to go to school. As a result, each morning the truck has been depositing its passengers in our driveway. All the parents are equally charmed by Maharaj and even though they protest and scold their children for skipping school, they have reluctantly given in.

The days are filled with great joy. Maharaj sings devotional songs in the afternoons and evenings and at the end of each session showers us with a variety of candies. Twice a day we go up to him to pay our respects by kneeling before him and bowing. He acknowledges our devotion by giving us delicious sweets and juicy fruits. His ring finger dips into a silver bowl containing the ashes of the sacrificial fire he lights each morning while performing his religious rites and rituals. He places the tip of his ring finger on our forehead, just above the center between the eyebrows, and our foreheads are marked by a black dot. Often, he places the palm of his right hand on our heads and for a second the world seems to disappear. We look up and see his beautiful eyes, limpid like a forest pool, and his radiant smile that lights up our hearts. It is true that he is the most beautiful human being I have ever seen, but there is something more. Each time I see him, I feel almost blinded by a luminosity that emanates from him. I do not think much about all this. They are just sensations that I experience. There must be something that attracts my friends, too, or why are we all so happy? We are just twelve years old and do not even know who Maharaj is. But when I am with him, a fountain of joy seems to be constantly bubbling within me.

Most of the time, we are in his presence. However, there are times when he shuts the door to his room and we leave him alone. Then I go out with my friends and play in the sunshine. It is my turn at hopscotch and as I hop along, trying very hard to stay within the squares, something distracts me. From the corner of my eye, I spy my uncle, Sankar, who is my mother's brother. He is sixteen years older than me, but I am good friends with him. I see him standing with a group of visitors and something about the body language of the group catches my attention.

"Out!" shouts a friend, and to my great disappointment I find that in trying to guess why my uncle is looking so nervous, I have stepped on the lines and been disqualified. As the next player excitedly gets ready for her turn, I walk up to my uncle and ask him why he looks so uncomfortable.

"Go away," he says. "You will not understand."

"Understand what?" I ask, refusing to budge. "What are you planning on doing?"

Uncle looks exasperated and finally says, "We are waiting to take *diksha*." And then seeing my blank look, he repeats, "*Diksha* means to be initiated."

"What does that mean? I have never heard that word."

"I told you this is not for you. Go away. This is serious stuff. Not for kids."

"I am not a kid," I retort before walking off in a huff.

I am not going to take this insult lying down, and I immediately go in search of my mother. The living room is filling up with devotees, followers, disciples, and newcomers. The hired photographer is getting his equipment ready. A family friend is placing a new spool in the brand new Grundig tape recorder Mother has bought to record Maharaj's songs. Mother's dear friend, whom we call Aunty Manju (Manju Mashi), is getting the sofa ready for Maharaj who has not yet entered the living room. Mother is nowhere to be seen. I next go to the kitchen and find her busy cooking the meal that is to be offered to the deities in the afternoon. I can tell that she does not wish to be disturbed.

"Mother. Mother?"

"What?"

"I want what Uncle is getting."

"What is that?" she asks furrowing her eyebrows.

"Something called *diksha*. He said the English word was initiation. I do not know either word."

Wanting to get rid of me, Mother says, "I cannot help you with that. Go and ask Maharaj."

Crestfallen, I make my way back to the living room where Maharaj is now seated.

Rushing up to the sofa, I kneel and bow to him before saying, "Maharaj, I want *diksha*."

He smiles and says, "You are too young for that."

Again, that smile which lights up the room. Again, that feeling of being submerged in bliss. I sit looking at him, mesmerized, unable to speak.

From somewhere far away, Aunty Manju's voice comes floating down. I look up and see she is standing right next to me. A devotee and disciple of Maharaj, she has a great sense of humor and often teases her guru. But our beautiful sage is very witty and quick with his retorts. No matter how hard one may try, no one can outwit him in words. He always has the last word, and we all laugh along with the person who started the exchange of witticisms. I am disoriented because Maharaj's presence stills my mind and I feel my brain has stopped thinking. I am aware that I am disappointed because I will not get what Uncle will receive today, but I am ready to move on to a battle of wits between disciple and guru.

"Why Maharaj?" asks Aunty Manju. "Why will you not initiate this little girl?"

Maharaj has a gentle nature and is very sensitive about hurting our feelings. I can see that he is being pushed into a corner.

"Well, typically in our society, husband and wife are initiated together. When she grows up and marries, what if members of her husband's family do not like the fact that she has already been initiated? What if her in-laws want her to be initiated by their family guru?" Maharaj's eyes are downcast, and he has a rueful smile on his face.

"But why can't you bless her so that her in-laws become devoted to you? Perhaps her husband may even wish to become your disciple," says Aunty Manju. "You know that anything is possible if you want it, Maharaj."

Maharaj finds himself in a tight spot and tries to wriggle out of it. But having found an advocate in Aunty Manju, I keep looking at him with pleading eyes. Finally, he caves in and I am told that I will be initiated that morning.

Standing on the sofa, Maharaj throwing candy after Kirtan
From left to right: Mother, Maharaj, Aunty Manju. Dehradun, 1971

Delighted, I rush out and proudly tell my uncle that he is not the only one involved in this initiation business and that I too am going to be initiated. Uncle does not believe a word of what I say, and I run off to play hopscotch.

Soon, one of the elders calls us in and Uncle is amazed to see me enter the house with him. I am too busy gloating over my victory to pay attention to any rituals that Maharaj may have performed before summoning us, one by one, into the shrine room. Since I am the youngest of the group and itching to go back to play outside—a desire that the All-Seeing sage scarcely needs his spiritual powers to discern—Maharaj calls me first.

I enter the shrine room and see Maharaj sitting on a mat on the floor in front of the altar. He gestures to me to sit on the mat across from him. Sunlight, streaming in through the two windows, pools on the cement floor. Smoke curls upwards from the lit incense sticks and a fragrance envelops the room. Everything inside me stills as I quietly sit down across from Maharaj. Taking a golden silk wrap, which has mantras and names of gods written in red letters across it, he places one end on my head and the other on his.

"Who is your favorite god or goddess?" he asks.

"Krishna," I mumble.

Maharaj leans over and whispers a mantra three times in my right ear, thus giving me the key to liberation.

I walk out in a haze and feel as though everything is in slow motion. I am clutching a slim book with a light pink cover in which my guru has written down my mantra in case I forget. I am not to tell anyone my mantra. If I need any help, I am to ask my mother. Each morning, after my morning shower, I must go to the shrine room and repeat the mantra a hundred and eight times while focusing on a picture of my favorite deity, Krishna. Each night, while in bed, just before going to sleep, I must repeat the mantra again a hundred and eight times. I am to ask mother how to keep count on my fingers.

My initiation. Dehradun, 1971
Seated (From left to right): I, Maharaj, Mrs. Majumdar
Standing (From left to right): Uncle Bose, Kul Bahadur, Uncle Sankar

The instructions slowly trickle through my consciousness as I try to process what has just happened. I am not sure what I was expecting when I had rushed forward with great gusto to get what Uncle would get. Perhaps, in my innocence, I had thought it was a special candy. But this turned out to be something different, and I do not know what to make of this experience.

An elderly lady, who seems older than my grandmother, beckons to me to come and sit with her in a corner of the living room.

"Did you take *diksha* from Maharaj today?" she asks.

I nod.

"Do you know what this means?" she asks.

I say, "No."

"From today Maharaj is your guru. He has given you a mantra and you must repeat the mantra every day and meditate. This meditation will lead you to God."

She asks me if I want to learn how to count my mantra on my hands. I nod and show my willingness to be her pupil. She teaches me and tells me to practice until I have it right. When she is pleased with my efforts, she lets me go, and I run off to play with my friends.

Twenty-seven years go by, and it is June of 1998. I live in the United States and am married to an American named Ralph Pyle. We met while studying for our doctoral degrees and got married after graduating from Purdue University in 1996. In 1997 we moved to Michigan where Ralph teaches Sociology at Michigan State University.

On this summer evening in 1998, I am alone in our University Village apartment because Ralph has gone to teach an evening class. I have just finished my evening prayers when the phone rings. I answer it and am surprised to hear my mother's voice. She is calling from Calcutta and gives me the shocking news that my father has passed away. My legs give way and I collapse on the living room carpet.

I cry for six months. As I mourn his death, it dawns on me that my father did not have to spend time being sick or bedridden, he did not have to suffer, and he did not have to be a "burden" on anyone. That is what he had wanted. However, in the throes of my bereavement, I still cannot come to terms with his death.

Mother calls and tells me that Maharaj is in the U.S. and I should try and visit him. I tell Ralph and he is eager to take me because he feels seeing Maharaj may help me process my grief. We leave for Du Quoin, a place in the state of Illinois. On the way, Ralph suddenly says, "Do you think Maharaj will be my guru?"

I am stunned to hear this. We have had conversations about the need for a guru earlier. Ralph has been reading books published by the Ramakrishna Mission and he has noticed that all the great teachers have emphasized the need for a guru.

"Where will I find a guru?" Ralph has asked me.

"I cannot help you with that," I have replied. "You have to find your own guru."

Not once have I told Ralph to take initiation from Maharaj. I have grown up with stories of disciples who went to a sage and asked to be initiated only to have the sage tell them that he was not their guru. Later, they found their guru. I understand that it is hard to find an Indian Hindu guru in the Midwest of the United States, but this matter is too serious for me to solve. This is a decision that must be taken by the guru and his disciple.

So, I am both delighted and apprehensive when out of the blue Ralph mentions Maharaj. While in Calcutta, just six months before my father's death, I had heard that Maharaj was no longer initiating anyone. But I do not say that to Ralph as we are driving to Du Quoin. Instead, I encourage him to ask Maharaj.

We arrive at the home where Maharaj is residing. It is afternoon and Maharaj has just closed his door to offer food to the deities. The host and his wife welcome us warmly. I know that we will not be able to see Maharaj now, but I ask the host about Maharaj's plans for the evening. As we are talking, I ask if Maharaj is initiating people because my husband would like to be initiated. The host looks at a group of men sitting at the dining table. One of them says, "Sorry, Maharaj is not initiating anyone these days. He is not keeping good health."

I find myself apologizing and saying, "Oh, I am so sorry to hear that. We would not dream of inconveniencing Maharaj. That's okay. We will go and check into our hotel now and return in the evening."

As we get up to leave, one of the men sitting at the table says, "Well, it is true that no initiation ceremony has been scheduled. But why don't you write a letter to Maharaj? When the door opens for us to take out the food offerings, we can give Maharaj your letter. Let us see what he says."

I experience a wave of gratitude towards this kind gentleman. I have paper and pen in my handbag and Ralph quickly writes a letter requesting initiation. The door opens and a couple of devotees go in to bring out the plates on which food offerings have been made. One of the men gives Maharaj our note. After a few minutes, we hear Maharaj say in a loud voice: "Tell them to come tomorrow. I will perform initiation."

The gentleman comes out with the good news, which we have already heard in Maharaj's own voice.

That evening, we go and meet Maharaj and listen to kirtan. When I go up to him, Maharaj looks sad and asks how Mother is coping with her grief. Naturally, he knows about my father's death. Once again, his compassion floods my being and I feel he understands how the human heart breaks when a loved one is gone. This is one of the many reasons for our loving him so much. Maharaj understands the human condition, he recognizes human suffering, he feels our pain. He sings devotional songs about the impermanence of life, the need to detach from worldly things, the wisdom in attaching to God, and the importance of our spiritual practice that will lead us to Self-realization. But at that moment when the human heart is shattered by the devastating news of a loved one's death, Maharaj's compassion embraces us like a mother's arms holding her child. It is the first time since my father died that I experience peace. I know it is temporary, but I am glad to feel it in my being because I had forgotten what it felt like.

The next morning Ralph and I are up at 4:00 a.m. After showering, I help Ralph to dress in Indian clothes. I am not quite sure about how to drape the *dhuti*, but we manage. Ralph must fast until the initiation is over. We drive over early, and I ask one of the male devotees to show me how to correctly wrap the *dhuti* around Ralph's waist. The gentleman teaches me how to do this, and Ralph is now properly attired. We sit in the living room waiting for Maharaj to open his door. I worry about what Ralph will say if Maharaj asks him which deity he likes. Ralph does not know anything about Hindu gods and goddesses. He is nervous, too. I try to train him.

"When Maharaj asks you which deity is your favorite, just tell him to choose for you," I say.

Ralph nods as he juggles the fruits and flowers we have bought for him to offer. I remind him that the monetary donation is in his right pocket. Just as I am about to confuse him further with more instructions, Maharaj's door opens and we clearly hear him say, "Tell them to come. I will first perform initiation."

A gentleman comes and tells us Maharaj has called for us to be initiated. I nudge Ralph to go ahead as, pointing at Ralph, I tell the gentleman, "He will be initiated today. I was initiated many years ago."

Ralph is ushered into Maharaj's room, but the gentleman comes back to me and says, "Maharaj wants to see you."

Maharaj and Ralph after Ralph's initiation. Illinois, U.S.A., 1998

I am surprised because during initiation only the guru and disciple are supposed to be present. No third person can be in the room. So, I cannot understand why Maharaj wants me. I enter his room and see Ralph seated on the carpet. Maharaj looks at me and says, "Go and sit next to him. I will initiate you both together."

Utterly bewildered, I go and sit next to Ralph. I wonder if Maharaj has forgotten that I have already been initiated. As this thought arises in my mind, Maharaj looks at me with those luminous eyes and says, "I gave you the Krishna mantra. I will give you both the Krishna mantra now." I am stupefied! Twenty-seven years ago, he initiated me in Dehradun. Since then, he has initiated hundreds of thousands of disciples. How could he remember?

He throws a silk cloth over his head and our heads and initiates us. He tells me to teach Ralph how to count on his fingers. Then he takes off his

10

silk stole and places it around Ralph's shoulders. It is a golden *namaboli*, a stole with the names of Krishna and Rama printed on it. Ralph looks beautiful. We leave the room, and everyone rejoices on seeing us. Later, while taking photos in the garden, Maharaj insists on taking one with Ralph sitting at his feet. We are both in a daze. We do not have cameras and do not even think of asking for copies of the photograph with Ralph. But someone takes down our address and mails us a copy.

Later, much later, I remember the conversation between Aunty Manju and Maharaj in 1971. Maharaj had hesitated to initiate me because I was just twelve years old. He had said, "What if her in-laws do not like me?" And Aunty Manju had said, "Maharaj, bless her so her in-laws like you and are all initiated by you." Well, Ralph's parents had passed when he was a teenager. They were officially Episcopalians, but they did not go to church.

While walking with Ralph one day in Philadelphia, he casually says, "I never got baptized."

I say, "Of course you did. You do not remember. Every baby is baptized."

Ralph replies, "No. When I was six or seven years old, I would hear my grandmother tell my mother, 'That little one never got baptized. We need to get him baptized one of these days.' But it never happened."

I have my mouth open in disbelief. That I had come all the way from India to the U.S. and met and married Ralph, who had then been initiated by my guru was indeed a mind-boggling thought. How did those words from a casual conversation made in the living room of our home in Dehradun come true after almost three decades? I still gasp in wonder when I think of it. Such is the grace of the guru!

When I ask Mother why Maharaj had initiated me a second time, she says Hindus like to initiate husband and wife together so they can both help and support each other on the spiritual path. Gradually, everything makes sense to me. For more than two decades now, Ralph has never missed his morning and evening meditations. He has been of immense support to me in my spiritual life. We come from two entirely different cultures, but our spiritual path has created a strong and abiding bond between us and is the foundation on which we have built our marriage.

Chapter 2: Maharaj and My Sister

It is 1972, and our family has moved from Dehradun to Calcutta. Father is back from the Bangladesh war and has spoken to the officials in the military headquarters requesting he be stationed in Calcutta for his final assignment before retiring. My maternal grandmother and my mother's sister, Aunt Dolly, live on the ground floor of my grandmother's two-storied house. The apartment upstairs has been leased by the Defense Forces and has just been vacated. We are very happy to know that the military has provided accommodation for us in the apartment they rent from my grandmother. To see our beloved grandmother and Aunt Dolly, all my sister Bonie and I have to do is just run down the stairs.

Several members of the family are disciples of Maharaj: Mother was initiated in 1969, Grandmother and Aunt Dolly took initiation in 1970, and Uncle Sankar and I became disciples in 1971. Father says he believes in God but is not interested in sages. Bonie is six years younger than I am and always wants to have what I have. She is miffed that she missed out on what happened in 1971 in Dehradun. How her elder sister got initiated without her knowing about it is a mystery my sister has yet to solve. But whenever we visit Maharaj, she never fails to ask him when he will initiate her. She is adorably cute and extremely naughty with big intelligent eyes sparkling with mischief, and her shenanigans always bring a smile to Maharaj's lips.

After we have settled down in our new apartment, we hear that Maharaj is visiting a disciple's home in Calcutta.

"Is this where he always lives?" asks Bonie.

"Not always," replies Mother. "He will stay for two or three days at this house and then leave."

"But where is his home?" asks Bonie.

"His ashram is in Deoghar," Mother says, "but he visits people all over the world. He usually does not stay in one place for more than three days."

Bonie looks bewildered on learning that it is not an easy task to find Maharaj. She is determined to make the most of this opportunity as my family prepares to visit Maharaj. We take a taxi to the house and climb the stairs to the roof where under a canopy many people are seated. There is a long queue of devotees waiting to meet Maharaj. Others have already paid their respects to him and are seated on the floor. We go and stand in line.

From left to right: I, Maharaj, and Bonie. Dehradun, 1971

Maharaj loves us all, but his face lights up with a childlike smile of appreciation whenever he sees children. Most children are either in their parents' laps or holding their parents' hands. As we stand in line to go up to meet Maharaj, the children fidget. They look around, shift their weight from one foot to another, chew on the free end of their mother's saris, and ask when they will go home. Occasionally a baby cries, and the parents try to stop the infant from disturbing others. Mothers scold the little ones and tell them to be patient while fathers rock the babies and try to make them sleep. In Calcutta, the crowds are huge and the line is long.

Finally, when the bedraggled family standing in front of us approaches Maharaj, all the carefully planned strategies fall apart. The little girl is confused and instead of offering the garland of marigolds to Maharaj, she wears it around her own neck. The mother scolds her in a whisper as Maharaj watches with his eyes twinkling. The father tries to balance the baby in his arms while bowing and somehow bumps the head of the sleeping baby who wakes up and screams blue murder. We are all watching and laughing. Everyone is enjoying the scene except for the beleaguered family. Maharaj's face beams with compassion as he leans over, blesses each member of the family, says soothing words to the baby, fills the little girl's hands with candy, and places his palm on each one's head. The family leaves rejuvenated. The long wait has been worth it.

Bonie and I are older and provide less trouble for our elders. Having always lived in the shelter of military cantonments, we are new to life in a big city. Visiting sages is not a novelty for us because we have gone with Mother to various places to meet holy men and women. But we have never seen such huge crowds. We are well behaved and stand patiently until our turn comes. Maharaj is happy to see that Father is back from the war. But before anyone can say anything, Bonie pushes herself forward.

"When will you initiate me?" she asks.

Maharaj's smile is radiant and he says, "You are little, now. You have to grow up and then we will initiate you."

"But you initiated my sister!" says my feisty sister.

Maharaj laughs and places his palm on her head and fills her cupped hands with candy. She moves away to take inventory of her goodies forgetting that she was going to insist on being initiated. The rest of us, one by one, go forward and bow to Maharaj.

Chapter 3: The Train to Deoghar

It is March of 1972, and Bonie and I are trying to adjust to our new school and the world of Calcutta. We go downstairs to our grandmother's room where we hear exciting news. The festival of Holi is approaching, and we will accompany Aunt Dolly to Maharaj's ashram in a place called Deoghar in the state next to ours. Bonie and I are familiar with the festival where we play with colors, but Bengalis call it Dol and not Holi. Mother tells us that Maharaj performs a great fire ceremony for several days at his ashram and then ends the ceremony with the celebration of Dol.

A couple of days before the start of the ceremony, we find ourselves in the crowded Howrah station waiting for the train we are to catch. Arrangements have been made for accommodations in Deoghar, and we will stay outside the ashram but within walking distance.

Bonie and I are excited. Travelling is fun, trains are fun, crowds are fun, and being away from school is always fun. We have a lot of luggage because we will be staying for almost two weeks and have to carry everything we may need. There are huge bedding rolls with mattresses and pillows and blankets and duvets; huge trunks with pots and pans and buckets and stoves; large suitcases with clothes and sweaters and jackets and footwear; and an assortment of bags carrying miscellaneous items ranging from storybooks to freshly cooked food to be eaten on the train. Aunt Dolly is sitting on a trunk and waiting for the train to pull in. We have reservations on the train and are not worried about the trip. While Aunt Dolly tells Bonie a story, I browse at the Wheeler bookstore.

As the train slowly chugs in, the scene around us changes swiftly. A sea of people swing into action and, pushing us out of the way, charge at the train. Some leap onto it while it is still moving, some scramble to find their footing on the steps, and some hoist themselves through the windows. Every entry is jammed with bodies and luggage. We stand there helpless until our porter tells us that we better get moving if we wish to get on board. We look at him helplessly. He realizes that we are novices at this and completely clueless as to what our next move should be. There seems to be no room on the train which is oozing bodies and luggage out of every window and door. The porter talks to a few other porters and suddenly we find ourselves being pushed and shoved into a compartment. How we get in and find our reserved seats, how we claim our rights to our reserved seats, and how we manage to get our humongous load of luggage into that overcrowded and splitting-at-the-seams compartment is anybody's guess. Somehow the porters push us through the door of the compartment and then slide our luggage in through the windows. So traumatic is the experience that even Bonie is quiet for the rest of the journey. As the train whistles and the conductor waves his flag to see us off, I see the porters moving away and wonder how on earth we will get off the train when we arrive at our destination. I wish that our resourceful porter had come with us because he really seemed to be well versed in the ins and outs of the Indian Railways.

The people around us begin to make themselves comfortable. Only a few of us are sitting on seats. Most of the passengers do not have reserved seats and are sitting on trunks and beddings or on the floor, depending on what is available to them. The passage used by vendors and passengers who wish to get up and use the restroom is blocked. Yet, whenever anyone needs to pass through, people move and shift and allow the person to proceed on his or her journey. Some are chatting, some are smoking, some are playing cards, and some are feeding their children. Looking at them, I feel as though they are sitting in the comfort of their homes. Their sense of ease calms me down and I begin to relax. Bonie asks Aunt Dolly if she has brought any snacks and soon we are munching on a packet of chips.

From time to time, the train slows down and stops at major stations where it disgorges a few passengers before swallowing up the crowds waiting on the platforms. The *chaiwala* (tea vendor) goes past our window with his huge kettle of tea crying out "*Chai garam* (hot tea)! *Chai garam!*" and passengers reach for their wallets and buy steaming hot tea which they sip in terracotta glasses called *khuris*. Other vendors come up to the compartment selling shiny baubles, toys, and cheap knickknacks. A vendor selling balloons goes by and Bonie wants a balloon. We tell her there is no room for one, but she insists. The vendor sells us one and Bonie plays with it. Within minutes we hear a gunshot that signals the demise of Bonie's balloon as it makes contact with the lit cigarette of a passenger. Bonie is ready to cry but the train stops her by jolting to a start and beginning to move.

I am immersed in my copy of *David Copperfield* when the vendor selling *jhal muri* (spicy puffed rice) shows up. Aunt Dolly gestures to him and he sets up shop near our seat as many passengers tell him that they, too, are interested in his wares. The vendor sells puffed rice spiced to the buyer's taste. We tell him to make ours mild because Bonie is not yet used to eating very spicy and hot food. I notice the dexterity with which he works.

Seated (from left to right): I, Maharaj, Bonie, Mother
Standing: Aunt Dolly. Dehradun, 1971

From what seems to be a belt around his waist hang many cans filled with various ingredients: chopped green chilies, sliced onions, roasted peanuts, fried vermicelli, trail mix, spices, and a variety of other delights. At the center of this circle of cans there is a large container from which he takes out the puffed rice and places it in an empty can. He begins by putting ingredients into the can. Then he tops it all with mustard oil. Putting a lid on the can, he shakes it vigorously. Then, taking a piece of old newspaper, he deftly twists it into a cone, pours the contents of the can into the cone and hands it to each customer. Bonie and I watch fascinated as he moves from customer to customer making them all happy with their demands of more spice or less spice or a little more peanut or slightly less cucumber. Each cone filled with spicy puffed rice is whipped up in a jiffy and handed to a drooling customer. The vendor pockets the change and gradually moves away from our compartment to the next. How he does all this in a space crowded with people and luggage and cigarette smoke and mewling babies is a wonder.

After a long and dusty journey, we arrive at Jasidih station where we get off the train with the help of the passengers who first push us out of the door, where passengers trying to get on the train threaten to push us back in, and then fling all our luggage out of the window. Before we can get our bearings, the train whistles and chugs away. Porters mill around us and carry our trunks and bedding and suitcases outside the station where we get into a *tonga*. Bonie and I have never been in a *tonga*--a horse drawn carriage--and we are excited and reinvigorated. We sit on either side of our aunt, with our backs to the horse, and carry a few bags with us. The porters hire another *tonga* to carry our luggage.

"Are you sure the horse can carry such a heavy load?" I ask the driver, anxiously, and he laughs.

It seems like a long ride to the ashram in Deoghar, but finally we are there and the second *tonga* is right behind us. Bonie and I get out of the carriage and run to see our accommodations. We find a small bare apartment with four wooden cots. The drivers carry in our luggage and we get busy unpacking. We still have the food we had brought with us for lunch because after eating the spicy puffed rice, we were too full to eat anything else. Aunt Dolly sniffs at the vegetables rolled up in *rotis* (tortillas) and after making sure that they have not spoiled, gives us dinner. The three of us eat because we are hungry by then. After having eaten, we drink the water we have carried with us in a terracotta *sarai* (water jar) which has a spout shaped in the form of a lion's head. Each time we tilt the *sarai* and hold the glass next to the lion's mouth, cool water gushes out. Now that our stomachs are satisfied, we help our aunt unroll the bedding and carry bedsheets, pillows, soft mattresses, blankets, and pillowcases to each cot to make up three beds. Even though hot weather has already arrived in Calcutta, it is quite chilly in Deoghar and we are cold. Tired after the long journey, I sleep well and dream of a night guard crying out in the night: "*Sab thik hai* (All is well)."

The early light of day wakes us up and I find Bonie in our aunt's bed. Apparently, my dream was real; there was a night guard crying out while on patrol duty and his voice in the dark night frightened our little Bonie who jumped out of bed and went whimpering to our aunt.

I laugh when I hear this and say, "Glad you did not climb into my bed, you silly girl."

Bonie scowls and replies, "Laugh all you want. You would have been scared, too, if you had heard him. And anyway, why would I go to you? You cannot protect me. You are just a wimp."

I am about to retort when Aunt Dolly says, "Stop bickering you two. We need to get ready and go to the ashram."

Chapter 4: A Tour of the Ashram in the Morning

After showering and eating breakfast, Aunt Dolly takes us to the Sri Sri Balananda Ashram which was founded by Maharaj's guru, Sri Sri Balananda Brahmachari. We find that we are a day early and Maharaj has not yet arrived. There are many monks wearing saffron-colored robes who are busy preparing for the arrival of Maharaj as well as the *yajna* or fire sacrifice he will perform once he arrives. Aunt Dolly takes us on a tour of the ashram.

First, we visit the Baleshwari Temple where we bow before the statue of Divine Mother bedecked with flaming red hibiscus flowers which, we are told, are her favorite flowers. Then we go to pay our respects to Divine Mother's husband, the great Lord Shiva. Here we do not see a statue but a Shiva Lingam.

"Where is Lord Shiva?" asks Bonie in a disappointed voice.

"This is a symbol of Shiva," explains Aunt Dolly while teaching us how to pour water on top of the Lingam and place three-leaved *bel* leaves and flowers on this sacred stone.

"I want to see Shiva with his dreadlocks and the crescent moon in his hair and the snake around his neck," whines Bonie, and our aunt gently shushes her because there are other devotees in the temple.

We come out into the sunshine and see the *Yajna Mandap* where the fire sacrifice will take place. We climb down the steps of the Shiva temple and walk into the *mandap*, which is an open pavilion-style pillared structure with a roof on top but no walls on the sides. There is an inner area, at the center of which is a large pit in which the fire will be lit for the sacrifice. Our aunt explains all this to us, and we do not enter the inner area where only priests and monks and Maharaj can enter. Surrounding this inner square shaped area is a larger square where laypeople can stand or sit and watch the fire ceremony.

"This will be a crowded place once Maharaj starts the fire sacrifice," says Aunt Dolly. "We will have to come early to find a place to sit."

"Why is this ceremony called a sacrifice?" I ask, having heard of animal sacrifice.

"Well, grains and cereals are poured into the fire as a sacrifice to please the gods so they bless this world and all of us," explains Aunt Dolly.

Many disciples and devotees of Maharaj are already there. Like us, they have come early so they are all settled before the ceremony begins. Others, who are not free to take so many days off from work, will come towards the end and see the fire ceremony culminate in the festival of colors. We look at the people around us and see that they range from little children to elderly women and men. Some have come with their families while others are alone.

There is a two-storied pink building called Mohan Mandir in front of the *mandap*, and we learn that Maharaj lives there when he comes to stay in the ashram twice a year: in March for Dol and in the autumn for Durga Puja.

"Will we come again in October?" I ask, knowing that in Calcutta we have a long holiday for Durga Puja.

Aunt Dolly gives a pleased laugh and says, "Let us first enjoy the present moment and then we will think about October."

As we walk, I notice several gigantic trees that look very old and have broad cemented platforms under them for people to sit.

"Can we sit on one of these and rest a bit?" Bonie suggests, and without waiting for our aunt's approval climbs onto a platform and breathes a sigh of relief. The ashram has many acres of land, and the sun has begun to get hot. My sister is tired.

"Should we go home and rest?" asks Aunt Dolly, but Bonie says she just needs a moment to catch her breath.

"Where will we go next?" I ask, and our aunt tells us that she will take us to a beautiful little cottage where Maharaj's guru lived.

"Who is he?" Bonie asks.

"Well, we call him Boro Maharaj and his name was Balananda Brahmachari. He was the founder of this ashram. He ran away from home when he was a little child, and he became a *sadhu*."

"What is a *sadhu*?" Bonie inquires.

"A holy man who leaves home in search of God."

"Did his mother cry when he ran away?" asks Bonie, looking as though she is about to cry.

"Many years after he ran away from home, his mother came and found her son when he was living here. She spent the final part of her life here and died here."

Happy that mother and son had been finally reunited, Bonie jumps off the platform to signal that she is ready to continue the tour.

Sri Sri Balananda Brahmachari

Soon we find ourselves in a secluded area with a huge pond before us and a small cottage. There is a hush in the air that makes everything inside us go still. Even Bonie is quiet. I feel a veil of peace descend softly on my head and I just want to close my eyes and sit down.

"This is Dhyan Kuthir," whispers Aunt Dolly, "and that pond is Narmada Kunda."

"What do those words mean?" whispers Bonie.

"*Dhyan* is meditation and *Kuthir* means hut or cottage."

We have many other questions to ask, but our tongues are still. Deeper than the silence resonating in the heart of a forest, deeper than the silence nestling in the peaks of the Himalayas, deeper than the silence reverberating among snowy glaciers is the silence of Dhyan Kuthir. We see the statue of a sage and know that that is Maharaj's guru, and the peace that emanates from the statue is so resounding that it almost hums in our ears. We bow and sit down on the floor. It is cool and soothing. Every sound is audible: the chirp of a bird, the soft stirring of a leaf, the gentle movements of the monk in charge of the cottage. I touch the floor and think how the sage must have walked on this very floor that is before my eyes. I feel a thrill go up my spine. Even my young heart knows there is something special about this place. The monk, who takes care of this temple, knows our aunt and nods to her as she puts a donation in the donation box. After we have sat in silence for some time, she gestures to us to get up. We obediently follow her wishes and leave after bowing one more time to both the sage, our guru's guru, and the monk in charge of the peaceful temple.

"Is there fish in this pond?" asks Bonie pointing at the pond and Aunt says there may be.

"What is Narmada? Why does this have such a strange name?" asks Bonie, and Aunt explains that the Narmada River is one of the many sacred rivers in India and people often go on a pilgrimage where they circumambulate the river.

"When I was four years old," I tell Bonie, "I almost drowned in that river. Our family had gone for a picnic with other families. I did not know how to swim. Some of the older children started wading in the river and I followed suit. Before I knew it, an undercurrent got hold of me and pulled me down."

Bonie's eyes are popping out of her head as she asks, "And then?"

"Father jumped in and fished me out."

"Yes," says Aunt as she smiles at Bonie "Your sister came to visit us and proudly told us this story except that she could not pronounce the name of the river correctly. Instead of saying Narmada she kept saying she had almost drowned in the *nardama*, and you know that *nardama* means a drain that carries sewage."

On hearing this story, Bonie bursts into laughter while I glare at her and fail to see any humor in the situation. At this juncture, a monk walking past us asks us if we have eaten lunch. We can hear a bell ringing and he tells us to go to the kitchen where lunch will be served. Aunt Dolly thanks the monk and heads towards the kitchen with us in pursuit. Suddenly, we are very hungry and need instant gratification.

We enter a large building and find people are already beginning to sit in rows on the polished floor. We, too, quickly sit down inside a huge hall as one of the workers in the ashram comes with a bunch of banana leaves and begins placing them in front of us. I see that mine is clean and freshly washed. Next comes a young boy with terracotta tumblers, and he is followed by an older boy with a large metal pitcher from which he pours cool water into our tumblers. Bonie and I are very thirsty, but not being sure of the etiquette in such a situation we watch our aunt's actions. We wait for the elders to drink first before giving in to the urge to quench our thirst. People sitting around us know our aunt and call her by her name.

"Dolly," they say. "So good to see you."

Aunt sits with great poise and dignity and smiles in return.

"Who are the children with you? Don't remember seeing them before."

"They are my nieces," replies Aunt, with a hint of pride in her voice. "They are my sister's daughters. You know my sister Lily, right?"

"Oh yes!" they say. "When will she come?"

"She and her husband will come towards the end of the festival. Perhaps my mother and brother may manage to come, too," says Aunt in a wistful tone. We know she is very fond of Uncle Sankar and misses him.

Mother (Lily) placing a garland on Maharaj. Dehradun 1971

All conversation comes to a halt as a booming voice announces the arrival of *khichuri*. We look up and see a muscular man carrying a large bucket and a ladle. He stops before each one of us and ladles a mound of steaming *khichuri* onto our banana leaves. This is followed by some fried vegetables and a preparation of mixed vegetables called *chanchra*.

"What is all this?" whispers Bonie to Aunt Dolly.

"You have eaten *khichuri* before this, haven't you?" asks our aunt.

"Of course, she has," I pipe in. "It is the lentil and rice dish Mother makes on rainy days."

"But I don't want to eat this messy vegetable dish," whimpers Bonie. "What is it? The man who served it called it some horrible name."

Aunt suppresses a smile and gently tells Bonie that even though the name of the dish is rather unappetizing, it is very tasty.

Bonie does not look convinced. She has a rebellious nature, and I am worried that in front of all these people my kid sister is going to throw a tantrum. What will people think! And what about the cook and his feelings? I really wish we had not brought Bonie on this trip.

"Just eat your food and stop making a fuss," I whisper to Bonie with clenched teeth. "This is an ashram, and the food is called *bhog* which means sacred food. Do not waste any of it."

I am tempted to add the "And you know how many people are starving in the world" bit that usually grownups fling at us each time we do not lick our platters clean, but I desist. What saves us from a scene is hunger. Bonie is hungry enough to try the food, and the minute she tastes it she realizes it is indeed delicious.

"*Amrita! Amrita!*" says the gentleman sitting next to me. And then turning to me, he asks, "It tastes like nectar, doesn't it?"

I smile shyly but do not know what to say because I have never tasted nectar. Aunt later explains that it was the gentleman's way of saying that the food was delicious.

For dessert there is *roshogolla* and Bonie has no questions regarding this item. She gobbles up the rich juicy sweet balls, soaked in syrup, and licks her fingers in delight. We now drink water, and the meal is over. The elders in each row announce that they are getting up, and we get up too and go out into the courtyard and wash our hands in the water streaming from a tap.

With clean hands we head home and jump into bed. Bonie and I are exhausted from our day's activities and our kind and gentle aunt, too, decides to rest a bit. She takes off her glasses and relaxes, and soon we doze off.

A short nap refreshes us all and Aunt decides that she should cook dinner before taking us out again. I read my book and Bonie takes out her drawing book and draws mountains and trees and a flock of birds with a house and a little girl.

Maharaj wearing a Nepali cap with a kukri pin on it. Dehradun, 1971

Chapter 5: The Ashram in the Evening

As evening descends, we are ready to go to the ashram again. We enter the precincts of this sacred place and hear bells ringing in the various temples as *arati* is being performed. We enter the temple closest to us and see the priest ringing a bell in one hand and holding a lit lamp in the other. He moves the lamp in circles before the deity and we all watch in silence. The fragrance of incense, the sound of conches being blown, crowds of people moving from one temple to another give the ashram an air of festivity.

Aunt takes us to a temple of impressive architecture called Jugal Mandir, which is built of marble and adorned with intricate carvings. Bonie and I are spellbound. Aunt explains that the temple is called Jugal Mandir because it houses the statues of Maharaj's guru and Gopal. The word *jugal* means "two." The temple is also known as Naulakha Temple because it cost nine lakh rupees to build the temple. At the entrance is the statue of Charushila Debi who was a disciple of the sage, Balananda. When her husband and son died, she used to come to her guru to listen to his words of wisdom which would lighten her heart and help her cope with her sorrow. Being a lady of great wealth, she constructed this temple where she placed the images of her two favorites: her Gopal (the baby Krishna she worshipped) and her guru.

"Why did Balananda . . .?" begins Bonie but Aunt Dolly interrupts her.

"We call him Boro Maharaj because he was Maharaj's guru," she says.

"Why did Boro Maharaj not reside in this beautiful marble temple instead of that small cottage we went to this morning?" asks Bonie.

"Well, he preferred the small cottage because holy men live simple lives and are content with very little," replies Aunt not knowing how to tell Bonie that temples usually house statues.

We admire the carvings, the statues, the majestic pillars, and the highly polished marble. Finally, when our feet are tired from all the walking and standing, we head home. The sight of the dinner Aunt had cooked before we left reminds us of how hungry we are, and we gobble up the food. As we get into bed, after changing into our night clothes, Bonie announces that she wants to sleep with Aunt or me because she is scared of the night guard. We laugh at her and tell her there is no need to be afraid because he is protecting us. By the time Aunt washes up and comes to bed, Bonie is already asleep in her bed. Our sweet aunt smiles affectionately and climbs into bed after turning off the light. We sleep so well that even Bonie is not awakened by the night guard's cry.

From left to right: Aunty Uma (Uma Mashi, a disciple of Maharaj and a friend of Aunt Dolly), Maharaj, and Aunt Dolly. Barkakana, 1989

Chapter 6: The Arrival of Maharaj

The next morning, Aunt wakes us up early and tells us to hurry and get ready. Bonie and I shower and wear clean clothes and rush to the ashram with our aunt. Outside the ashram many more vendor stands seem to have sprung up overnight selling flowers, incense sticks, garlands, *malas* made of sandalwood and *rudraksha* beads, bright shiny knickknacks, souvenirs, food, snacks, and an assortment of goods that I do not remember seeing the day before. There are cycle rickshaws honking and vendors hawking their goods. Young shopkeepers cry out, asking us to buy flowers for the temples. Others beckon to Bonie and me and point at delicious looking sweets called *peda*, which are famous in Deoghar. But we have already eaten breakfast and are not tempted. As we walk through the gates of the ashram, the noisy hustle and bustle of the world outside the boundary walls of the ashram subsides and we feel our hearts fill with peace and joy.

As we did the day before, we pay our respects to goddess Baleshwari and Lord Shiva and then go and sit on one of the circular platforms under a giant tree. Aunt asks a passing monk when Maharaj will arrive, and he tells us that they are expecting him any minute now. Quite a crowd has gathered near us and there is an exciting air of anticipation. There are women clad in white who remind me of my grandmother. I know she wears white because she is a widow. I guess these elderly ladies are also widows. There are others who are wearing white saris, too, but with broad red borders. They wear vermillion in the parting of their hair, and that is a sign that their husbands are alive. Having lived all my life outside Bengal, there are many things I do not know about my own culture. I quietly observe and learn. I try not to talk too much because my cousins in Calcutta laugh at my Bengali and say I have an accent. I am self-conscious and embarrassed that I am not quite conversant in my mother tongue, so I listen to others as they speak and try and make note of the correct pronunciation of Bengali words.

Suddenly we hear cars honking and before we know what is happening several cars drive into the ashram, one after the other, and we see Maharaj in the first car. Bonie and I jump off the platform and the crowd surges forward. Maharaj gets out of the car and looks at the devotees with his radiant smile. I experience that moment of stillness, once again, as everything seems to be filled with a blinding light. Bonie has made her way through the crowd by weaving in and out of the legs of the adults. She runs to Maharaj, tugs at his robe, and asks, "Won't you initiate me now?" Maharaj's face lights up with an even bigger smile as the crowd laughs at the antics of this little girl. I am ready to curl up and die of embarrassment.

Holding Bonie's hand, Maharaj walks swiftly through the crowd and into the pink building called Mohan Mandir where he stays when he comes to his ashram. The crowd begins to disperse, but Aunt and I wait until a monk brings Bonie back to us.

"He says I am still too little," says a glum-faced Bonie, her hands full of the candy which Maharaj has given her to assuage her disappointment.

"When will I grow up?" she whines, as she counts her candy. "I want to grow up right now."

Maharaj standing against a backdrop of the Sivalik range. Dehradun, 1971

Aunt Dolly laughs and I scowl at my sister and tell her to stop pestering Maharaj each time she sees him. We roam around within the confines of the ashram and feel at home. Even though we see the same people, something is different. It feels as though the ashram is full. I think of how I had once witnessed a ceremony during which the priest chanted mantras and performed rituals to invoke life in the statue of the goddess Durga. I had asked my mother the significance of the rituals, and she had said it was called *pran pratistha*, which meant giving life to the statue. After the ceremony, the belief is that the statue is alive with the presence of the goddess. This is a common ceremony performed in India when a new statue of a deity is placed in a temple. The memory comes back to me, and I feel that the whole ashram has sprung to life with the advent of Maharaj.

"Maharaj is the heart of the ashram!" I exclaim in surprise, and my aunt agrees with me.

After lunch at the ashram, on our way back home, Bonie buys a flute from a vendor who entices her with his beautiful melody. We come home and she immediately begins to play the flute. The sounds that emanate bear no resemblance to the vendor's melodies and my sister is getting ready to bawl. Aunt Dolly quickly diverts her attention by saying, "Did you know that Maharaj was a young boy when he came to this ashram?"

Bonie and I sense a story coming and settle down to listen to our aunt as she tells us how Maharaj was studying at Scottish Church College in Calcutta when one day he decided to be a monk and left Calcutta and came to Deoghar. His parents were disciples of Balananda Brahmachari, and the young student wished to become a monk.

"Was his name always Maharaj?" asks Bonie.

"No," Aunt replied. "His name was Manmohon Bandopadhaya. After he became a monk, his name was changed to Mohanananda Brahmachari."

"But why do we call him Maharaj?" asks our bewildered Bonie while I roll my eyes in despair at all her interruptions.

"We address all holy men as Swamiji or Maharaj or Baba to show respect to them," Aunt explains.

"Okay, that's enough," I say, glaring at Bonie. "Can we go on with the story, please?"

"Well, Balanandaji told Maharaj that this was a very difficult path, but Maharaj was determined. Then Balanandaji sent for Maharaj's parents. Maharaj's father gave his son his blessings, but Maharaj's mother was very sad. She could not imagine her son living the life of an ascetic and facing all the hardships one faces as a monk."

"Did she cry?" asks Bonie in a whimpering tone.

"Well, I am sure she did cry," says Aunt, "but when she saw her son's determination, what could she do but give in?"

Seeing that Bonie was getting ready to bawl again, Aunt hurries on to say that Maharaj worked so hard to become a good monk that when Balanandaji left his body, he appointed Maharaj as the monk in charge of the ashram. This brightens up Bonie's spirits and brings a smile to her lips. She turns to her flute and starts playing with it while I pick up my book and read a few more pages of Charles Dickens.

Maharaj sitting in our garden. Dehradun, 1971

Chapter 7: The Fire Sacrifice

From the next day onwards, time seems to fly by as we try to participate in a variety of activities. Waking up early each morning, we bathe, eat breakfast and rush to the ashram with our beloved aunt. We do not stop at all the temples as we did the first two days. Aunt Dolly is in a hurry to get to the *Yajna Mandap*, the pavilion where the fire sacrifice will be performed by Maharaj. Some elderly widows are already there, sitting right behind the railings of the inner sanctum from where one can get the best view. Bonie and I rush to sit behind them and find bricks and stones and rags and sheets of old newspaper and moldy pebbles and even leaves. Wondering why these things are scattered here when all the ashram is so clean, we are about to brush them away when the elders caution us and tell us not to touch them. Apparently, these items have been placed by devotees who woke up at the crack of dawn and came to the pavilion to reserve their seats.

"But that's not fair," I mutter, turning to my aunt, but she tells us to listen to the elderly women because the people who have reserved their seats can be quite feisty.

"God help you if you take someone's seat," says one widow. "Even Maharaj cannot save you from the clutches of an enraged devotee if you encroach on her turf."

Bonie and I look down and keep silent, but once we are seated with Aunt in the third row we ask her to explain what all this means.

"I understand you are upset," she says. "But just think of how devoted these people are to have come and reserved their spots early in the morning. You must always see what is good in people."

Bonie and I do not quite agree with her, but soon we are distracted by the conversations floating around us as more and more people begin to join us. I note that by and large there are fewer men attending the ceremony than women. Most of the men are standing around the *mandap*. The devotees sitting in our section of the *mandap* are all women. There are grandmothers, mothers, children, widows, and single women. The conversations range from gossip regarding domestic issues to the glories of being a disciple of Maharaj. When the gossip seems to be getting out of control, often someone shushes the participants and tells them to focus on spiritual matters. There are elders who are constantly giving advice and quoting from the scriptures. There are mothers-in-law complaining about daughters-in-law and vice versa. The children get restless with the endless waiting and are soundly rebuked by the mothers. Grandmothers are kinder and distract the children by telling them stories. There are siblings who are playing with each other and others who are bickering. Bonie and I are quiet and do not trouble our aunt. Some of the devotees notice this and compliment her by telling her that her nieces have good manners.

The crowd begins to swell, and soon the outer circle of the pavilion is packed. There is no room for latecomers to sit, so they stand outside the pavilion. Some climb onto the porch of the Lord Shiva temple from where they can see the inner sanctum which is also filling up with monks carrying items for the fire sacrifice and priests getting ready to chant the ancient mantras from the holy scriptures. Suddenly, there is a mixture of commotion and restrained jubilation as Maharaj walks swiftly from his residence to the pavilion. He sits down on a raised seat which is directly in front of the *Yajna Kunda*, the cavernous pit in the floor where the fire will be lit. Maharaj's name truly suits him, I think, as he is dressed like a king. Clad in a golden cloth, adorned with luminous gems sparkling with the luster of a million suns, he sits regally as a hush falls over the crowd. I feel immersed in calmness and yet there is a fountain of joy bubbling within me. I do not understand what I feel but I know it is connected to the presence of this radiant being.

A hush has fallen on the ashram and soon we hear crackling sounds as tongues of fire begin to lick the air above the hollow in which the fire has been lit. Maharaj dips a long-stemmed ladle into a bowl of *ghee* and pours the clarified butter into the flames. The fire ritual has begun. Monks and priests sitting on both sides of the fire begin to recite Vedic mantras, ancient verses that have been chanted through the ages at such ceremonies. The leaping flames tower at least ten feet high, and a blaze of blinding light falls in white cascades illumining the pavilion. Sweat begins to gleam on the holy faces of the saffron-clad ascetics who have left their homes in search of God. With the chanting of each sacred verse, more butter is poured, and with each mantra more sizzling is heard, and with each utterance of the word *swaha* the flames roar louder. The mixture of ghee, wood, and the various offerings poured into the fire gives rise to a fragrance which is typically unique to fire ceremonies.

We, the laity, hover on the outskirts of the inner sanctum inhaling the rich perfumes of incense and burnt wood. Even though we are far from the holy fire, the smoke still pricks our eyes, the heat almost seems to singe our hair, and sweat drips down our backs under the onslaught of the intense heat. As

I feel myself wilting, I watch Maharaj through the flames. He sits unperturbed at arm's length from the blaze. Ignoring the juices offered to quench his thirst, refusing the towels brought to mop his brow, hour after hour he sits feeding the flames, chanting the sacred words, and performing the rituals handed down to us eons ago by hoary-headed sages. Through the quivering flames, we see his radiant face dazzling brighter than the flaming fire.

The morning session ends with Maharaj and the monks circumambulating the sacred space chanting the Peace Mantra. They walk on the outer square where we had been sitting and from where we had all hurriedly moved out when the time came for the circumambulation. We stand on the outskirts of the pavilion and watch the monks as they go around the inner sanctum three times sending out peace to Heaven, Sky, Earth, Water, Plants, Trees, Gods, Brahman or the Supreme Being, and Everything and Everybody including themselves. I listen quietly and love the rhythm, the cadence, the intonation, and the Sanskrit words which I do not understand and yet am drawn to. I am filled with peace.

The crowd waits until Maharaj leaves the *mandap* and goes back to his residence and then there is chaos and confusion. Mothers are looking for their children, fathers are telling their sons to run to the kitchen and queue up for lunch, grandmothers are asking if someone has seen their purse or spectacles or other such items they have mislaid. Aunt Dolly grabs Bonie and me and makes a beeline towards the kitchen where one batch of devotees has just finished lunch and the floor is being washed and swept dry before the next batch can sit. Suddenly we find that we are all famished. Mesmerized by Maharaj, none of us had realized that it was way past our lunch time. I vaguely recall some announcements being made on the loudspeaker requesting people to come and get lunch, but no one had budged as long as Maharaj was in front of their eyes. Hence, the long lines now and the frustrated public. All the patience displayed at the pavilion appears to have vanished. I hear a few children crying and parents threatening dire consequences unless the little ones behave appropriately. Bonie and I are very hungry, but we stand silently and Aunt is proud of us. Finally, we do get squeezed into the next batch and sit down as we have done the past two days.

The kitchen is bustling with activity. Huge cauldrons boil over with *khichuri*. The hall fills with scores of devotees, and we sit in rows facing each other, staring at the green plantain leaves and the bright red terracotta glasses. Saffron-clad monks scurry along with buckets of steaming aromatic *khichuri*, ladling golden heaps of delicious *bhog* onto our plates. At the end of the meal, there awaits a special treat. A pair of rosy feet gently pass between the rows of plantain plates, anklets tinkling gracefully. Cupping our hands, we look up to receive the gift of the Radiant One. Showering love, radiating brilliance, smiling sweetness, into each hand He drops a sweet juicy *roshogolla*. No sweet ever tasted so sweet as the one we received from Maharaj.

Gone are the heavy silks and brocades, gone are the jewels and ornaments. Dressed in a simple saffron-colored robe, he is busy feeding us when I thought he would be resting. After the long morning, I am ready to take a nap. But there is no trace of fatigue on Maharaj's luminous face as he looks at me and drops the sweet into my hands.

Bonie nudges me and I turn to see her eating her sweet. In a daze I realize that my sweet is still in my cupped hands even though Maharaj has gone on to the next row. I cannot forget the glance that lit on my upturned face as Maharaj stood in front of me for a second. Love streamed from those serene eyes like moonlight on a full moon night. I thought of a comment one of the elderly widows had made in the morning while we were watching the fire ceremony. "He is the ocean of compassion," she had said, and I had not quite understood what she meant until this moment.

"Are you okay?" asks Aunt, and I just nod to reassure her. But I have no words to describe the impact Maharaj's presence has had on me.

After lunch, we go home and rest a bit before getting ready, once again, to go to the ashram. This time Aunt takes us to the Narmada Kunda, the huge pond in front of the cottage in which Maharaj's guru used to live. We find clusters of grown-ups standing distanced from each other, and we join a group of Aunt's friends. We know one of them because she had gone to Dehradun in 1971 when Maharaj had visited us and I had taken initiation. We call her Aunty Reba (Reba Mashi) and she is very happy to see us. As we are catching up, there is a stirring among the clusters and the voices become subdued. We see Maharaj walking on the wide path that goes all the way around the pond. Since he is very tall, he walks fast with long steps and the monks on either side of him are focused on keeping up with him. As he passes each cluster of lay devotees, some join him while others are content to stand and watch. Bonie, I see, is getting ready to join. Aunt Dolly whispers and tells me that she will wait for us and that once we are done, we must come back to her. Maharaj and his group are just going past us when Bonie and I and a few others from our cluster join them. Bonie, of course, runs ahead and is right next to Maharaj. To keep up with him, she must hop, skip, and jump but she is undaunted. I pray she does not bother him with her request for initiation. Luckily, she is too busy keeping up with Maharaj's pace as he circumambulates the pond three times walking as swiftly as the wind. I am glad that I can keep up, but by the time Bonie and I get back to our aunt, we are both panting. Maharaj goes back to his residence, and we head for the pavilion and get ready to watch the evening rituals.

Group photo with Maharaj. Aunty Reba is standing third from the right. Dehradun, 1971

We are early and get good seats, but Bonie is getting tired and sleepy by now and asks, "When does Maharaj rest?"

"Rest?" pipes in the grandmother with the *mala* which she is using to count as she silently repeats her mantra. "Maharaj has no rest. Don't you see how he is everywhere? Performing the fire ceremony, feeding people in the kitchen, circumambulating the pond at dusk, taking care of a variety of administrative matters. He only knows how to give, and he spends all his time working for the welfare of humanity. Yogis like him have the power to do this. They do not get tired like you and I do"

Bonie realizes that there is not much rest for Maharaj and that means there may not be much rest for her. Sure enough, after the evening ceremony is over and Maharaj has left the pavilion, the crowd surges towards Mohan Mandir which is Maharaj's place of residence. A queue forms outside the entrance, and Aunt explains to us that we will have to stand in line if we wish to pay our respects to Maharaj that night.

"If you are too tired tonight, we can go home," she says.

Even though Bonie is very tired, she does not want to miss this chance of getting some candy and reminding Maharaj that he has promised her that she will soon be initiated. So, we go and stand in line. Aunt goes to the man who sits in the courtyard with a basketful of garlands strung with marigolds and tuberoses. She buys three garlands and we each hold one in our hands. After some time, the queue begins to move, and we enter the building. There is an enclosed veranda at one end of which is a staircase that takes Maharaj to his room upstairs. At the other end of the veranda is the door that leads to the room where Maharaj will receive us. When we enter the room, I am surprised to find that it is quite small. Maharaj is sitting on a chair and is flanked by two monks. One is giving fruits and sweets to the devotees and the other is placing the black dot (*vibhuti*) on each devotee's forehead. When it is our turn, Maharaj leans over so we can put the garland around his neck. We bow down and touch our forehead on his feet. When we straighten up, Maharaj places the garland back around our necks and places his palm on our heads. He asks Aunt Dolly when Lily, my mother, will come. He asks me if I am missing school to be here and I give him a sheepish grin and hang my head as the crowd titters good humoredly. Bonie steals the show by asking when he will initiate her, and everyone laughs loudly. Maharaj fills her hands with candy and sends her off.

The routine of the first day of the fire ceremony becomes our routine for the rest of our stay. Some evenings we do not go for the Narmada circumambulation because we are tired and need a nap. Some nights we do not get to pay our respects to Maharaj because he is busy attending meetings regarding the administration of the ashram and other important matters. However, most of our mornings and evenings are spent watching the fire ceremony. We eat lunch at the ashram and Aunt cooks us a simple dinner at night.

Chapter 8: The Baidyanath Temple

One morning, while we are in Deoghar, Aunt tells us that she will take us to the famous Baidyanath temple of Lord Shiva.

"But haven't we already seen so many temples?" whines Bonie.

"Yes, we have," says Aunt, "but this is a renowned place of pilgrimage, and it would be disrespectful if we did not go and pay our respects. They say Ravana worshipped Shiva where the temple stands."

Both Bonie and I are excited. We know all about Ravana from a thick illustrated book we have at home. "*Ramayana* is one of the greatest epics in the world," Uncle Sankar had said to me when he had given me that book. I was five years old and fascinated by the pictures. I would beg all the elders to read the story to me because I could not read Bengali and the words were written in Bengali. In a couple of weeks, I had memorized the whole book. So fascinated was I with the stories that I would even have dreams where I was a character in the epic. Later, I would tell Bonie the stories and show her the pictures.

"Is Ravana the one who slept for six months?" asks Bonie.

"No, silly," I say, "that is Kumbhakarna. Ravana is the one who kidnapped Sita."

Bonie is a little scared of Kumbhakarna, who is shown in the pictures gobbling up everything in sight, including the soldiers of the opposing army led by Sita's husband, Rama. Reassured that the temple we are about to visit is in no way associated with the voracious demon, Bonie gets ready. We hail a cycle rickshaw and tell the driver to take us to the temple.

When we arrive at the temple, Aunt is at once surrounded by a group of men called *pandas*. They are priests who guide pilgrims at most Hindu temples by helping them visit the shrine and perform the necessary rituals. Aunt Dolly chooses one of them and he immediately barks out orders to a group of his assistants, and before we know what is happening, we are surrounded by these men. They all hold hands and form a tight circle around us. Aunt has flowers and incense and money which she will offer to Lord Shiva, and she gives us some flowers and tells us to hold tight. The place is teeming with pilgrims who are carrying huge pitchers of water on their heads. There are men in traditional Indian garb and women in saris. There are old people who can barely walk and toddlers who need to be carried by their parents. Everyone seems to be enclosed in circles formed by *pandas*, and each group is moving towards what I presume is the entrance to the shrine.

Bonie and I are not quite sure what will happen next. Suddenly, our circle is inside the temple and it is quite dark and extremely congested. It feels as though a small space that can hold only ten people has been stuffed with a hundred pilgrims. They are all chanting words that honor Shiva, such as *Om Namah Shivaya* and *Bum Bum Bhole* and *Hara Hara Mahadeva*. The words bounce off the walls of the small space, which seems to me to be some ancient cavern, and then resound with a might that is overwhelmingly deafening. Amidst the chaos and confusion, our circle is ripped apart and *pandas*, pilgrims, Bonie, Aunt, and I are separated as the crowd surges and pushes us this way and that way. Might has the right of way here and the men push their way towards the shrine. They are strong and so are their wives from working in the fields all day. Aunt, Bonie, and I do not stand a chance unless Shiva performs a miracle, which He does. He places us in front of the aggressive pilgrims, and as they move towards the Shiva Lingam, we find ourselves being inadvertently pushed forward. Soon I am in front of the Lingam representing Lord Shiva. I bow down to place the wilted flowers on His head and find cascades of water almost drowning me. Apparently, my head is in the way and the pilgrims who are pouring water on Shiva do not bother to wait for their turn. Some more pushing whirls me out of the temple and I find Aunt and Bonie waiting outside for me.

"What happened to you?" asks a concerned Aunt Dolly, "You are drenched!"

Bonie keels over with laughter as she points at me and says, "Look at you! You look like something the cat dragged in."

Glaring at her, I collapse on a platform at the base of a huge tree and relate my sorry tale.

"Well, I am glad you were able to pay your respects to Lord Shiva," says Aunt, and I can tell that the whole experience has been quite traumatic for her. Paying the *pandas* their dues, even though they have failed miserably at their job, we climb into a rickshaw and go back to our apartment. There is still time to go to the ashram for the morning ceremony even though we will not find a place to sit. I quickly change my clothes and we run to the safe world of our ashram, where we always feel at ease.

Chapter 9: Holi at the Ashram

The days go by swiftly, and as the end of the ceremony nears Mother and Father arrive with Grandmother and Uncle Sankar. Bonie and I are delighted as our whole family is now present. They have brought a lot of food with them, and we eat a delicious dinner. The next day, which is our last day at the ashram, is also the festival of colors. After the end of the fire ceremony, we line up to pay our respects to Maharaj. The crowd has almost doubled as many people have taken a couple of days off to see their guru and visit the ashram. Maharaj is very happy to see all the members of our family who have just arrived. As we bow to him, we sprinkle some colored powder on his feet in celebration of the festival of Dol (Holi). He showers us with his blessings and fills our hands with fruits and sweets. Even though we are sad that our happy time with Maharaj has ended, his presence fills us with an indescribable joy. We say goodbye to Aunt Dolly's friends, who are all busy talking to my mother, and then we go back to our apartment, pack, and leave for the station.

Father buys tickets as we wait in the waiting room of Jasidih station. These waiting rooms are huge with high ceilings, old fans whirring above us, and lounge chairs where one can stretch out and even take a nap. When it is time for our train to arrive, we go to the platform where a small crowd of people waits. Stray dogs sleep in the sun, and a vendor comes by selling cigarettes and chewing gum. Bonie is about to ask for a packet of gum when the train chugs in. We get on board with our luggage. As we settle down, Bonie and I excitedly start telling stories about our train journey to Jasidih and how our luggage entered the compartment through the windows because of the dense population. The elders are laughing as we tell them about how I got drenched while visiting Lord Shiva at the famous Baidyanath temple. Bonie complains that even though she has diligently pursued the matter of her initiation, Maharaj has not yet agreed. We all laugh while Bonie scowls. Stories of the fire ceremony, eating lunch at the ashram, sitting in silence at the cottage of Maharaj's guru, admiring the architecture of the temple built with marble, walking fast with Maharaj to circumambulate the pond, and being frightened out of our wits by the cry of the night guard make the train journey short, and before we know it, we are in Calcutta.

Chapter 10: The Munnar Trip

A couple of months later, school closes for the summer and Mother announces that she and Aunt Dolly are going to take Bonie and me to Madras to visit Maharaj. Father has work and cannot get leave and Grandmother will stay home to take care of all that is required to run a household. Uncle Sankar, after his brief visit to the Deoghar ashram, has gone back to Dhanbad where he is posted as an officer in the Eastern branch of the Indian Railways.

After hearing stories of our perilous train journey to Deoghar, my father makes sure that we have reserved seats in a first-class compartment of the train that we will take to Madras. As such, our journey is peaceful and without event. Maharaj is staying with a judge and his wife. They are very kind people and are hosting a small group of Maharaj's disciples. We are well looked after and spend as much time as possible with Maharaj. After a few days, our group leaves in a bus to go to a beautiful hill station called Munnar. The place reminds me of Dehradun with its serene hills and dense forests.

Mornings in Munnar are often spent with Maharaj who enjoys walking up and down the front lawn of the guest house where he is residing. Bonie skips ahead of all of us and holds Maharaj's hand as he walks. Maharaj gives her an amused smile, but I am worried that she will bother him with her demand to be initiated. After his walk is over, Maharaj asks us to gather in a group so he can take pictures. I remember him doing this in Dehradun. This is one of his hobbies and he has a variety of cameras. The one that excites us the most is the Polaroid camera. Within minutes, our photo is right before us, and we find that magical. No waiting for the roll to finish, no going to the store to get the pictures developed. There we are, all grouped around Maharaj who sets a timer and joins us each time before the camera makes a whirring sound and clicks.

In the afternoons, we sit in the living room waiting for Maharaj to sing kirtan or devotional songs. Maharaj is busy either writing letters to his many devotees who have written to him or dictating letters to a devotee sitting on the floor next to Maharaj's chair. Another disciple is sitting at the harmonium, singing beautifully. His name is Ajit but everyone calls him Ajitda to show respect. *Dada* is the Bengali word for elder brother and *da* is a short form of *Dada*. We are all listening to Ajitda. Sometimes Maharaj looks up and tells someone in the audience to sing. The person gets up and comes to the harmonium and carries out Maharaj's request.

Maharaj reading letters while Govinda Gopal Mukhopadhyay sings in our home. Calcutta, 1997

Bonie and I know only one Bengali song, which we learned when Maharaj came to our home in Dehradun. Having grown up outside Bengal, we did not know how to read or write Bengali. So we wrote down the Bengali words in Hindi and memorized a song so we could sing in front of Maharaj. Each day, during his Dehradun visit, Bonie and I would sing the same song. Ours was a song by Rabindranath Tagore and began with the words *Aguner poroshmoni*. Having been asked to perform more than once on this trip, we live in constant dread that Maharaj's glance will alight on us and we will have to plague the audience with our rendition of this well-known song. Most Bengali girls are trained to sing and can sing beautifully. We are ashamed of never having taken a single music lesson and knowing just this one Rabindra Sangeet.

After several singers have sung, Maharaj picks up his *khonjoni*, a pair of small hand cymbals, and begins to sing. Devotional songs in India are usually sung in the form of call and response. So most of the time Maharaj sings a couple of lines and we repeat after him, but sometimes he sings a solo and a hush falls on the audience. Bonie and I are too young to understand the

43

profound philosophy embedded in each song, but we do not complain. Something seems to be conveyed but we lack the words to vocalize our feelings. My sister, who is usually restless and full of mischief, becomes quiet. I experience the vastness of the blue ocean in my being. Both of us sing along with the Hindi songs that have a catchy beat, but during the chanting of Sanskrit verses or Bengali songs we become quiet because we are not familiar with all the words.

At the end of each kirtan, Maharaj stands up on his seat singing "Radhe Radhe" and throws sweet sugar candy called *batasha*, toffees and lozenges, fruits, and Indian sweets such as *laddoos* into our laps. This, I have learned, is a tradition called *Harir Loot*, and it is common to end kirtans in this way. Maharaj throws with gusto and makes sure that everyone gets a fair share of the items he is throwing. Adults and children rush to grab the sweets, and we have an exciting time trying to outdo each other. Some we catch in our hands, others fall in our laps, and still others fall on the ground, and we rush to pick them up before anyone else can get them. There is much laughter and fun. Maharaj's face beams with smiles as his joy at giving and our joy at receiving mingle to fill the room with ecstasy. After all the items have been given away, the host brings a small bucket of perfumed water and a water gun, and Maharaj squirts us with water. As the drops fall on our heads, the devotees sing "*Shanti, Shanti.*" The elders pray that with Maharaj's blessings we will all have peace. I am too young to understand the importance of this desire because my life is both peaceful and happy. Bonie and I just find the "peace water" fun.

Finally, Maharaj ends the kirtan with his hands folded and his eyes closed, singing "Radhe Radhe." The crowd is mesmerized by the magic of the kirtan and the presence of this illumined being. In the silence that follows, Ajitda begins to thank everyone. We start off with Maharaj, and then there is a long list which includes the host, the devotees, and all who have participated in the kirtan. Referring to a list of names, Ajitda announces a name and then together we all enthusiastically say, "*Jai*" which literally means "victory" but in this context a better translation could be "in praise of." So, for instance, Ajitda says, "Sri Sri Guru Maharaj *ki,*" and he pauses as though asking a question, and we respond with a resounding "*Jai.*" After kirtan is over, Maharaj leaves us to go to his room while Bonie and I take inventory of all the sweets we have gathered and wonder which one to eat first.

In the evenings, Maharaj goes for a ride in his car. Some devotees who have cars follow him. Others pile into the backseat of his car. A couple of times, Bonie and I are ushered into Maharaj's car. He sits in the front

Maharaj ending a session of kirtan. Dehradun, 1971

passenger seat, next to the driver, while we are in the back seat with a couple of grownups. To my surprise, I find that Maharaj spends his time in the car in silence. One of the adults sitting next to us tells us that Maharaj likes to say his evening prayers in the car, so we must maintain silence. We drive up and down the mountainous roads breathing in the spectacular scenery of green plantations and rolling hillsides. When we come back to the rest house, we are greeted by the devotees who did not go for the ride. They act as though we have been away for days. Such is their deep love for their guru that they do not wish to lose sight of him even for a minute.

Maharaj and his devotees, with Bonie standing to the left of Maharaj. Burnpur, 1970s

Smiling at the eagerly waiting devotees, Maharaj goes to his room to complete his prayers. We rush to get dinner and then come and sit on the carpet in the living room where we wait for Maharaj. I listen to three women chatting about their experiences with Maharaj. Each has a lovely story to tell of how he has been gracious, compassionate, and benevolent to her in times of crises. As each woman tells her story, her face is flooded with devotion. The stories reveal how close, how dear, how special Maharaj is to his devotees. Ajitda sits down and begins to tune the harmonium. As he starts singing a devotional song, the chitchat ends and we all settle down for kirtan. Finally, Maharaj comes and takes his seat. By now the little ones are getting sleepy, and some of the elders are tired from the day's activities and excitement. But Maharaj looks fresh and radiant in a blue silk robe as he casts

46

his glance around the room taking in the faces of his beloved disciples. Aunty Manju, who has been with us on this trip, goes up to Maharaj and kneels next to him.

"Maharaj," she says. "I am giving you this small bottle of perfume. It is very expensive. My brother brought it for me when he went abroad. I have saved it for you. Please use it a little and then I will take it back."

Maharaj takes the tiny bottle, looks at it with eyes brimming with humor, and puts it on the table next to him. He does not do what Aunty Manju requested him to do, and we all wait eagerly to see how this story will end. With a nonchalant look, Maharaj picks up his small cymbals and begins to sing. The lights are turned off. Moonlight streams in through the windows and a soft light from a small lamp throws patterns on the walls. Maharaj sings song after song and the audience is sucked into a vortex of divine bliss. How the hours fly by we do not know. Some of the solos are heartrending in their yearning for God and my young heart responds to the sorrows of the devotee longing to be united with the Beloved. Perhaps if I had heard these songs on the radio or on a record player, I would not have paid much attention to them. But the pathos lingering in each word is highlighted and enhanced by Maharaj's sweet voice and his pure-hearted rendition of the lyrics. I find tears streaming down my cheeks and am glad that no one can see me in the dark.

Too soon it seems to us that the lights are turned back on to signal the end of the kirtan. Maharaj stands up on his seat and begins *Harir Loot*. As fistfuls of candy and other treats fall into my lap, I feel I am still in a daze and need time to switch gears. I sit quietly and watch as the room springs to life with adults and children animatedly lunging this way and that way to catch a fruit or grab a piece of candy. Finally, it is time for the *shantir jal* or "peace water." I see Maharaj stoop down and whisper something to the host who goes to another room and returns with a small bucket of water. Now, in front of everyone, Maharaj gleefully opens the stopper of Aunty Manju's perfume and dumps the whole bottle of perfume into the bucket. The room fills with the most heavenly fragrance as Aunty Manju cries out in horror.

"No, Maharaj, no!" she exclaims. "Please, please don't do that. Just a drop is enough."

Maharaj's smile is as wide as the rainbow, and we are all laughing at this beautiful interaction between him and his devotee. We all love Aunty Manju because she is not only a lovable person but also has a great sense of humor. By now she, too, is laughing even though she tries to plague Maharaj with mock protests. In the meantime, we are being drenched with the water from the water guns that Maharaj is squirting on us and our clothes smell of expensive perfume. After kirtan is over and everyone has been thanked, Maharaj gets up to go to his room. As he walks past Aunty Manju, he drops the empty bottle in her lap. Once again, we all roar with laughter. It will take me many years to realize that with that simple act Maharaj had taught us many lessons of which renunciation and impermanence were the most significant.

The next day we get on our bus and go to see Periyar Lake. Our group gets on a large boat with Maharaj and we are taken on a tour. Suddenly, there is some excitement on the deck, and I see people pointing at something in the distance. The owner of the boat slows down as we begin to approach a herd of elephants. When we are still at some distance from the elephants, the owner of our boat cuts off the motor. It is a memorable sight. The elephants are in the water, bathing and playing. There are mothers and calves. The adult elephants are sucking in water through their trunks and spraying the babies with the water. At times, two adult elephants spray each other. If they are aware of our presence, they ignore us. We do not wish to intrude upon their privacy and are happy to watch from afar. Perhaps a couple of devotees take photos, but ours is not the world of selfies or cell phone cameras and there are no frenzied attempts to capture the moment. We watch almost hypnotized by the beauty of the spectacle, until it is time to turn back.

Chapter 11: From Munnar to Cochin

From Munnar we go to the densely populated port city of Cochin where Maharaj is besieged by many disciples and devotees and, suddenly, we find ourselves deprived of the quiet closeness with our guru that we had enjoyed in the hills. Those of us who are traveling with Maharaj are housed in comfortable lodgings situated on the waterfront. Our focus is still on spending as much time as possible with Maharaj, so we see little of the city. A bus takes us back and forth each morning to the house where Maharaj is residing. There we spend the day, coming home at night after kirtan. The hosts are generous and kind and take good care of us. In the evenings, Maharaj often visits the homes of other devotees, and we accompany him or stay back depending on whether we get a seat in one of the many cars following Maharaj's car.

On the waterfront. Left to right: A young boy who was with the group, I, and Bonie.
Cochin, 1972

One evening, a kind lady who I know is a resident of Cochin gestures to me and says I can go with her in her car. I tell her I can go only if there is room for my sister. She looks at Bonie and agrees. I tell Mother and Aunt Dolly that we will be following Maharaj, and they tell us to keep close to the lady who is taking us and to not get lost. Maharaj visits four homes that evening and we watch the same rituals performed in each house.

Maharaj enters the first house and is asked to sit on a divan that has been decorated with a colorful cloth. The host and his wife are on their knees performing what is known as *charan puja.*

Mother washing Maharaj's feet (*charan puja*). Burnpur, 1970s

Maharaj places his feet in a large silver bowl, and the host and his wife wash his feet with water which has been mixed with rose water. I am sitting close to Maharaj and see how beautiful his feet are. I have this sudden insight into the words "lotus feet" that Hindus often use to describe God's feet. I could easily call Maharaj's feet "lotus feet" because they remind me of a pink

50

lotus. Now the host's wife is drying her guru's feet with a soft towel. Next, she anoints Maharaj's feet with fragrant essential oils called attar; then she dips basil leaves and marigolds in a small bowl of sandalwood paste before placing them on his feet. Having finished these rituals, she prostrates before Maharaj by touching her forehead to his feet. She moves aside and allows her husband to perform the rituals. I look up to see Maharaj's face and he has the same benign expression he usually has. I experience a strange wish arising in me: I wish my heart were a pool of crystal-clear water in which the Radiant One would wash his feet. As the thought arises, the host, who has finished his rituals, looks at me and asks if I would like to perform the ritual. I look up and see benevolence shining forth from my guru's eyes. I pull Bonie to my side and the two of us dip the flowers in sandalwood paste and place them on Maharaj's feet before prostrating to him. A sigh of contentment ripples through the audience as Maharaj taps us both on the head. Then he gets up and goes into the bedroom of the host where he will offer food to the deities in the host's shrine room and change into the new silk robe presented by the host's wife.

Everyone bursts into conversation now that Maharaj is in another room and the door is locked. The host and his wife have disappeared because they have much to take care of. The plate in which the feet washing ceremony was performed lies on the floor in front of me. The lady, who is giving us a ride in her car, comes and sits next to us and smiles warmly.

"Well, you two did a good job," she says. "Were you nervous?"

"No," I reply, shyly.

"We have done this before," says Bonie. "Maharaj came to our house in Dehradun and stayed for a week. We did this every morning."

The lady laughs at Bonie's words and looks at the flowers on the plate and says, "Look at those flowers. Aren't they lucky? I wish I were a flower, and someone placed me on Maharaj's feet." She sighs a blissful sigh as though her wish has already been fulfilled.

I smile and am not sure how to respond when the door opens and Maharaj walks to his seat dressed in a purple robe with a silver border. People stand in queue and come to pay their respects to him. After he has blessed them and filled their hands with sweets and fruits, he gets up to leave and we all rush to our cars so we can follow him to the next house. The same rituals are performed in each house. The feet washing ceremony is followed by Maharaj leaving the devotees to go and change into the new set of clothes offered by the host. Then he comes out and the people in the room get a chance to pay their respects and be blessed by Maharaj. By the time we leave the second house, Bonie and I are tired.

However, there are no signs of weariness on Maharaj's face when we see him in the third and fourth homes. Looking vibrant and radiant, he gives everyone his time, patiently listens to people and their problems, generously feeds everyone, and showers an abundance of blessings on all present. Wherever we go, there is joy that is palpable. Maharaj enters homes that are brimming over with joyous expectation. He spends a little less than an hour and the house hums with joy. When he says goodbye, he leaves behind a trail of joy. We, who are going with him from house to house, are intoxicated with joy that is indescribable and inexpressible. This is evident from our faces which reflect his radiance. When Bonie and I are safely deposited back with our mother, she takes one look at us and hugs us in joy because she knows what we are experiencing.

From Cochin, our group returns to Madras. After bidding goodbye to Maharaj and thanking our hosts, Mother, Aunt Dolly, Bonie, and I take the train to Calcutta and come home to my grandmother's house. There we spend days and weeks telling her and Father all the stories of what comes to be known in our family as the Munnar trip.

Chapter 12: Devotees and Disciples

My grandmother's home is always full of people. She is a favorite aunt to many of her nieces and nephews, and they all flock to see her. They sit on her bed and share their problems with her because she is a sympathetic listener. Upstairs, my parents often have their military friends over, and there is much wining and dining as well as telling of stories of heroic battles fought in the past. Bonie and I have many friends and they like coming to our house, too.

Left to right: Bhishmada, Aunt Dolly, Maharaj, Aunty Reba, Chaya Boudi.
Dehradun, 1971

I enjoy spending time with everyone, but I am most excited when Maharaj's disciples come to visit us. Some are close friends with Mother and Aunt Dolly and very fond of Bonie and me. There is the singer whom Mother calls Bhishmada and his wife Chaya Boudi. Bhishmada was responsible for teaching Bonie and me the Bengali song that we perform each time Maharaj tells us to sing. Then we have Aunty Reba and her husband Uncle Arun. We have known Aunty Reba since the Dehradun days because she accompanied the singer and his wife when Maharaj visited us. But when she comes to visit us in Calcutta, she brings her husband whom we call Uncle Arun (Arun Mama). Bonie and I like him a lot because he has a great sense of humor. He brings special candy for us and tells us stories of how this candy is the only food astronauts are allowed to eat in space. We are thrilled with this discovery, and only when we see Aunt Dolly's eyes twinkling with merriment do we realize that Uncle Arun is teasing us. Aunty Reba has a brother whose name is Debkumar Ray (but who is known as Chorda in Maharaj's circle) and he, too, becomes a regular visitor to our house and tells us fascinating stories of his childhood spent in the Deoghar ashram. Aunty Reba's parents are disciples of Maharaj's guru, so their family has been visiting the ashram for a long time. In fact, her father is the architect of Jugal Mandir, the fabulous marble temple we have visited in Deoghar. Many a long afternoon is spent with disciples of Maharaj as, over snacks and multiple cups of tea, they tell us stories of times spent with our guru.

I listen to them and realize that their world centers around Maharaj. When faced with a crisis, they turn to him; when sorrow darkens their day, they turn to him; when sickness creeps into their homes, they turn to him; and when death deprives them of a loved one, they turn to him. They fumble with their words as they try to describe what Maharaj means to them. He is their guru, and yet he is more; he is their parent, and yet he is more; he is their friend, and yet he is more; he is their God, and yet he is more. Maharaj is not just princely, majestic, regal as a king should be; nor is he just stern, firm, and awe-inspiring as a guru should be; he is as full of laughter as a baby's crib, he is as full of song as a bumble bee, he is as full of joy as a rainbow in spring. Words fail and silence stills their tongues as tears wet their lashes and they become quiet. We all understand what each one is trying to convey. But this is a language of the heart and their thoughts are communicated silently.

Chapter 13: Celebrating the Guru on Guru Purnima

It is July and Aunt Dolly tells us that we must get ready early in the morning to go and pay our respects to Maharaj on Guru Purnima.

"What is Guru Purnima?" asks Bonie.

"Purnima means 'full moon,' and there will be a full moon tomorrow," says our aunt. "But this day of the full moon is dedicated to all gurus. On this day we pay special respects to our guru."

Getting ready early in the morning is not a problem for us because Bonie and I are ready at 7:30 a.m. for the school bus that comes each weekday to pick us up. But we are shocked when we are told that we will have to wake up at 4:00 a.m. and get ready as soon as we can so we can get in the queue that will form to see Maharaj. Grandmother, Mother, and Father will go in the evening because it is a weekday and Father has work during the day.

So the next morning Bonie and I are woken up by Mother before dawn. We rush to the bathroom, shower, get ready, eat a light breakfast and run downstairs. A taxi has been summoned and we get in with Aunt Dolly. We finally arrive at a grand mansion and see a man sitting on his haunches on the pavement. He gets up and comes towards us. Behind him we see many pairs of slippers, sandals, flipflops, sneakers and shoes of all sizes. Aunt tells us to take off our slippers and the man ties all three pairs into a bundle, puts a slip of paper on our bundle and gives us a matching ticket. Soon we are entering the gates of the grand house where Maharaj is residing at present.

It is 5:30 a.m. and already there are quite a few devotees crowding around the flower seller. His name is Rishi. Dark complexioned and thin, clothed in spotless white garments, he sits on the cemented driveway with his basket brimming over with a profusion of colors. The brilliant hues and the heady perfumes of his wares set our hearts aflame as we stop to buy a garland that has been painstakingly strung by the flower seller's hands.

"Which one do you want, little sister?" he asks Bonie, who chooses a garland with bright orange marigolds. I want one with tube roses, and Aunt Dolly prefers jasmine.

As we are about to move away after paying him, Bonie asks the flower seller, "Won't you come with us to see Maharaj?"

Rishi laughs and says, "Not now, little one. When everyone has paid their respects, then I will go with the last garland and offer it to Maharaj. You run along now and get in the queue."

Wondering if he has a special garland that he keeps aside for himself, we follow Aunt Dolly's lead and find ourselves at the entrance of what seems like a maze constructed by strong bamboo poles. A large open area has been covered with canvas to prevent us from getting wet in case it rains. After all, July is a monsoon month and the weather is unpredictable. The area is divided into two halves: on the right, we have women and children, while the left is open to all. We enter the right side and go zigzagging all the way until we find ourselves in the third row from the front. High up before us is a raised platform, as big as a stage, where Maharaj will come and sit. Devotees have arrived before us and are sitting in the first two rows. Aunt tells us to sit down with her because we are going to be there for a long time. There is a constant stream of devotees entering the covered area, and I notice that our side is quickly filling up.

"Why are there so few people on the other side?" I ask my aunt.

"Well, that side is for men and for families who wish to be together when they see Maharaj. Most men are at work. In the evening, that side will be full. When your parents come with your grandmother, they will stand on that side."

Bonie and I sit quietly and listen to all the chatter around us. Most of the women who arrived before us are elderly. Many are clad in white saris. Some have a dot of sandal wood paste between their eyebrows. Others have little cloth bags with prayer *malas*. My sister and I are familiar with the scene. We have already witnessed this in Deoghar. In fact, we recognize some of the elders. Everyone knows Aunt Dolly and they call out to her. Some smile at us and ask us if we are well. Bonie and I politely smile back.

The elder in front of us complains to her friend: "I tell my son and daughter to not miss these opportunities of seeing Maharaj. But no! Who listens to me? My daughter says she is too busy with her children's exams, my son complains about his bad tempered boss and how he may lose his job if he took a day off, and my daughter-in-law says, 'Who will cook for your son and your grandchildren if we all went and sat at your guru's feet?' Such cheek!"

"Let them be, Didi (elder sister)," says the friend. "One day they will realize how precious these moments are and then they will come. You were able to come today, and that is what matters. When we come to Maharaj, we should just leave our worldly attachments behind."

The elder behind us is chatting away even though the *japa mala* with which she is counting her mantra is sliding through her fingers. "I try so hard to focus on Krishna's image when I meditate at home, but my mind keeps wandering off," she says. "With age, I find it harder and harder to concentrate. It is easier for me to come here and see Maharaj. Once he is before me, I forget the world. I don't need to concentrate. I am mesmerized. When I go home, for days I am in a trance. Each time I close my eyes, I see him."

"Whom do you see?" asks the person sitting next to her. "Krishna?"

"No, Maharaj. Oh! So beautiful and so full of life! I think I am going to tell him that from now on I will meditate on him and not on Krishna. I love Krishna, don't get me wrong. But I have not seen him with these eyes of flesh and blood. But I do see Maharaj as often as I can. And I can close my eyes and focus on him and meditate for hours. Sometimes I even forget to recite my mantra, you know?"

"It is all the same, dear sister," says her neighbor. "You know how the great sage, Kabir, said that if God and Guru come and stand before me at the same time, I will first touch my Guru's feet because he has shown me the way to God. So, if it is easier for you to focus on Maharaj, just do that."

Now I hear voices in the fourth row and look back to see a woman in her forties talking to an elder: "All day long I meditate, perform rituals, go to the temple, make merit, read books on the Dharma, and listen to Dharma talks. But when Maharaj comes, I drop everything and run to see the Living God."

"Of course," says the elder. "My sons live in England. I see their photos and the photos of my grandchildren. But when they come to visit me, do you think I even remember the photos? No. I have the original, right? That's how it is when we come here. We see the original."

At this point, we hear an uproar that is coming from the far end of the enclosed area. We hear voices raised in objection and then a pleading voice begging to be heard. Gradually the commotion dies down and we see a young girl making her way gingerly through the maze, stopping every now and then to explain that her grandmother is waiting for her in the first row. We look towards the front and see a white-clad figure vigorously waving her arms and shouting, "Poonti! P-o-o-onti!" Bonie and I hide our smiles at this funny name. Poonti flushes with embarrassment. I am sure she has a beautiful formal name, but this is what they call her at home. Finally, the girl is united with her grandmother and the crowd sighs with relief even though they are not sure that Poonti should have been allowed to be in the first row when she had obviously had a full night's sleep and taken her time to show up while the rest of us had been sitting here with our aching knees forever. But all negativity is put aside as we notice some movements on the stage. A couple of saffron-clothed monks have arrived to prepare for Maharaj's arrival and seeing them gives us hope of seeing our guru soon.

Two men carry a large sofa and set it at the center of the stage. Two women begin to drape the sofa with colorful cloths. They fluff pretty cushions and bolsters encased in silk and satin and place it on the sofa for Maharaj's comfort. More monks begin to appear with lamps and conches and bells and sticks of incense and flowers and many other things that will be needed for the rituals. The stage, by now, is a place of busy activity with monks and lay people scurrying around to get everything ready before Maharaj arrives. Below the stage, where we are, the crowds have begun to thicken. The maze is full on both sides and the queue is now stretching beyond the main gate through which we had entered. This news is brought to us by an officious looking young man, who is trying to look very important. He has a badge on his shirt and Aunt Dolly tells us he is one of the "volunteers" who will help to ensure that the queue moves efficiently once we begin to line up to meet Maharaj. More volunteers begin to show up and a few come and stand near the stage while the rest are at the entrance to the maze.

At noon, Maharaj appears on the stage and a roar of happiness ripples through the devotees. He stands, looks around, and smiles at us and even though we are too far for him to see each of us, we feel that he does see each and every one of us. Gone is the weariness of the more than six hour long wait; gone are the aches and pains in the knees from sitting with little room to move; and gone are all the silent complaints about the hardness of the ground, the mugginess of the weather, and the fidgetiness of the devotees around us. A hush falls on the crowd. I look around and see the multitudes and am reminded of the Pied Piper of Hamelin who played his pipe and the town was emptied of its children. It feels as though every home has been emptied of its people today. Old and young, fathers and mothers, rich and poor, sick and well, married and single, one and all have come to fill their hearts with joy.

We continue to sit as Maharaj first pays his respects to his guru by performing a series of rituals. Bonie and I feel close to Maharaj's guru because we have been to his ashram in Deoghar and seen where he lived. Since this is a day when we worship our guru, Maharaj, too, must participate in this ceremony before we pay our respects to him. After he has completed the rituals and bowed to the picture of his guru, the monks get ready to worship Maharaj. They also perform a series of rituals while Maharaj sits quietly.

Maharaj in our home. Dehradun, 1971

After the monks have completed their rituals, there is a flurry of activity on the stage. Maharaj stands up and comes close to the edge of the stage. A monk brings a basket of candy and Maharaj begins to throw candy at us. The crowd roars with happiness as we all scramble to pick up a lozenge here and a toffee there. I think of how compassionate Maharaj is to try to shower us with his blessings even though we are sitting far from him. The people on the stage are close to him. Perhaps those of us who are at a distance from Maharaj might be wishing that we, too, were on the stage. Lest we feel hurt or deprived, this is his way of letting us know that we have not been forgotten. Of course, these are just speculations on my part, but they make my heart go soft with a sense of being loved. A monk places a long water gun in Maharaj's hands and soon jets of water are being sprayed at us. People in the front rows are overjoyed but the water gun is powerful and even Bonie and I get a light spray. Inside the hot and humid enclosed area, the cool water is refreshing. But what steals our hearts is the joy emanating from the radiant figure standing on the stage and reaching out to the masses who have been waiting for him since the crack of dawn.

Now all the people on and around the stage are moving quickly. Maharaj's sofa is placed close to the edge of the stage and he sits down. On both sides of Maharaj are monks who will help the devotees make their offerings to Maharaj and also place the black dot of sacred ash on our forehead in case Maharaj is unable to do that. The volunteers are gearing up to control the crowds. Sometimes a devotee wants to spend a lot of time in front of Maharaj. This is when a volunteer must firmly nudge the devotee to move on. At other times, people may become impatient. Then the volunteers have to calm them down and tell them that they will soon be in front of Maharaj. On rare occasions, someone may faint or there may be a medical emergency. The volunteers are responsible for taking care of such situations by moving the patient to a safe place before calling a doctor.

We get up from the ground and stand up. Before we can stretch our legs and shake off the cramps, the crowd surges. Space has opened since it takes more space to sit than to stand. Gaps must not be allowed because they may encourage unethical and undisciplined devotees to crawl under the bamboo poles and make a beeline for the front row. Bonie and I have been raised to treat people with respect and are not prepared for all that happens in the blink of an eye. We are found guilty of providing the dreaded gap and a toothless hoary-headed grandma grabs the opportunity and fills up the void to our great consternation. The veterans in the crowd do not scold the culprit. Instead, Bonie and I are thoroughly scolded for being derelict in our duties. Aunt Dolly is red in the face and upset that we are being scolded. She protests that we are new to all this and are not used to such unethical behavior. Now the crowd turns on her and tells her she needs to train us. Bonie and I are aghast. How can these elderly ladies, who are supposed to be spiritual, behave in this fashion? We are up to our necks in righteous indignation.

At this point, our attention is distracted by yet another elderly lady who is trying to follow in the footsteps of the usurper of our space. But unfortunately, she has underestimated her size and is stuck under the bamboo pole. The crowd turns on her and roars its disapproval. But our hearts melt on seeing her plight and our anger is diffused. Merriment and compassion rush in and after quickly deciding that she should not be rewarded for her transgression, the devotees in the row from which she was trying to escape grab hold of her. With considerable heaving and tugging, she is once again back where she belongs. All this happens in the blink of an eye, and when we turn to face Maharaj again, we find that the line has started moving.

On a dais placed between the two mazes sit a group of kirtan singers who start singing *bhajans* or devotional songs. Some of these are familiar to us and others are new. From time to time, the lead singer relinquishes his or her role to a new singer and in this way a constant stream of songs keeps us distracted from the aches and pains creeping up our legs. One song catches my attention. It is a Bengali song in which an elder is complaining that Krishna plays his flute and everyone leaves his or her task and runs to him. Apparently the elder has told Krishna to not play his enchanting music, but we all know that Krishna does not listen to anyone. I stand and daydream and think of how the cowherds must have been keeping an eye on the cows grazing in the pasture and how the milkmaids must have been milking their cows and churning their butter when suddenly, this enchanting music came wafting through the dense forests of Vrindavan and they all dropped what they were doing and moved towards the source of the music. I wonder how many household chores have been neglected today as the devotees around me have come to see their enchanting Lord. The song haunts me and I feel I do not have to go to Vrindavan to witness the devotion of Krishna's playmates because I see it before my very eyes.

Gradually, we inch along on both sides, zigzagging through the maze, heading towards our final destination: Maharaj. At the exit points for both sides is a space where the volunteers reign supreme. Trying to be fair to both sides, they allow one person from the left and one person from the right to approach Maharaj. Of course, in many cases there are couples or families who wish to see Maharaj together. We watch a family with seven members exiting the maze to our left and taking up a lot of time as each member pays his or her respects to Maharaj. We watch with envy and resentment as the queue in the left maze seems to move fast because it has just disgorged a large family. Our queue seems to be stuck. We crane our necks and see one solitary widow exit from our maze before the volunteer turns to the left and says it is now their turn. We grumble inwardly and argue that this is just not fair. Suddenly, a cluster of lozenges hits us and we look up with joy. While we have been busy looking left and right and counting the number of people who have been allowed on each side, we have forgotten to look at Maharaj.

Perhaps reading our minds, he has decided to take a break and fill our laps with goodies. This is followed by peace water, and by now Bonie, Aunt Dolly, and I are close enough for generous sprays of water to land on our heads. Once again, we are focused on our goal: Maharaj. Gone are the worries, the jealousies, the resentments, the complaints as our hearts sing with joy and our heads buzz with his blessings.

Finally, Aunt, Bonie, and I exit the maze and find ourselves under the strict control of a volunteer who gestures to us to wait. We see an elderly lady diving into her bag and trying to get something out of it. She has already placed a garland of marigolds around Maharaj's neck. She has a box of sweets, packets of incense sticks, and some money. All this is taking up a considerable amount of time and the volunteers are urging her to hurry as thousands of devotees are still waiting. Maharaj is looking at her with a benign smile. The lady seems to be wrestling with something that is too big and which refuses to come out of her bag because the mouth of her bag is too small for the item. The bag refuses to cooperate and the lady refuses to give up. A tug of war appears to have ensued as we are chomping at the bit and our patience is running thin. Suddenly, the lady's frail legs give way and she sits down on the ground. As she hits the ground, her fisted hand emerges from the bag in a show of victory.

"Here it is!" she says, triumphantly. "I bought it especially for Maharaj. How can I not offer it to him?"

We see what looks like a handful of potatoes.

Utterly bewildered by this, I ask my aunt, "Why is she giving potatoes to Maharaj?"

"They are not potatoes," says Aunt. "It is a fruit called *sobeda*."

Relieved to find that the lady's fall has not given rise to a medical emergency, the volunteers haul her up and she offers the fruit to Maharaj before placing her forehead on his feet. Everyone is most irritated with her, everyone but Maharaj. He takes the garland she has placed around his neck and places it around her neck. He places his palm on her head and gives her a smile that lights up the stage. He puts a dot of sacred ash on her forehead and fills her cupped hands with sweets and fruits. All this time, the elderly lady is looking at him tenderly with her eyes streaming with devotion and gratitude. Finally, she is pried away by the volunteers and sent to the lunch table where devotees can pick up a lunch packet.

Eventually it is our turn and Aunt ushers Bonie and me to the stage. We quickly offer our garlands to Maharaj. Bonie offers sweets, Aunt offers incense, and I offer oranges. We place our foreheads with reverence on his beautiful feet, and receive garlands, sweets, sacred ash and blessings from him. I look up and see that winsome smile and know that I have never seen anyone more beautiful than Maharaj. The volunteers gently prod us to leave and we move away.

After picking up our lunch packets, we come out of the gates of the mansion and look for the man who was keeping an eye on our slippers. We give him our ticket and he retrieves our slippers for us. While waiting for Aunt to pay him, I ask a devotee who is just entering if he could tell me the time. He says it is 3:30 p.m. It is hard to believe that we have been there for ten hours. We were tired and worn out by the time we exited the left maze, but the brief interaction with Maharaj has wiped out all the strain of the arduous wait. We feel rejuvenated, as though waking up after a long rest. I wonder if Bonie and I feel this way because we are young. But when I look at my aunt, her cheeks are glowing and her eyes are shining with happiness. Feeling almost light-headed with joy, we hail a cab and go home.

Chapter 14: The Festival of Goddess Durga

It is October 1972 and this will be the first time Bonie and I will be in Bengal during Durga Puja. This is the most important festival for Bengalis, and much effort goes into the preparations preceding this celebration. The artisans of Kumortuli spend months sculpting clay images of the group of gods and goddesses who will visit the makeshift pavilions or *pandals* of Bengal. Every neighborhood of Calcutta will host a celebration or *puja*. The young men of our Keyatala neighborhood go from door to door raising funds for Durga Puja.

I am thrilled to hear that school will be closed for several weeks during this time. We hear from our friends about how their mothers will buy many new clothes for them, how they will go from *pandal* to *pandal* feasting their eyes on the beautiful images of the goddess, Durga, how the *pandals* will be illuminated with multicolored lights, how the priests will chant mantras during *anjali* when lay people will offer flowers to the goddess, how the boys of the neighborhood will dance the *dhunochi* dance to the rhythm of the *dhakis* playing the drums, how Durga will finally slay the demon Mahisasura, and how the festival will end on the tenth day of Vijaya Dashami with everyone saying goodbye to Goddess Durga and people paying respects to their elders and feeding the children delicious sweets.

Bonie and I listen with open mouths as we learn that Durga will arrive on a lion and will be accompanied by her two daughters and two sons: Lakshmi, the goddess of wealth; Saraswati, the goddess of learning; Kartik, the god of war; and Ganesh, the remover of obstacles. Durga is famous for having killed the demon Mahisasura, but in Bengal this festival is celebrated as a homecoming. Durga is seen as the daughter coming home to visit her parents with her children. During this festival, many daughters leave the homes of their husbands and come to their parents' home to visit the relatives and friends with whom they spent their childhood.

My sister and I are looking forward to these holidays when Mother tells us that we will spend Durga Puja at Deoghar. So, once again, we board a train to Jasidih and go to our ashram. As in March, Aunt Dolly leaves early with Bonie and me and the rest of the family arrives later. The events are similar to what we have experienced during the fire ceremony in March except that in one corner of the inner sanctum of the pavilion is a statue of Durga riding on a lion with her trident spearing the chest of the demon. Her four children are with her. The image is placed so that it has its back to us when we sit in the corner where we had sat during the fire ceremony.

"I cannot see the goddess," complains Bonie, but Aunt Dolly tells us we are sitting in the best spot.

As in March, there is a rush for seats and many of the faces we became familiar with earlier this year start surfacing. The elders are very happy to see my aunt with her two obedient nieces. Maharaj arrives dressed in brocades and silks, bedecked with jewels from top to toe, and begins to perform the rituals that are needed for the ceremony. We watch from where we are sitting, and I realize why my aunt has placed us in that corner. We can see Maharaj. We have forgotten all about the clay goddess as we watch the divine radiant form of our guru before us.

Maharaj in my grandmother's house. Calcutta, 1990s

Each morning, during the festival, we offer flowers to the goddess while repeating the mantras after Maharaj. At the end of each session, Maharaj stands in front of the image and performs *arati* by waving in circular motions a variety of objects before the goddess: lit lamps, a conch with water in it, a cloth, a hand fan, and a flower are some of the things I note. He is just a couple of feet away from us and we can see him clearly. His face glows as he moves his right hand delicately in circles with the lit lamp all the while ringing the small bell held in his left hand. Other monks and novices are playing a variety of percussion instruments, including drums, cymbals, and gongs. Some are blowing the conch while women are ululating. These are all sacred and auspicious sounds in Bengali and Indian culture. Maharaj, in the meantime, continues with the *arati* and seems to be almost swaying. It is a gentle swaying, as though he is shifting his weight from one foot to another, but there is something more to it. He seems oblivious to the rest of the world--all the hundreds of people watching him, all the noises surrounding him, all the rituals he seems to be performing with the utmost perfection. He is there and yet not there. It is almost as though he has merged with the goddess he is worshipping. There are times when we cannot tell who is the goddess: Maharaj or the clay image?

There is the usual rush to the kitchen for lunch in the afternoons and Maharaj often comes to drop a sweet *roshogolla* into our cupped hands. At night, we line up to pay our respects to him. We do not have to worry about whether our mother bought new clothes for us because, along with many other devotees, Bonie and I receive new saris from Maharaj. On the eighth day of the festival, one of the monks tells Aunt Dolly to bring Bonie to the ashram for *Kumari puja*. Aunt takes Bonie to the ashram at the appointed time and my sister is dressed in a sari over which she keeps tripping even though she is excited to be the center of attraction. That evening she is worshipped as the goddess Durga. Apparently, this is a ceremony that is commonly held during Durga Puja. After she returns in her red sari and some tacky costume jewelry, my sister has her nose high up in the air and barely condescends to speak to me. I tease her mercilessly until she gives up acting superior and regains her normal self. I help her change into a frock, and we run to see what is happening at the ashram.

As the festival nears the end, my parents, grandmother, and uncle arrive. On the last day, after we have all witnessed the final rituals of the *puja*, we stand in a long line to pay our respects to Maharaj. Bonie and I are very proud of ourselves as we are dressed in the saris that Maharaj has given us. Many people in the queue are also wearing saris given to them by Maharaj, but my sister and I usually do not wear saris and today we feel all grown up. Maharaj is glowing with the gentle luminescence of the full moon and our hearts are full of bliss. We pay our respects and come home with our hands filled with sweets. We are sad to say goodbye to Maharaj and the ashram as we head back to Calcutta and school, but we have no regrets that we did not spend Durga Puja in Calcutta.

When we come home, we hear about our friends' thrilling experiences, but we do not know how to even begin to explain to them our experience of being with Maharaj during the festival. Even at that young age I know that no one will understand how I feel. This inexpressible feeling must be experienced. Words fail me when I try to convey the happiness we bask in when we are in Maharaj's presence.

There are years when we are unable to go to the ashram for Durga Puja and have to be content with celebrating the festival in Calcutta. But none of the attractions the city offers can hold a candle to what we have witnessed at our ashram. The bright lights cannot rival the radiance of Maharaj, the Hindi songs played on loudspeakers are jarring to ears that have heard Maharaj reciting sacred mantras, the priest's *arati* pales in comparison to our guru's worship of Durga, and the joy of attending the entertainment provided by the local clubs cannot compete with the joy we experience while running around in our guru's ashram as we go from event to event. It is only after we have witnessed Puja in Calcutta that we understand why our elders take us each year to witness Maharaj's Durga Puja.

Chapter 15: Celebrating Maharaj's Birthday

The months slide by and towards the end of the year we attend another event similar to what we experienced on Guru Purnima. At this event, we celebrate Maharaj's birthday. Bonie and I learn that his birthday is on a different day each year because the event is calculated according to the lunar calendar. This is a new concept for us. However, as we begin to participate in various events and festivals, we note that all these important days are calculated according to the lunar calendar. Only Christmas is on the 25th of December, but that is a Christian holiday even though our family celebrates it with gusto.

On Maharaj's birthday, Bonie and I go in the evening with Father and Grandmother because Mother and Aunt Dolly have gone to visit Uncle Sankar in Dhanbad. Father comes home early from work, and we take a taxi to the same house where less than six months ago Bonie and I had gone with Aunt Dolly for Guru Purnima. By now, we know what to do and after depositing our shoes and sandals we head to Rishi and buy four flower garlands for Maharaj. This time we will line up in the maze which is on the left side because Father is with us and we are going to see Maharaj as a family. Crowds throng the venue. Since we have come in the evening, we have missed the morning schedule of events during which various rituals were performed to worship both Maharaj's guru and Maharaj. At this time of the day, thousands are lined up on both sides with the sole purpose of paying their respects to Maharaj, who is sitting on the dais receiving people as they come up to him to offer their respects.

"Looks like it will be a long night," says a man behind us and Father acknowledges his comment with a smile.

On the platform between the two mazes, the kirtan singers are singing one song after another and that gives us all the energy to keep going. Father has a good sense of humor and keeps us entertained with stories, Grandmother has tremendous patience and is willing to stand for hours to see her guru, and Bonie and I are young and happy to be with our loved ones.

"I am sure Mother and Aunt Dolly are missing not being here," says our grandmother.

"We can call them tomorrow and tell them that we did come," says Father.

Aunty Reba and Uncle Arun are leaving the arena when they see us and come to talk to us.

"Where is Dolly? Where is Lily?" they ask, and we explain their absence. They say they have been in line for almost six hours, and we tell them to go home and rest. Wishing us luck, they leave.

The devotional singing stops and there is a long pause. Father wonders aloud why the singing has stopped, and I tell him that they are waiting for the next singer to get ready to sing. Bonie starts narrating our experiences from when we came for Guru Purnima and has everyone laughing with her story of how the elderly grandma got stuck under the bamboo. Just as this story finishes, a wavering sound begins to blare from the microphone. At first, we think there is a technical problem. But soon we realize that the person who is the lead singer is obviously very nervous, and she is singing in a tremulous voice.

"This person cannot sing at all," says a matronly woman in a loud voice standing in the row before us. Hearing this, the woman standing next to her begins to laugh loudly in a strange and rather unbecoming manner. This triggers a wave of laughter among those of us nearby and a couple of volunteers come to our section of the crowd to find out if all is well. We try to stop our giggles and look serious. But others behind us keep asking what happened.

It is around this time that I see a woman I have seen on almost every occasion when I have gone to see Maharaj. Aunt Dolly had told me that someone had given her the nickname "The President." She is a devotee of Maharaj and there is something striking about her. As poor as a church mouse, as old as the moon woman, she goes to almost every house Maharaj visits in Calcutta. No one knows who has named her or when she got that name. No one knows who she is or where she came from. As I see her hovering outside the maze, it seems to me as though she has always been there with her silver mane and her beautiful ancient face wrinkled like cracked porcelain. Not saying much, she finds a spot from where she can see Maharaj. On those old bones she stands for hours, afraid to blink for fear she will miss even a glimpse of the Radiant One. With all her heart and soul she watches, undistracted by the crowds around her. I wonder at her amazing concentration and her devotion to her guru. She is always alone in her widow's sari. Perhaps she has no one--no one but the only one who matters to her: this luminescent being from whom she cannot tear her eyes away. There is a quiet dignity about her that is charming and makes me respect her.

The queue has been moving quite fast all this time, and the tremulous voice has been replaced by a robust voice which is belting out some devotional songs with catchy beats and rhythms. The crowd is invigorated and some of us sing along. I notice that the maze on the other side is not as full as ours because women and children unaccompanied by a male wish to get home before the city buses stop running. As I am wondering about why I am always in the slow queue, a cluster of lozenges hits me on my chest and we look up to see Maharaj standing at the edge of the dais throwing sweets and candy at us. All boredom and fatigue vanish, and I see that we are just three rows away from Maharaj. Father catches several apples and Maharaj sees him because my father is very tall. After spraying peace water on the crowds, Maharaj sits down and the queue begins to move.

A holy lady, dressed in saffron robes, is in the second row. We presume she is holy because of her robes, but what follows makes us doubt her piety. Suddenly, without warning, she ducks under the bamboo poles and makes a beeline for Maharaj. Before we can process what is happening, she is already offering her garland to Maharaj. The crowd roars its disapproval but it is too late. I am shocked because as a teenager I have high standards and am extremely judgmental.

"How could she do that?" I exclaim.

"Perhaps she wasn't feeling well," says my older, wiser, and more compassionate father, but I am outraged. Bonie is laughing and I glare at her.

She says, "What?"

I say, "It is no laughing matter."

Bonie says, "Don't be silly. I am laughing at the woman with the odd laugh."

Only then do I hear the same woman laughing and laughing her strange and highly inappropriate laugh. Laughter is infectious and it puts a smile back on my lips.

I look to see if my grandmother is laughing, but what I see shocks me. My grandmother is as tall as my father and very strong. Her face has a strange look on it. She is light-skinned and I can see that her face is flushed. Her eyes look glazed. I have never seen her ill, and I feel a chill run down my spine as I realize she is about to faint. I grab my father's attention and he at once realizes the gravity of the situation. My mind races on as fear grips me. What are we going to do? What if she dies? We are still three rows away from the dais and it will take us at least an hour to get to Maharaj. She cannot wait that long. But even if we decide to go home without meeting Maharaj, how can we get out of the maze? How will we take her home?

Seated from left to right: Mother, Maharaj, Father, Aunt Dolly
Standing: Uncle Sankar and my grandmother. Malda, 1980s

As these thoughts race through my mind, a strange thing happens. Suddenly, three or four volunteers come rushing to us and say, "Come, come. Maharaj is calling you." We are amazed! No one knows us and no one knows that my grandmother has taken ill. Maharaj is far from us and cannot even see us because he is sitting on his sofa and we are obscured from his view. But there is no time to ask these questions or wait for answers. The bamboo of the side of the aisle is lifted, and we are rushed to the front to Maharaj. We pay our respects to him and he showers us with many blessings, smiles, fruits, and sweets. His palm lands on all our heads and we are on Cloud 9. As we are ushered out by the volunteers, I look at my grandmother and see that she is looking normal. We sit on the steps of the veranda and I ask her what happened. She says, "I don't know. I felt I was blacking out."

Father says we need to go because it is close to midnight. We get up and stretch our tired legs. A few stragglers are still walking in and buying garlands.

I wonder when they will finish paying their respects to Maharaj. Bonie goes to Rishi and asks, "When will you go and see Maharaj?"

"Very soon, little sister, very soon," he replies.

The man who has been keeping an eye on our shoes laughs and says, "He is usually the last one in the line, but he keeps the best garland for himself." We all laugh, and Rishi looks happy.

"How long will this go on?" asks Father.

"Sometimes until dawn," says Rishi.

We retrieve our shoes and sandals and head out. The streets are dark and lonely, the shops are shuttered for the night, the rickshaw pullers are asleep on the sidewalks, a stray dog howls. Stepping into what seems to be almost a menacing world after having spent six hours in a safe space throbbing with songs, filled with people, and lit by Maharaj's presence is challenging, but we feel safe because Father is with us. Grandmother is nervous and repeating two words under her breath: "*Jai Guru, Jai Guru!*"

Before we step any further, a taxi halts in front of Father and we pile in. He is relieved and says, "I am glad we could get a taxi or else we would have had to walk home. I could have easily walked home but it would have been too much for you all."

"We should not worry about these things because Mother says that Maharaj always takes care of us," I pipe in.

"But when does Maharaj rest?" Bonie asks, puzzled with the timeline of events. "He comes to the stage around noon. And Rishi says people keep meeting him until dawn!"

"Well, that's what makes him special," says Grandmother. "He can do what we cannot. Great yogis like him can do many things if they want to."

"Like Superman in my comic books?" asks Bonie, and we all laugh.

"Yes," says Grandmother. "Maharaj is our Superman."

I reflect on how this great yogi, as Grandmother calls him, can spend hours blessing people, allowing thousands to touch his feet, filling their hands with sweets and fruits, accepting their garlands and then placing them around the necks of the devotees, getting up from time to time to throw goodies to the waiting crowds, putting the needs of his devotees before his own needs, and trying to bring joy and peace to all of us. He seems to me to be the epitome of patience and compassion. I have noticed while standing in line how each devotee receives his or her due. How can he treat everyone equally and go through the same rituals again and again so that we all feel that our long wait has been worth it? And how did he know that

Grandmother was about to faint? My thoughts overwhelm me, and I know what I have witnessed is special.

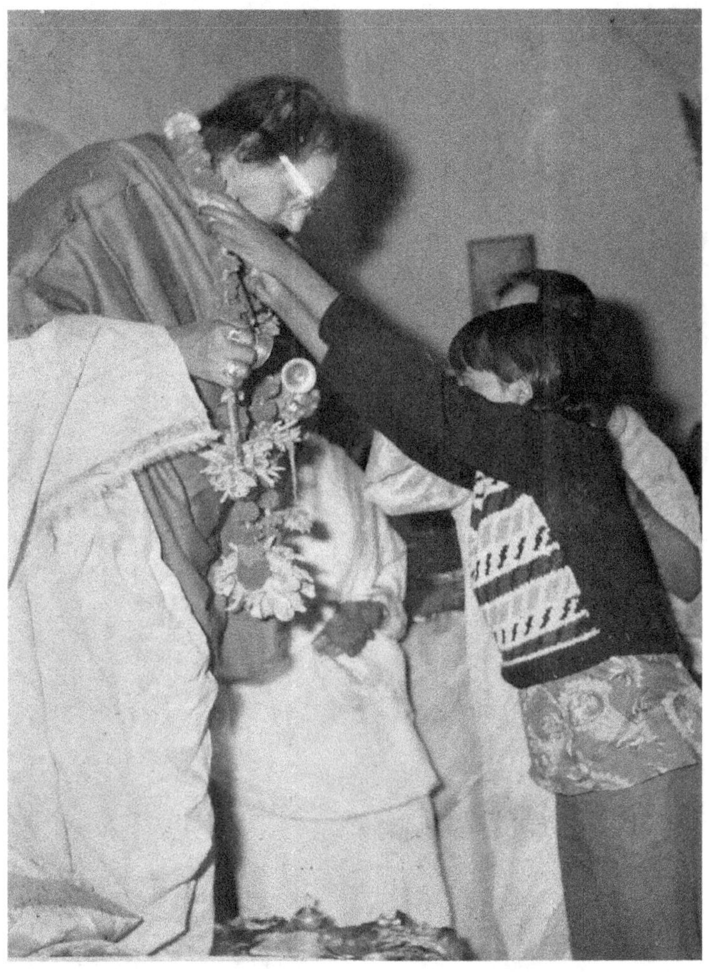

Offering a garland to Maharaj after kirtan. Dehradun, 1971

Chapter 16: Maharaj at the Airport

Often Maharaj is out of town as he roams all over India staying in each place for three days or less. There are devotees in various cities and small towns. Sometimes devotees follow Maharaj and go from place to place to savor his presence. Mother and Aunt Dolly often go on such trips, sometimes alone and sometimes together. Father has work, Bonie and I have school, Uncle Sankar is posted outside Calcutta, and Grandmother stays home and runs the household. But whenever we hear that Maharaj will be in Calcutta, we do not miss an opportunity to see him.

Bonie's sketch of Maharaj wearing a Nepali cap. Maharaj's signature can be seen partially on the right.

There are times when we cannot wait for him to arrive at the house where he will reside, and we run to the Calcutta airport and find a small group of devotees waiting for him. Maharaj travels frequently and the airport staff are familiar with the sight of his devotees lining up in the airport lounge to meet him. While waiting for him, the teenager in me feels self-conscious as strangers, who are there to catch a plane, stare at us and wonder what we are doing with flowers and garlands and boxes of sweets and baskets of fruits. I look at the people who have come to see Maharaj. It is a motley crowd ranging from highly sophisticated wealthy devotees to poor elderly widows in flip flops. There are men discussing politics, women comparing notes on their children's educational progress, elders counting their *malas*, and children running around playing hide and seek; there are grandparents speaking lovingly to grandchildren and parents rebuking their children and men breaking out into loud arguments and women complaining about the long lines. So much is happening around me that I am thoroughly entertained.

Aunty Reba, who is a good friend of our family, comes and stands with us. She is excited because she has made something special for Maharaj. She takes it gently out of her bag and shows us a delicate sandalwood *mala* which she will offer to Maharaj. I watch in wonder and think of how many days it must have taken her to make this mala. She tells us how she sprinkled drops of water on the sandalwood disc and then rubbed the sandalwood stick on the disc in circles to make sandalwood paste. Next, she twirled the paste into little balls and then dried them to form little beads. Before the beads had fully hardened, she pierced them with a needle so a string could pass through each bead. Then she strung the beads on a fine string to make this fragrant *mala* to offer to Maharaj. I am in awe of her patience, perseverance, and devotion. Knowing that Maharaj will wear it only for a few moments before giving it back to her or to someone else, I am amazed by the fact that someone would go to such lengths to make something that would give her only a few moments of happiness.

At this point, Aunty Reba's brother catches her attention by waving to her. Telling us to keep her place in the line, she goes away. Given an opportunity to voice my misgivings, I whisper to Aunt Dolly and ask her why Aunty Reba would take on such a gargantuan project when she knew that the *mala* would be around Maharaj's neck only for a couple of minutes. My aunt laughs and tries to explain that the happiness is not confined to the few moments when Maharaj is wearing the *mala*. The happiness lies in the whole project. Aunty Reba was excited when the idea came to her to make such a *mala*. All the long hours of work she put into it were filled with joy. At each stage, her joy increased as the progress of the project became associated with her seeing Maharaj. Each step seemed to bring her closer and closer to Maharaj. Finally, her task was finished, and she put the sandalwood *mala* carefully in a plastic bag and put the bag in her purse. Now the *mala* is waiting for its final destination.

"Everything is impermanent," says my aunt. "Even we will die one day. But that does not mean we do not live each day, does it?"

I like what she says even though I do not fully understand it. I am relieved that Aunty Reba's feelings will not be hurt when Maharaj gives the *mala* to someone else. Years later I will remember this conversation when I hear the saying "It is not the destination but the journey that matters."

Perhaps Maharaj reads my mind when Aunty Reba places the *mala* around his neck. He gives her a garland of marigolds and the sandalwood *mala* sits around his neck for a long time until it is my turn to touch his feet. As I lift my head to look into his eyes, time stands still. He has a way of looking at me, not really looking at me but looking through me. It feels as though with those luminous eyes, he perceives the whole: my past and my present, my mind and my soul. All this happens in the blink of an eye, and I get up and move away as the person behind me kneels down to receive Maharaj's blessings. I feel disoriented and go and sit on one of the airport chairs. Something is missing. I come out of my daze and remember that I had offered a heavy garland of marigolds. Usually, Maharaj gives back the garland we offer him. But my shoulders are light. I reach up and my fingers close on small fragile beads. I look at the *mala* that hangs around my neck and am overjoyed as the fragrance of sandalwood gently kisses my nose.

Aunt Dolly comes looking for me and sees the *mala* and laughs. All she says is, "See?" Words are not needed to explain such happenings and by now I know not to talk about such experiences.

Aunty Reba comes up to me and is happy to see her *mala* hanging around my neck. She does not know about my misgivings. I watch her face and see that there is not the slightest attachment to the *mala* she has painstakingly worked on for months. I marvel at all I see and know there is much to learn from Maharaj's devotees. On the surface they behave like ordinary human beings. They can be angry and kind, joyous and miserable, humble and arrogant, obedient and feisty. But under the surface hides something that I glimpse from time to time. They have been coming to this great sage for so long, that some of his qualities have seeped into them. I see glimpses of his energy, strength, compassion, kindness, joy, contentment, and love in this crowd of many faces. These qualities may not be permanent, but I see sparks of them as certain situations arise and I think, "Some of these devotees are supermen and superwomen, too."

Preparations for feet washing ceremony (*charan puja*). Dehradun, 1971

Chapter 17: Trip to Badrinath

It is 1973 and Maharaj will be going with a small group of devotees to Badrinath, a sacred place high up in the Himalayas. Maharaj has ashrams, hospitals, schools, and charitable institutions in many places in India. This year he will attend the inaugural ceremony of his new ashram in Badrinath. Most of my family members have already seen this place visited by pilgrims from all over India. To be present while Maharaj performs the fire ceremony for three days in a place as sacred as Badrinath is a temptation Mother cannot resist. Grandmother stays back in Calcutta to hold down the fort while Father, Mother, Aunt Dolly, Bonie, and I take the Doon Express from Calcutta and arrive at Dehradun.

After a short stay in the military cantonment, where Maharaj had visited us and initiated me in 1971, we are on our way to Badrinath by road. Father's friends have arranged for a military jeep to take us, and on the way we stop overnight at places where the Army has rest houses. The journey is picturesque. As the road begins to wind up the majestic mountains, I note that on one side we have the rising mountains and on the other side is the gorge. The roads blasted into the Himalayas are narrow with hairpin bends. Buses loaded with passengers, luggage, goats and chicken come careening around the bends and it is a wonder that they do not slide into the gorge. Apparently, sometimes they do. The very thought sends a shiver up my spine. As we climb towards our destination, we stop from time to time and look down at the magnificent scenery. Deep down in the gorge runs my namesake. Finally, I have seen the river I have been named after. The family story is repeated. I have heard it many times, but this seems to be a fitting location to hear it again.

"When I was an instructor at the Indian Military Academy in Dehradun," says my father, "I used to bring the cadets up these Himalayan mountains for trekking. When I first saw this river, I told myself that if I ever had a daughter, I would name her Alaknanda."

"Were you and Mother married at that time?" asks Bonie.

"No. That was long before I met your mother. But I never forgot."

We stand silently, drinking in Nature's abundance. The puffy cumulous clouds sailing in the azure sky, the emerald Alaknanda snaking its way down below, the mountain slopes draped in green foliage, the wildflowers sporting flamboyant colors, and, above all, the humming drumming almost deafening sound of silence.

A bus with passengers spilling out of its windows blares its horn and breaks my reverie. We munch on a few snacks and climb back into the jeep. There are times when two buses are negotiating a bend. One is going up and the other is coming down the road. We stop and watch with our hearts in our mouths. One false step and the bus on the gorge-side of the road will plunge into the Alaknanda. Fortunately, everyone is safe, and we do not witness any accidents.

Mother outside the temple of Badrinath

After an overnight stay at Rudraprayag, we drive on to Badrinath and arrive there in time for a late lunch. The military has provided us with accommodation in their guest house. After we have checked in and eaten

79

lunch, Mother takes us to Maharaj's ashram where we meet a monk whom she addresses as Bhabanida. He is in charge and has supervised the construction of the ashram. He seems to know my parents and gives us a warm welcome. He says that Maharaj is scheduled to arrive the next day and tells us to come in the afternoon. We go back to the guest house, eat dinner, and go to bed.

We are up early next morning and after a quick shower and change of clothes, we visit the famous temple of Badrinath. The temple is very impressive with a colorful façade. A flight of stairs takes us to the main arena. In the background stand Himalayan peaks where the snow never melts. A priest, who knows my parents, smiles when he sees them and takes charge of our group. At that time of the day, the temple is not very crowded, and I am glad that there is no shoving and jostling from energetic pilgrims. We pay our respects to the deity before circumambulating the temple three times.

Father enthusiastically decides to take Bonie and me to the hot springs because it will be a novel experience for us. Mother and Aunt Dolly head back to the guest house, while my father leads the way to a bathing pool where the water is bubbling and steaming. We are amazed at what we see and want to bathe. Promising to bring us another day, Father takes us to the guest house where after a quick lunch we go to the ashram to wait for Maharaj's arrival. A few devotees have arrived, and they introduce themselves to us and ask us about our accommodation. As the elders are chatting, suddenly there is a commotion at the gate, and we run out to see Maharaj's car pulling up followed by a motorcade. Maharaj steps out looking as fresh as a rose. His smiling eyes light up as he surveys the small crowd of devotees. My father is right in front of the crowd. Maharaj asks my father, "When did you arrive?" as they make their way into the ashram. We all follow as Maharaj sits down on the chair in his room. Monks and lay people, who have travelled by car, come in and the room that had seemed large and empty is now full.

We watch the monks performing *charan puja*, and then we form a line to pay our respects to Maharaj. Afterwards, we all sit close to him and some of the elders ask him about his journey. Maharaj says a few words. Bonie, who is sitting right near his feet, begins to massage Maharaj's feet. The adults laugh gently, and I hear whispers of approval. Maharaj looks at Bonie with an amused smile. I am embarrassed by my kid sister pushing herself into the limelight and am worried that this act of hers signals the start of her never-ending campaign to get initiated. With her little eight-year-old hands, Bonie is kneading Maharaj's feet as though her life depends on it. Maharaj's eyes begin to twinkle with merriment as he tries and fails to hide his amusement. With a smile, he says, "*Eto pada seva! E to na porei pash.*" Everyone bursts into laughter. I whisper to Aunt Dolly to ask what he had said. She replies, "Maharaj said Bonie is doing such a good job massaging his feet that she will pass all her exams without studying." Maharaj is witty, and Bonie and I are still young and not quite versatile enough in Bengali to catch his witticisms. Strangely enough, my sister does not mention initiation. After spending some time with all of us, Maharaj retires.

The next day will be a busy day when the fire ceremony will begin. We are all about to leave the ashram to go back and rest at our guest house when Bhabanida, the monk we had met on our arrival, calls Mother and says something to her. Mother comes away looking pleased. That night when we are in bed, she tells us that Maharaj wants Bonie to be the *Kumari* next day.

"Will I get lots of jewelry like I did in Deoghar?" asks a sleepy Bonie.

"Badrinath is a sacred place," says Aunt Dolly. "To be a *Kumari* at the fire ceremony held here on the auspicious occasion of the inauguration of Maharaj's ashram is a great honor." Bonie and I nod our heads without quite understanding, turn over and fall asleep.

The next morning, we get ready quickly because we must be at the ashram before the activities start. It is very cold and both Bonie and I are wearing sweaters and slacks. Mother goes inside the building of the ashram to dress Bonie in a sari, while the rest of us wait with other devotees at the *mandap* or pavilion where the fire ceremony will be held. After some time, Bonie comes dressed in a sari with some bangles and necklaces that a devotee has provided. She looks very proud of herself, and I try to stifle my giggles.

"What?" asks Bonie, looking at me suspiciously, and I burst out laughing. The sari is a little wide for her and the pleats that have been tucked into her waist make her look funny.

"You are the funniest looking *Kumari* I have ever seen," I say, unable to resist the temptation to tease her.

"You are just jealous because Maharaj did not choose you," says Bonie and walks off in a huff.

Mother glares at me and I wipe off the grin from my face. The audience loves Bonie. The women go to her and admire her jewelry. One fixes Bonie's sari while another adjusts the fake tiara on her head. The monks begin to come to the *mandap*, signaling Maharaj's arrival. We watch as Maharaj joins the monks. They stand in a group led by Maharaj. Bonie is made to stand in front of Maharaj. He bends down and tells her what she must do.

The Himalayan winds are blowing, and we are all snuggling inside our coats and jackets while poor Bonie is shivering. Maharaj turns to a young monk and says something to him. The monk comes running to Mother, takes Bonie's jacket from her and gives it to Bonie to wear. My sister looks relieved. Once again, Maharaj says something to the same monk. This time he goes into the building of the ashram and comes back with a couple of large leaves. The small brass pot that Bonie was holding in her hands is now covered with the leaves before it is placed in her hands again. The winds bite at our fingers and we all have our gloves and mittens on, but Bonie was holding the cold metal pot with her bare hands until Maharaj saw her shivering and tried what he could do to provide her with some relief. Finally, the group seems ready to go.

Chanting in chorus, led by Bonie the *Kumari*, the group of monks slowly circumambulates the inner sanctum of the *mandap* three times while we watch from outside the pavilion. Bonie is very careful and takes each step with great deliberation so as not to trip on her sari. She looks really cute and everyone falls in love with her. I, of course, am terrified she will drop the pot or trip and fall or start crying or do something that will be considered catastrophic and then how will I ever show my face to the world! But thankfully, all goes well and my sister is relieved of her duties as Maharaj enters the inner sanctum and sits down to start the fire ceremony.

Bonie walks up to me showing off her fake jewelry and looking as proud as Punch while everyone is patting her on her back and telling her what a good job she has done. Aunt Dolly takes her into the main building to change. Putting the sari and accessories into a bag, my aunt dresses Bonie in her regular clothes. By now the ceremony has begun and we are all focused on Maharaj. Surrounded by snowcapped Himalayan mountains, we listen to the chants that have been chanted for centuries and watch Maharaj sitting in the midst of a group of saffron-robed monks performing oblations and saying *swaha* while pouring ghee into the fire. The wind whips the branches of the giant evergreen trees, and patches of sunshine paint patterns on the ashram grounds whenever the sun peeks out from behind the clouds. I feel as though I have been transported into the world of ancient India where, thousands of years ago, great sages sat and performed the fire ceremony in this manner, chanting the same hymns while offering worship and oblations.

That night, when we go to pay our respects to Maharaj, his palm lands heavily on Bonie's head and we all laugh because we know that Maharaj is pleased with her performance. He looks at Mother and tells her that he will be initiating a small group of people the next day and she was to bring Bonie

Maharaj blessing Bonie. Boston, 1990

so he could initiate her. Bonie gives him a sheepish grin. It has taken almost two years of constant nagging on her part for her wish to be granted. I do not know if my sister will walk or fly home when we go back to our guest house. After being the star of the show as a *Kumari* in the morning and now with Maharaj's special blessings, will she even deign to look at a puny mortal like me? But secretly I am very pleased and happy for Bonie because she may be my pesky kid sister, but I love her. We go home and I drift off to sleep thinking about Maharaj's compassionate actions in trying to protect Bonie from the biting cold.

Bonie is initiated the next day and we are all very proud of her.

"I bet you have already forgotten your mantra," I tease her.

"No, I have not," retorts Bonie. "And anyway, Maharaj wrote it down for me and told me that I could ask Mother if I forget. So there!"

83

"I bet you can't count on your fingers the way you are supposed to," I say, remembering that it took me a little time to learn how to count 108 times on my fingers.

Bonie looks a little confused and begins to count on her fingers as fast as she can. Seeing her look of consternation, I say, "I'll teach you, silly! It's very easy. Come here. Let me show you. I was just teasing you."

I am happy to have the upper hand at this and start showing off in front of Bonie. I tell her not to share the mantra with anyone even though it may be hard for her to keep a secret and she may be dying to tell her best friend. I tell her that friends at school may tease her and try to provoke her into revealing the mantra but no matter what, she is not to tell anyone what Maharaj had whispered in her ear. Then I show her how to count on both hands and how to stop at 108.

All day long, while others watch the fire ceremony, Bonie furiously repeats her mantra while keeping count on her fingers. She is worried that she will forget her mantra or forget how to keep count on her fingers. At night, when we are sitting at Maharaj's feet, he sees her intent on counting and suppresses an affectionate smile several times.

On the third and last day of the fire ceremony, we get up early and go to bathe in the hot springs. It is a unique and exhilarating experience for Bonie and me, and we do not wish to leave the pool. Eventually, we go back to the guest house and then to the ashram to enjoy our last day with Maharaj. The elder devotees at the ashram ask Bonie if she remembers her mantra, and she gives them a shy smile and nods. "I even know how to count," she says proudly, and everyone laughs and some even reach down and pinch her cheeks.

That night, when we are saying goodbye to Maharaj, he asks my father to join his motorcade and follow his car on our way back to the plains. So, the next morning we wait in our military jeep for Maharaj's car to start and then follow him as his motorcade winds its way down the Himalayan mountains. Savoring the spectacular scenery of the tall mountains and the snaking Alaknanda River, we drive for a couple of hours before stopping for a break.

Apparently arrangements have been made for Maharaj to stop at a rest house for an hour or so. We go to the rest house and enter the room where Maharaj is sitting. After paying our respects to him, we sit on the floor. Maharaj is giving instructions to someone, and soon devotees who are part of our group begin to bring lots of food from their cars. There are sweets and fruits and a variety of other goodies that Maharaj loads us with before making *jhal muri* or spicy puffed rice. He places a big bowl on his lap and fills it with puffed rice. Into this he pours several spicy ingredients and mixes it all up with a look of delight on his face. Then he asks us to come and get it. One by one, we go and kneel with cupped hands and he fills our hands to the brim. Everyone is eating and no one needs lunch after this. I notice that Maharaj does not eat anything.

Maharaj giving sweets to devotees. Barkakana, 1989

Someone brings in crates and crates of Coca Cola and Maharaj gives us each a bottle. Among the group are two elderly widows who are fasting that day and who refuse to break their fast even though Maharaj keeps trying to feed them. They take what he gives them and put it all away in plastic bags to be eaten after their fast is over. But when he gives them the bottles of Coca Cola, they do not know what to do. The bottles are not sealed and cannot be stored like the rest of the food because the beverage will spill. Maharaj's eyes are twinkling with merriment. He knows he has the widows in a fix. They look helplessly at him, protesting and at the same time covering their faces with the loose end of their saris and laughing. We watch this beautiful play between these two devotees and their God. These ladies belong to very conservative families, and they will never break the rules imposed on them by society. Yet their guru is their God and how can one refuse God? Finally, the lady who is sitting closest to Maharaj takes a bottle in her left hand and with her right hand she grabs Maharaj's big toe, much to his surprise. Next, she holds the toe against the mouth of the bottle while we are all watching in befuddled amusement. Then she tilts the bottle so the beverage touches Maharaj's toe.

"Here you go," she says to the other lady, giving her the bottle before going on to perform the same act again with her bottle.

All this happens in the blink of an eye. Even Maharaj is not quite sure what is happening. As for us, we are speechless.

"Go ahead," she says to her friend. "Drink it now. *Charan Amrita*. It has been sanctified. We will not be sinning." The crowd bursts into uproarious laughter. Maharaj is trying his best to suppress his smile because his feisty devotee has managed to get the upper hand in this case.

I find the situation funny but do not quite understand why the drink has become sanctified. In a whisper to Mother I ask her to explain and she says, "When we bathe the deities or the guru's feet, we often drink that water. It is called *charan amrit* and regarded as sacred or holy water. As a widow the lady is not supposed to drink any beverage because she is fasting today. So, she turned it into holy water by dipping Maharaj's toe in the drink. Anyone can drink holy water."

I remember that priests give us holy water called *charan amrit* to drink when we visit temples. We cup our hands and the priest gives us a spoonful of the holy water. I also remember Mother calling us each day and pouring a spoonful of *charan amrit* into our mouths when Maharaj was visiting us in Dehradun. That was water with which his feet had been washed during the *charan puja* or feet washing ceremony. Now I have some insight into the event I just witnessed. I think of how intelligent this elder is and how devoted. Throwing all caution to the wind, she has risked her reputation to drink the beverage given by her guru.

After spending a couple of hours at the rest house, we get ready to continue our journey. Suddenly, Maharaj turns to my father and expresses a wish to ride in our jeep. We are thrilled! Father tells our driver to get in the back with the rest of us. Placing Maharaj in the passenger's seat, Father drives for the next couple of hours. All the other cars follow us. Finally, Maharaj gently tells my father to stop. After blessing us, he goes back to his car. We drive on in silence to Rudraprayag, where we are going to spend the night. By riding with us for a part of the way, Maharaj has showered us with blessings beyond our dreams and we are brimming over with joy and gratitude.

Maharaj and the other devotees are all staying that night in Rudraprayag. After checking into our Army guest house and freshening up, we eat a quick dinner and then go to the guest house where Maharaj is residing. The house has a wide porch from which one has a spectacular view of the Alaknanda shimmering in the moonlit night. The mountains are awash in the light of the full moon and the air has a velvet feel to it. We sit on the porch, around the chair reserved for Maharaj, enjoying the splendor of the Himalayas as we wait for him. He comes, dressed in a white pure silk, looking as radiant as the moon hanging up in the sky. What follows is pure magic. He sings for a couple of hours, and we all join in as we sit at his feet amidst the breathtaking wonders of Nature.

The next morning, after paying our respects and saying goodbye to Maharaj, we drive down to Dehradun where we visit our old house and enjoy the company of our friends. But Father has to get back to work, so a couple of days later we board the Doon Express and go back to Calcutta. After we have rested from our trip, friends, family, and Maharaj's devotees flock to our house for many days to listen to stories of Maharaj and our trip to Badrinath.

Chapter 18: My Father's Initiation

By 1973, everyone in our family has been initiated by Maharaj except my father. Father says he believes in God and respects Maharaj but is not ready to be initiated. As his retirement from the military draws nearer, Father worries about how he will support us on his pension. Bonie and I hear our parents arguing.

"If I don't get a job, we will be out on the streets," says Father.

"You will get a job," says Mother in a calm voice. "Stop worrying. Maharaj will take care of us."

"I do not think your Maharaj can perform miracles," retorts Father, irritated by what seems to him to be Mother's blind faith in her guru. "I am fifty years old. Who will hire me? It will need a miracle for someone to hire me."

Mother is miffed that Father has referred to her guru as "your Maharaj." She pouts and then says in a challenging voice, "Okay. What will you do if Maharaj gets you a job?"

Father rolls his eyes in disbelief and says, "Whatever you say."

Mother pounces at this opportunity and says, "Will you take initiation from him?" Father does not hesitate to agree because he does not believe in miracles.

Soon after this argument, my father applies for the position of Chief Security and Vigilance Officer at the Indian Iron and Steel Company (IISCO) in Burnpur and goes for an interview. He comes home looking despondent. There is a younger candidate, and father is sure that the interviewers will choose the younger applicant. Maharaj is in town and Mother goes to see him. Sometimes it is hard in the huge Calcutta crowds to talk to Maharaj, so she writes a short note informing Maharaj of Father's situation. She gives him the note when she meets him and makes sure that Maharaj reads it. A week later Father is offered the job. We are all delighted, and he keeps his word. In 1975, he retires from the Army, joins IISCO, and goes to Deoghar in March to be initiated by Maharaj at the festival of Dol (Holi). Many devotees are initiated by Maharaj at the Baleshwari temple that year, and my father is one of them.

When he joins IISCO, our family moves to Burnpur which is three hours away by train from Calcutta. The steel plant provides our family with accommodation in a spacious flat in a complex called Palm Court Flats. However, Mother has been waiting for Maharaj to visit us as he did in

Maharaj with Father. Burnpur, 1970s

Dehradun. He does visit us a couple of times in our Calcutta house, but those are just one-hour long visits in the evenings when Maharaj goes out to visit his devotees either at their homes or in the hospitals if they are ill. Thousands flock to see Maharaj in Calcutta and the house that hosts Maharaj must be big enough to accommodate the devotees. Most of these houses have a large rooftop which is covered by a tarp to protect everyone from the sun and rain. In the 1970s, we think our house in Calcutta is too small to invite Maharaj to stay for three days. So, Mother has been praying every day, with all her heart, for an opportunity to serve her guru. She is disappointed when we are given a flat instead of a bungalow in Burnpur but Father assures her that he is on the waiting list for a bungalow. Mother continues to pray with the passion of a devotee whose request God cannot ignore.

Chapter 19: Maharaj in Burnpur

After a year or more of living in Palm Court Flats in Burnpur, Father is allotted a bungalow with spacious lawns in front and a large area behind the house. Ever since we left Dehradun in 1971, Mother has been waiting for this day. Now that we have a house that can accommodate Maharaj and his devotees, she begins to invite him each time she sees him. Maharaj is booked through the year as he goes from place to place, usually staying only for three days at any given location. He travels all over India and also flies abroad to visit his devotees in the U.K., Europe, and the U.S. In addition, there are train tours, privately arranged car tours, festivals in Deoghar, and various obligatory meetings he must attend with the trustees and board members of hospitals and schools and other charitable institutions he runs or sponsors. Just listening to all that Maharaj has to do can make one feel exhausted. So, it is hard for him to find time to visit us at Burnpur since his schedule is already full. But Mother refuses to be daunted by all these insurmountable obstacles that seem to provide her with no opening. She has full faith and confidence in the power of prayer, and she prays day and night for Maharaj to come to her home. She comes to Calcutta whenever Maharaj is in the city and goes to see him in person to request that he find a way to make room in his schedule for a visit to Burnpur. And then, one night, the power of prayer is revealed to us.

It is around eight o'clock on a December night in 1977, and we are all chatting in my grandmother's room. Father is in Burnpur but the rest of us are in Calcutta. I live with Aunt Dolly and Grandmother because I attend a college in Calcutta, and Bonie and Mother are visiting us even though they live in Burnpur with Father most of the year. Suddenly we hear a loud voice calling from the streets, "Lily! Lily!" Mother jumps up from the bed and runs to the main door. We are baffled as to why the person is calling Mother's name instead of ringing the doorbell. We all get up and follow Mother as she opens the door and greets a woman who is a devotee of Maharaj. Her name is Tara and I call her Aunty Tara (Tara Mashi). She is a widow who wears a dot on her forehead made with sandalwood paste, and I have seen her in Deoghar and in many other places when I have gone to see Maharaj.

We are surprised to see her because she has never visited us before. Moreover, we all know that Maharaj is leaving on a train tour next morning and most devotees would be spending the evening with Maharaj because they will not see him again for a month. Both my mother and aunt had gone to see him in the afternoon and had just returned a few hours before this incident. But there is not much time to think because we are all listening to our visitor who has good news for us.

"Baba is going to your house tomorrow," she says to my mother, and we all gasp in surprise. Maharaj's devotees often call him Baba or Father and we immediately understand what she means. Apparently, at the very last moment, there was a hitch and the train tour was cancelled. As mentioned earlier, Mother has displayed great perseverance in inviting Maharaj to Burnpur and that day, too, she had mentioned the idea to him while paying her respects. When Maharaj found out that the tour organizers had run into some obstacles, he asked if someone would contact my mother and tell her that he had decided to go on a car tour instead and his first stop would be Burnpur. Aunty Tara was present when he said this, and she had hurried over to our house to give us the news. She knew where we lived and was also aware that we needed to start preparing as soon as possible.

Mother's face is beaming with joy while the rest of us are still in a daze. After our visitor leaves, my mother immediately takes a taxi to Howrah station and catches the first train that will take her to Asansol station, near Burnpur. She arrives in the dead of night and calls my father from the Stations Master's office and tells him to come and pick her up at the station.

Father is alarmed to hear that she is calling from Asansol station. "What are you doing there at this time of the night?" he asks.

"Come and pick me up," says Mother. "Maharaj is coming to our house tomorrow."

"WHAT?" exclaims Father. "Oh no! How are we going to get ready for him?"

"Don't say anything negative," says Mother. "It will all work out. Now come and pick me up. We do not have a minute to waste."

This conversation will be repeated through the years and will become a favorite family story. The Bengali word Father had used, when he heard the news, was *shorbonash*, which means "disaster" or "catastrophe." He will always be teased for using such an inappropriate word when he should have said, "Wonderful" or "We are indeed blessed." However, my father was not wrong in feeling nervous. Hosting Maharaj requires a great deal of preparation because with him come many devotees who will need accommodation, food, and transportation. But Mother has been preparing for years. Her devotion has made Maharaj choose her home for his first stop. He will stay in Burnpur for three days before going to the next place. All the other hosts will have several days to prepare. Mother, however, has just a few hours.

Back in Calcutta, Grandmother and Aunt Dolly spend the whole night packing after Mother leaves, and early next morning they take the train to Asansol along with Bonie and me. Father picks us up at the station and tells us that Mother is moving like a "whirlwind." By the time we arrive in Burnpur, our home is ready to receive Maharaj and his devotees. The large living room has been emptied of all furniture except the sofa on which Maharaj will sit. Colorful thick rugs have been placed on the floor for devotees to sit. The sofa, which is draped with rich cloths, is adorned with blue and gold satin cushions and bolsters. My parents' room has also been rearranged. Maharaj's bed, which Mother has carried with her since his trip to Dehradun, has been readied for him. All the things he used in Dehradun have been carefully and lovingly preserved by Mother and now we see them arrayed in the room. It is December and Burnpur is cold, so a warm duvet in a silk cover sits at one end of the bed.

Aunt Dolly begins to unpack her bags and a variety of items pop out which will be of use. I wonder when she bought all these things, and she says she has been stocking up through the year. There are vials of Indian perfume called attar; small containers of finely sliced sweetened betel nut, called *mishti supari*, mixed with fennel seeds which act as mouth fresheners; and bottles of digestive tablets called *hajmi guli*. Mother and Aunt Dolly are well versed in everything needed to host Maharaj and between the two of them all the remaining finishing touches are given to Maharaj's room, the shrine room, and the bathroom.

Father rushes off to bring back another group of devotees; among them is my grandmother's aunt, whom we call Phul Dida. She is a devotee of Maharaj and has known him since he first arrived at his guru's ashram to become a monk. It is Phul Dida who initially encouraged Aunt Dolly to accompany her to Maharaj's ashram in Deoghar and then, one by one, we all followed suit and became disciples of Maharaj. Phul Dida arrives with some of my mother and aunt's friends. They immediately take charge of the kitchen where food will be prepared for Maharaj to offer to his deities.

Out in our backyard, some men are putting up a tent that will house the dining area. A small truck roars in with tables and chairs which are quickly unloaded and will later be placed inside the tent. At a distance is a very large kitchen which we have never used. It was probably used during the times of the British but later a smaller kitchen was attached to the house. Mother usually cooks in the small kitchen but now it has been handed over to Phul

Dida and her assistants. The larger kitchen has been cleaned and dusted and this is where the cook, who has been hired for this occasion, has set up his domain. Everyone who comes to visit Maharaj during the day and at night will be invited to eat at our house. The cook is preparing food for hundreds of devotees.

Father's friends are running around making arrangements to accommodate the devotees who will be accompanying Maharaj. The Burnpur Hotel is within walking distance of our house and my father has booked some rooms there. Several devotees of Maharaj who live in Burnpur offer to accommodate as many devotees as they can house, and Mother is grateful to them. There is a palpable joy in the air as everyone works together to do what he or she can do to make Maharaj's visit a success. This involves not just pleasing Maharaj but also making sure that his devotees are well looked after.

Suddenly, Mother calls Bonie and me and tells us to go in Father's jeep to a certain crossroads and wait there until we see Maharaj's car. We are then to guide Maharaj's driver to our house. Bonie and I quickly eat lunch and then hop into our father's jeep. The driver knows where to go and soon we are at the spot on the highway where we will meet Maharaj's car. After an hour or so, we see the car. Maharaj has also seen Father's jeep and tells his driver to slow down. Bonie and I wave at Maharaj and a big smile breaks across his face. Once again our world is illumined. Our driver goes and says something to Maharaj's driver and soon we are guiding Maharaj's car to our house. As we enter the gates of our house, our driver takes the jeep to the backyard so Maharaj's car and the cars following him have enough room to park in the front driveway. Bonie and I jump out and run to the front of the house where all our elders have gathered to welcome Maharaj. Father runs and opens the car door and Maharaj steps out looking resplendent in a saffron-colored silk which has "Hare Rama Hare Krishna" printed all over it in Bengali. He looks around in the crowd and sees Bonie and me. Smiling, he holds Father's hand and enters the house.

Maharaj sits in the living room on the sofa that has been readied for him. On the wall behind him hangs a photo of his guru. My parents start the *charan puja* and call Bonie and me to participate. After we are done, Aunt Dolly, Grandmother, Phul Dida, and Aunt Dolly's close friends participate in the feet washing ceremony. Once this is over, Maharaj's feet are wiped with a soft towel. Then, one by one, the devotees who have been waiting come forward to pay their respects to Maharaj. It is a small crowd because word has not yet spread of the sudden change in plans. However, we are expecting a larger crowd at night because many of the people who were booked for the train tour have decided to join the car tour and will soon be arriving by road.

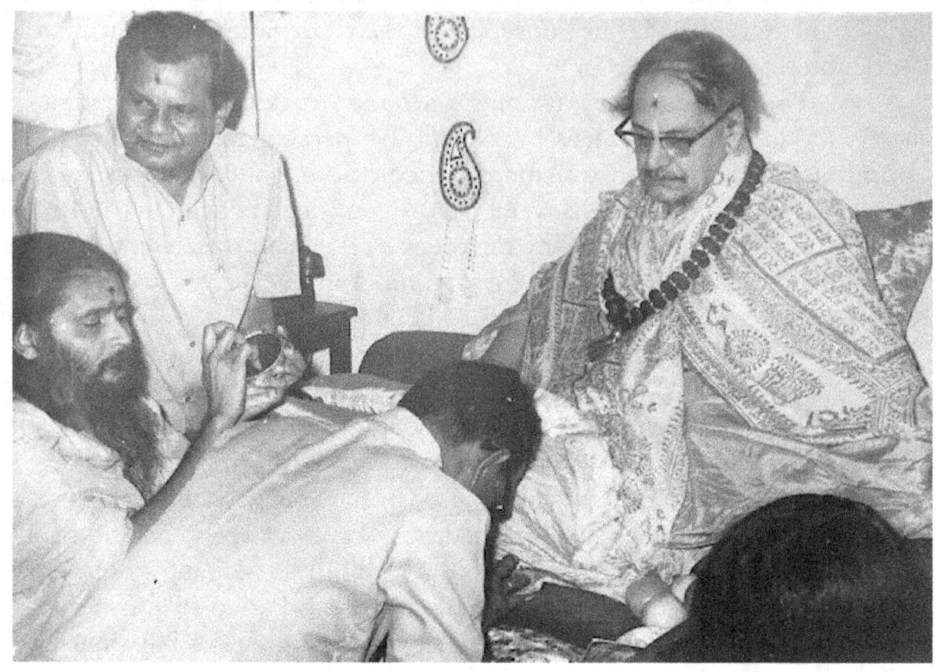

A devotee bowing to Maharaj in our living room. Burnpur, 1970s

Afterwards, Maharaj goes to his room, and Aunt Dolly and her friends unpack his things before bringing in the food which Maharaj will offer to the deities in the shrine room and then partake of. When Maharaj closes his door, the devotees who are not staying in our house go home to rest before coming back at night.

Father has been busy taking some of the devotees to Burnpur Hotel where they will stay for three days. Other devotees keep arriving in batches. Some have arranged for accommodation and others have not. My father finds accommodation for these devotees in the homes of his friends who have offered to act as hosts if needed. By evening, it seems everyone is settled and has a place to spend the night.

Just before dusk, Maharaj goes for a drive. Some cars follow him. Bonie and I are in his car. Mother and most family members stay back to get the house ready for the night's kirtan. Maharaj's car does not stop anywhere as we drive for a couple of hours in silence while Maharaj says his prayers. When we come home, the place is buzzing with activity. Maharaj walks in and goes to his room to finish his prayers. It is late in the evening and Father requests the devotees to go to the dining tent for dinner. Many devotees from out of town decide that this might be the best time to eat dinner. Others live near us and have already eaten. Bonie and I go and change our clothes. Both of us wear saris now in Maharaj's presence, and we feel very grown up even though I am still a teenager and Bonie is just a kid.

Maharaj entering our living room where devotees are waiting for him. Burnpur, 1970s

The living room is filling up with devotees who are ready for the night's kirtan. An area in the shape of a semicircle has been left empty for members of the family and the harmonium player. I will sit on Maharaj's left and be in charge of the sweets and fruits while Bonie will sit on his right with the silver bowl that contains the sacred ashes with which Maharaj will bless his devotees as they bow to him. We are all waiting in silence for Maharaj's door to open when Mother comes and gives me a Philips tape recorder and some blank cassettes and tells me to record Maharaj's kirtan. I put a blank tape in and keep the recorder under the sofa and close to me.

Maharaj's door opens and we all stand up out of respect for him. He wears a blue sari that Mother has offered him and new sandals that Aunt Dolly has bought for his feet. He looks enchanting and charms all of us with a shy smile. He takes his seat, and the devotees line up to pay their respects. One by one they come, and Maharaj places a dot of sacred ash on their forehead, takes the sweet from me and gives it to them. Sometimes, he also gives the devotees a fruit. Most of the times he places his hands on the top of the devotees' heads. Some give him garlands they have made with flowers that are now wilting, others give him packets of sweets, and still others give him money. People talk about their problems, and he listens to everyone carefully. He knows all the devotees by their names. He also remembers the names of their relatives. He asks a man, "How is your mother?" He asks a woman, "Was your husband unable to come?" The devotees pour out their hearts to him. Someone's father has cancer, someone is entangled in a litigation case, someone wants a good husband for her daughter, someone wants a job for his son. Little children who are yawning away because it is past their bedtime ask for candy and their mothers scold them and say, "Ask Guruji for good grades, silly!" and Maharaj laughs and taps the kids on their heads while looking for candy. Mother is quick on her feet and gets him some candy to give. Some mothers say they will have to go home to put their children to bed, but they promise to come back the next day.

Sitting so close to Maharaj, I am privy to most of the interactions between Maharaj and his devotees. Some wish to be initiated and Maharaj tells them to talk to my mother about the details. An elderly woman comes and begins to sob as though her heart has broken. Maharaj's face is filled with compassion as between broken sobs she tells him how her only son died in an accident. So heartrending are her sobs that I have tears in my eyes. Many come and pour their suffering at his feet. I notice how some are rich and others are poor. I see how they are all suffering and I realize that sorrow does not discriminate. Wealth cannot provide one with a way out of suffering. I see how Maharaj treats everyone with equal compassion. A gentleman with a questionable reputation receives the same blessings as my angelic aunt. When later I ask my mother about this, she tells me that great sages like Maharaj see everyone equally. I learn a new word: *samadarshi*. Mother explains that *sama* means equal and *darshi* is seer. Enlightened beings see God in everyone, she says. They do not see the miser exploiting his workers or the embezzler cheating his firm. They see the divine *Atman* (Soul) in all.

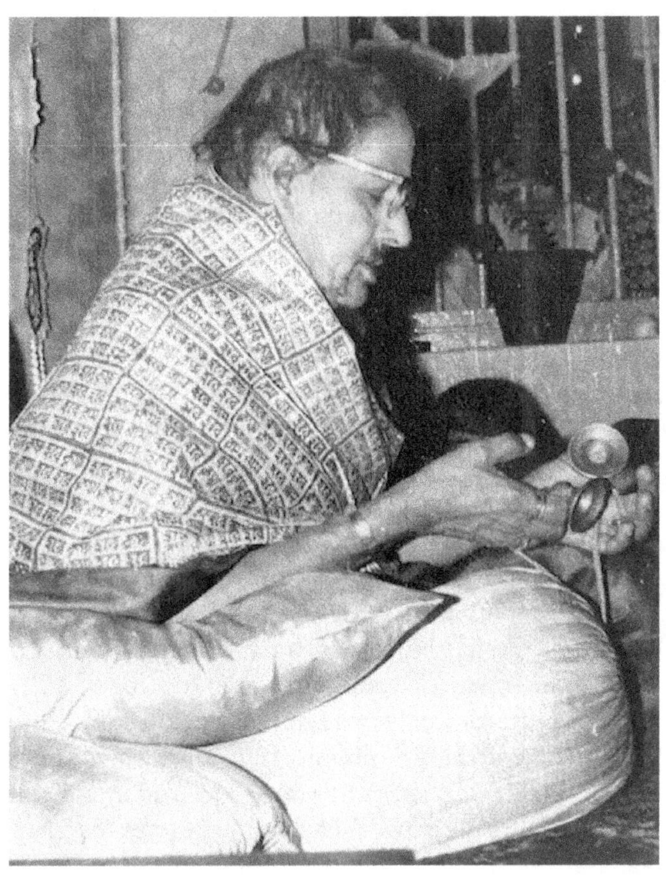

Maharaj singing kirtan at night. Burnpur, 1970s

After all the devotees have paid their respects to Maharaj, the lights are dimmed and we get ready to listen to Maharaj's divine songs. While the devotees have been paying their respects to their guru, the singers in the audience have taken turns singing devotional songs to Maharaj. So the mood is already set and now a lady, whose name is Kasturi, and whom I call Aunty Kasturi (Kasturi Mashi), takes charge of the harmonium and Maharaj slowly picks up his tiny cymbals. His eyes close and the room fills with the celestial music of devotional songs. As I sit mesmerized, I recognize some of the songs written by great composers of India and some which I know have been composed by Maharaj himself. The style of kirtan is one of call and response. Maharaj sings a line of the song he has chosen to sing and we repeat after him.

Aunty Kasturi is adept at keeping up with Maharaj as he moves from one song to another. Sometimes we stumble over the words of a song we are hearing for the first time, but she seems to know every word. On rare occasions, Maharaj breaks into a solo and the audience forgets to breathe. Such is the yearning for God in these songs that tears stream down the cheeks of those who are truly attuned to both Maharaj and music. The poetic lyrics emphasize the devotee's longing and thirst for the Divine, but it is Maharaj's soulful rendering of the song that fuels its intensity. During such solos, Maharaj's voice becomes heavy and sometimes he pauses when the song has ended as though he has merged with the Divine and is unaware of his surroundings. A couple of times it seems as though he needs a few minutes to gather himself, and he tells Aunty Kasturi to continue. As she gently begins to sing something easy, such as "Hare Krishna Hare Krishna, Krishna Krishna Hare Hare," Maharaj comes back to earth and resumes kirtan.

Through the hours, I kneel next to the sofa and hold the recorder high so that we have the best possible recording. Since I am young, kneeling for a couple of hours while holding a heavy recorder is not an arduous task for me. Mother has given me a job and I am doing this for her. Perhaps because of the intense concentration with which I am recording or perhaps because of my proximity to Maharaj, I am completely absorbed in the kirtan. I listen to the words and begin to realize the profound truths embedded in them. I realize that this is Maharaj's way of teaching us. Other teachers give Dharma talks, but Maharaj sings. Each song is meaningful and teaches us about how to live life and how to love God. The tapes hold only thirty minutes of recording on each side, so I have to flip each cassette as it comes to an end. I am glad Mother has given me several cassettes because the cassettes seem to be filling up at a rapid pace. As Maharaj ends that night's kirtan, I find I have recorded two hours of his singing. Mother will be pleased. Kirtan ends with the usual *Harir Loot*, and after everyone has collected all the sweets and candy and *batasha* and fruits they can, Maharaj goes to his room and the devotees leave. Most of them know where to go. There are a couple of people who arrived late that evening and Father manages to find accommodations for them even though it is past midnight.

Phul Dida and her assistants are rushing back and forth between the kitchen and the shrine room as the food that has been prepared for the deities is brought into the shrine room. Maharaj enters the shrine room and closes the door behind him. We wait while he offers the food to the deities and then eats a little. Maharaj is a small eater, and the platters and bowls almost always seem to come out untouched. He opens the door and Phul

Maharaj distributing sweets and candy (*Harir Loot*) after Kirtan. Burnpur, 1970s

Dida's assistants hurry to bring all the plates and bowls and glasses out of the shrine room.

Now it is time for the family members and a few close friends and relatives to sit in Maharaj's room and spend some time with him. We gather at his feet. My father and mother start massaging our guru's feet. Maharaj has an array of Indian mouth fresheners beside him, and he gives us fistfuls of it. We munch on these sweet concoctions in which fennel seeds dominate. There are also bottles of *hajmi guli*, little balls of sweet and sour tangy tamarind reputed to help digestion, which Maharaj generously distributes.

Mother says, "Maharaj, now that you have finally come to Burnpur, you must come every year."

Ignoring my mother, Maharaj looks at my father and says, "When I went to Dehradun, we missed you."

Father smiles and replies, "Yes, Maharaj. I was in Bangladesh at that time."

In a persuasive voice, Mother says, "Maharaj! Promise that you will come each year."

Seated (left to right): Mother, Maharaj, Aunt Dolly
Standing (left to right): Phul Dida, my grandmother, Father. Burnpur, 1970s

Once again, dodging her request, Maharaj looks at Bonie and asks, "Are you reciting the mantra I gave you?"

"Yes, Maharaj," says Bonie, hastily gulping down her *hajmi guli.*

Mother insists, "Maharaj, I am only asking for three days each year."

Maharaj hides his smile and says, "Three days! That's a lot! Soon it will be just one day in each place. And then it will be half a day."

"No, Maharaj, you can't do that to us. When you came to Dehradun, you stayed for seven days. This time it is only three days. Okay. I accept that. But you must come each year and you must stay for a minimum of three days."

"We will see what can be done about that," says Maharaj as he gives my mother a gentle smile and places his palm on her head.

Mother motions to us to get up. It is time for Maharaj to retire and we vacate the room. As Maharaj shuts the door to his room, I look at the clock and see that it is 2:00 a.m.

We go to the kitchen where the food offered to Maharaj awaits inspection. Aunt Dolly and her friends are checking to see if Maharaj ate anything. There are exclamations of happiness when evidence is found that he has nibbled at something, and there are signs of disappointment when it is clear that some dishes have remained untouched. The food is seen as *prasad* or sacred food because it has been offered to the deities and Maharaj. We are all given a mouthful of *prasad*.

As we are munching on the food, we hear raised voices coming from the dining tent. Father goes to investigate and finds our cook very upset about the treatment he has received from a demanding guest. It is 2:00 a.m. and she wants him to make her some fritters. The cook does not know that this woman must be placated because she is our guest. Father takes the cook aside and calms him down. The problem is brought to my mother's notice, and she coaxes our sleepy cook to do what must be done. The fire is lit, vegetables are chopped, a batter is made with gram flour, fritters are deep fried in bubbling oil, and the guest is appeased.

Not much of the night is left since Maharaj will be up at 4:00 a.m. My parents sit on the veranda for a couple of hours while the rest of us get some sleep. At 4:00 a.m. sharp, Mother gently opens the back door to Maharaj's bathroom and slides in two buckets of hot water. Winters are cold in Burnpur and there is no running hot water in this old bungalow. The light is on in Maharaj's bedroom. Father and the cook take cups and a huge kettle of tea and go to wake up the guests, who are staying at Burnpur Hotel, with hot tea. Father may hold a high position in the steel company, but here he thinks of himself as someone who is happy to serve not just Maharaj but his devotees. I hear these stories from the cook the next morning when I wake up.

This is the start of a series of joyous occasions when Maharaj visits Burnpur each December until my father retires from his job in IISCO in 1982 and we move, once again, to Calcutta.

Seated (from left to right): Grandmother, Maharaj, Aunt Dolly
Kneeling (from left to right): Bonie and I
Standing (from left to right): Mother and Father. Burnpur, 1970s

Chapter 20: Trips with Maharaj

Members of my family make use of every opportunity they get to visit Maharaj in Deoghar, Calcutta and other places. Twice a year, we go to Deoghar for the fire ceremony and for Durga Puja. When Maharaj comes to Calcutta, I try to see him as many times as possible. Sometimes Bonie and Mother are in Calcutta and they go with us. Aunt Dolly and Mother go on month-long train trips with Maharaj and visit sacred temples and places of pilgrimage with him. These trips are organized by a gentleman whom everyone calls Babu. He and his close relatives, along with cooks and servers, take many devotees on these trips. When booking reservations for these trips, Babu tries to book a saloon coach—which is like a moving house--for Maharaj and sometimes asks my uncle for advice. Uncle Sankar works for the Indian Railways and is usually able to help. If a saloon coach is not available, Babu books a first-class passenger coach for Maharaj. Those traveling with Maharaj who can afford a first-class ticket travel also in the saloon coach or the first-class coach, but there is a third-class passenger coach for other devotees.

We eagerly wait for Mother and Aunt Dolly to come back with their bags full of stories. When they arrive, they look radiant with joy and spiritual fervor. We listen to stories of hours and hours of kirtan, happy times spent with Maharaj at famous places of pilgrimage such as Vrindavan, worshipping deities with Maharaj at ancient temples, and visiting Maharaj in places where he detrained for a couple of days and stayed at a devotee's home. When Maharaj was not on the train, the saloon coach and passenger coach were detached from the train temporarily and stationed in the railway yard so the devotees had a place to stay. They went back and forth between the now stationary coach and the house where Maharaj was residing. There are stories of the good food that was served on most days, stories of waking up at 4:00 a.m. to get to the bathroom for a shower before others woke up, and stories of devotees who were disciples of Maharaj's guru and had seen Maharaj from the time he first came to his guru's ashram. There are always funny stories of feisty devotees who could be very demanding, and others who liked to gossip, and still others who snored through a kirtan, and others who got lost while visiting temples and kept everyone waiting. Mother and Aunt Dolly's friends come, and we spend long afternoons making our pilgrims tell and retell these stories until we feel that we have spent the whole afternoon in Maharaj's presence.

Several of these devotees were on a train tour with Maharaj when he stopped for a few days at Uncle Sankar's house. Barkakana, 1989

I am not able to go on the train trips with Maharaj because they are usually in the winter, and I am under academic pressure due to exams. However, in 1979, I do have the privilege of accompanying Aunt Dolly on a trip with Babu's organization to North Bengal where we visit Maharaj in Darjeeling and Kurseong. This is a very pleasant trip. We take the train to Jalpaiguri and then travel in jeeps that take us up the winding roads to the picturesque town of Darjeeling. We spend several days with Maharaj, paying our respects to him, singing kirtan, and going for walks with him. At night, the local people who are Nepalese line up to pay their respects to Maharaj. Babu has us housed in a lovely cottage, but we are at Maharaj's home most of the time and come back to our residence only to sleep at night. Each morning, after a quick shower and breakfast we walk to Maharaj's home which is close by.

It is April and the weather is pleasantly cool. On my birthday, Aunt Dolly gives me a beautiful sari, a packet of incense sticks, a bag of fruits, and a box of sweets to offer to my guru. Maharaj comes into the living room where we are waiting for him. He is dressed in golden silk with a light pink shawl draped around his shoulders. When it is my turn to touch his feet, I shyly offer him all the things my aunt has provided. Maharaj smiles and as I bend to touch my forehead on his feet, I hear my aunt saying, "It is her birthday today."

"Oh, now I understand. That is why she is giving me so many things," says Maharaj with a beaming smile as he places his palm on my head and blesses me. I am about to move away to make room for the next person when I hear Maharaj say, "Wait." I look at him and see him taking the shawl off his shoulders and offering it to me. I bow and he drapes the shawl around my neck. Everyone in the room is happy for me and I am in bliss. (See the pink shawl in my photo on the back cover of this book.)

Maharaj with his right hand on my head. Indiana, 1992

From Darjeeling we travel in jeeps to yet another beautiful place in the mountains called Kurseong. The host owns tea plantations, and we are taken to the factory to taste the best tea in the world. Here, too, we have a very memorable stay as we enjoy our time with Maharaj. I have been in bliss ever since I received my birthday gift from Maharaj, and nothing can go wrong for me. Others around me complain about this and that from time to time, but I cannot see any problem with anyone or anything. After a week, which seems to have flown by a little too fast, we head back to the plains and take the train back to Calcutta.

This time it is my turn to tell stories as everyone comes to listen, including Mother and Bonie who come from Burnpur. My aunt and I tell the stories together, but the story of my birthday is told by me. At the end of the story, I dramatically bring out the shawl and everyone says it is truly beautiful.

Another memorable trip I make with Aunt Dolly is to a place called Pakur where Mother and Aunt Dolly have visited Maharaj on several occasions. Everyone says seeing Maharaj in Pakur is the experience of a lifetime. I am not quite sure what to expect but am happy to accompany my aunt. We stay with a devotee of Maharaj who knows both my mother and my aunt and whom I call Aunty Lali (Lali Mashi). Maharaj is residing elsewhere, and we go back and forth between our host's house and Maharaj's residence.

Soon after our arrival, to our surprise we find lots of young girls coming to see us. They seem to be looking at me and giggling among themselves. When I go out for a walk, I find a group of young boys and girls following me. They point at me and whisper and giggle. Coming from the city, Pakur seems to me to be a rural area and I do not understand why these children find me so amusing. Finally, my aunt finds out the cause of the amusement. The children have never seen a girl with short hair! At first, they tried to ascertain whether I was a boy or a girl. When they repeatedly saw me wearing a sari, they concluded that I was a girl. But why did I have such short hair? Widows often shave their heads but since I am wearing colorful saris, not white, they rule out the possibility of my being a widow. Then why do I not have long hair as any girl or woman should? No matter how hard we try to explain to them that nowadays many girls and women wear their hair short, they still giggle. I find I am quite the star in Aunty Lali's home.

When we go to visit Maharaj, however, I no longer feel conspicuous since all eyes are focused on our guru. The crowds are huge, and it feels as though all the people of Pakur have shown up to pay their respects to this great sage. Old and young, men and women, rich and poor are all pouring in with gifts for Maharaj. Eager to touch his feet and receive his blessings, eager to listen to hours and hours of his ecstatic singing, eager to jump up and catch all the flying candy, sweets, and fruits Maharaj throws after kirtan, and eager to be drenched with the peace water he sprinkles at the very end of each session, the people of Pakur flock to see their guru during the day and also at night. The air is pregnant with joy. It feels as though we are basking in a joy that is as high as the sky, as vast as the ocean, as deep as the forests, and as sweet as a mother's love for her child.

Group photo with Maharaj shielding his face from the sun. Malda, 1980s

The people of Pakur love Maharaj with all their heart and he returns their love. In the evenings he goes from house to house to visit devotees who have requested that he bless their homes with his presence. Some homes are in locations where unpaved roads have turned into muddy slush from heavy rains. The alleys are too narrow for Maharaj's car to enter, and he must walk in the mud with his velvet slippers. Devotees in his car discourage him from getting out of the car, but he gets out and walks through the muddy alleys in his rich brocades and silks and enters the humble abode of a devotee. Many of us do not venture from our cars. After a while, Maharaj returns in a simple saffron-colored cotton sari and gets into the car. His face is peaceful and radiant. I look at the householder whose home he has just blessed, and words cannot describe the happiness of the man whose eyes are streaming with tears of joy. Wherever we follow Maharaj, people come pouring out from their neighborhoods. From palaces to slums, Maharaj reigns in the hearts of the people. Now I understand why my mother and aunt do their best not to miss Maharaj's annual visit to Pakur. They are enthralled by the symphony of joy that floods Pakur during Maharaj's visit.

Maharaj with a bottle in his left hand to spray devotees with peace water at our house.
Calcutta, 1990s

Chapter 21: The Chariot Festival

After my father retires from the steel factory in Burnpur in 1982, once again our family moves to Calcutta. We live in the apartment above our grandmother's apartment in her house on Keyatala Lane. Maharaj's visits to our home stop because Grandmother's house is too small for the gigantic crowds of Calcutta. But Mother is on the prowl, looking for ways in which she can entice Maharaj to visit us. Since Uncle Sankar is posted in a town called Malda, Mother invites Maharaj to come and stay with us in my uncle's home. In the late 1980s, Maharaj visits us twice and stays in Uncle's railway quarters for three days. Later, Uncle is posted to Barkakana and Maharaj visits us there, too. Each visit lasts for three days and is filled with the utmost joy--long hours of kirtan, drives in the evening, brief visits to the homes of devotees, and endless blessings from our loving and compassionate guru.

On one memorable occasion, we celebrate Ratha Yatra at Barkakana. Ratha means chariot and Yatra means journey. Ratha Yatra is the festival of the chariot of Lord Jagannath which is held each year in June. The main festival is celebrated in Puri, a renowned place of pilgrimage in the state of Orissa. In this sacred place, the ancient temple dedicated to Lord Jagannath (Krishna) welcomes millions of pilgrims each year who come to pay their respects. In the temple one sees three statues as Jagannath is worshipped along with his brother Balaram and his sister Subhadra.

On the day of the festival, three gigantic chariots are brought out on the streets of Puri and each carries a statue of one of the deities. These chariots are pulled by thousands of devotees and taken to a temple called Gundicha Bari. The streets are lined with pilgrims and tourists. Every house's balcony, rooftop, and windows are filled with people eager to view the journey of the chariots.

As Lord Jagannath drives through the town with his siblings, everyone can see him and pay their respects to him. After reaching his destination, he stays in the Gundicha temple, which is also known as his Mashir Bari or his aunt's house, for seven days and then the chariots bring him back again to his temple. This journey is called Ulta Rath or Return Journey and people come to see him again.

Even though the main festival is held in Puri, people in Bengal also celebrate this festival. Children have a little chariot with three small images of the deities, and they tie a rope to the chariot and pull it on the sidewalks and streets of their neighborhoods. Big chariots from one or two major organizations are also seen on the streets of Bengal's towns and cities.

In 1990, Maharaj is on a train tour and his saloon coach has been disconnected at Barkakana so he can stay with us at my uncle's home for three days. All the devotees travelling with him come to Uncle Sankar's bungalow and other devotees from the surrounding areas come by road. Out of these three days, one day happens to be the auspicious day of the Ratha Yatra. On this day, after Maharaj opens his door around 10:30 a.m., we all pay our respects by bowing to him. It is still too early for kirtan, so Maharaj tells everyone to go to the garden and get ready to be photographed.

Father holding the door open for Maharaj. Barkakana, 1989

Uncle Sankar's bungalow has a well-kept large garden that is oval shaped. Around the garden runs a wide gravel driveway. When we come out with Maharaj, we find that the devotees have decorated his car with flowers and have tied ropes to the car. Maharaj is ushered into the passenger seat. A few of us standing close by, including Aunt Dolly and myself, are ushered into

110

the back seat. I am not quite sure what is going on until the devotees begin to pull the car. The driver has not started the engine. He just sits with his hands on the wheel and his foot poised over the brake. That is when I understand that Maharaj's devotees are celebrating the great Ratha Yatra with our very own Lord Jagannath.

Tears of joy stream down our cheeks. Aunt Dolly holds my hand tightly. She cannot believe our great fortune to be in the car with Maharaj on this auspicious occasion. Finally, after everyone has had a chance to pull the car, the car is brought to a halt in front of the house and Maharaj gets out. He then goes to the garden and looks for his camera bags. Taking out his cameras, he asks us to gather around his chair to pose for each photograph. After focusing the camera lens on us and setting the timer, he comes to us with quick long strides and sits on the chair. I notice that while we are all still reeling from the joy of having celebrated this great festival with Maharaj, he continues going from one task to another as though it were just any other day.

Maharaj in our garden with his cameras. Dehradun, 1971

Chapter 22: Maharaj in the United States

The years slide by, and one by one, first Bonie and then I leave for the United States in pursuit of higher studies. Of course, we have both asked Maharaj for his permission to go abroad, and he has wholeheartedly given us his blessings and encouraged us to go. In Boston, Bonie sees Maharaj whenever he visits the suburbs. In 1993, she marries Jim and they both go to India in December when Maharaj visits our home in Calcutta and stays for three days. From 1993 to 1997, Maharaj visits our Keyatala home in the winter.

I am at Purdue University from 1990 to 1996, and Mother calls me to tell me when Maharaj will visit Indianapolis. I am a student and do not have a car. Indianapolis is 65 miles away from Purdue, but I find friends to take me to see Maharaj. The first time I meet him in Indianapolis, his eyes light up with recognition and his lips burst into a smile. Usually quiet when he is among new devotees, Maharaj tells the few people in the room how he has seen me grow up from when I was a little girl. He showers my friends and me with many blessings and plenty of fruits and sweets. Gradually, Ralph begins to go with me. Maharaj takes to him at once. So when I give Maharaj a letter sent by my father informing him that my family would like me to marry Ralph if Maharaj agrees, my guru is pleased. Ralph and I get married in 1996.

That summer my parents come to the States and stay in Bonie's apartment in Boston. Ralph and I fly to Boston to spend time with my parents. We know that Maharaj is in the Boston area, and we go to visit him. As we enter the living room of the house Maharaj is residing in, my father is the last one to enter as it takes time for him to take his shoes off. Maharaj looks up from the letter he is dictating, and he seems to be searching for someone. His glance alights on each of us and moves away, still searching. It is the look of a mother who has momentarily lost sight of her child in a crowd. And then he finds the person he has been looking for and his face beams with happiness.

"There you are," he says, looking at my father. "How is your health?"

Father comes forward with tears in his eyes. Maharaj makes him sit next to him on the sofa. Such compassion flows from Maharaj that many of us are tearing up.

Seated on bed: Father and Maharaj at our house. Calcutta, 1997
Seated on the floor (left to right): Mother, I, Aunt Dolly, Uncle Sankar

My father has severe pain and stiffness from his waist down. In 1991, he had become bedridden from gout, which had led to arthritis. Maharaj had come to see him, and Father had told Maharaj that he did not wish to live if he had to remain confined in bed. Maharaj had blessed him, and my father had recovered. Mother gives Father some homeopathic medicine each day, and he is able to live an independent life, but we all know that he owes his mobility to Maharaj's blessings. This is probably the reason for my father's intense devotion and love for his guru towards the end of his life. What we do not know at this time is that my father's time is coming to an end, and he will leave us in 1998. Perhaps Maharaj senses this and showers my father with love and blessings.

We spend wonderful days with Maharaj in Boston. Ralph has rented a car and we go wherever Maharaj visits. The crowds are small, and we are able to spend quality time with him. Sometimes, in the afternoons, on weekdays, we seem to be the only visitors. We listen to hours and hours of kirtan. I am worried that Ralph may be bored. He is a jazz musician and is very choosy about what music he will listen to. Moreover, he does not know the language. But Ralph is spellbound by Maharaj's singing. When we come home, Ralph says that even though he does not understand the words, he feels Maharaj is conveying an important message to him.

I am curious and ask, "What is this message?"

Ralph says, "No matter what life brings to us, we must accept it with equanimity."

While we are in Boston, one day, Maharaj turns to Bonie and me and says, "Why don't you two sisters sing?"

Even though there are just a few people in the room, Bonie and I are petrified. We have not sung in years. We look at each other in panic.

Maharaj says, "How about *Aguner parashmoni*?"

We are stunned. Twenty-five years ago, we had learned the song in Dehradun. How could Maharaj remember? We have forgotten that there is a song we sang so many times as children that even now we can sing it without any help. A very sweet lady, whom we call Aunty Gayatri (Gayatri Mashi) and whom we have known for years, plays the harmonium and we sing the song we had first sung in 1971.

Such happy moments are in abundance as we spend time with our guru. Even though all this is very new to Ralph, I can tell that Maharaj has made a deep impression on Ralph. Perhaps it is this time that he spent with Maharaj in 1996 that eventually leads to Ralph's initiation in 1998.

In the summer of 1998, after Ralph's initiation in Du Quoin, Illinois, we visit Maharaj in many places. I become an expert in dressing Ralph in a *dhuti* and Ralph becomes an expert in handling the *dhuti*. Maharaj pours his affection on Ralph and gives him a beautiful name: Rameshwar. I explain to Ralph that as far as I know, Rameshwar is a name for Lord Shiva. This happens at a disciple's house in the Detroit area. Our guru also asks me to teach Ralph a song Maharaj often sings:

> Jaya Krishna hare Sri Krishna hare
> Dukhiyon ke dukh dur kare
> Jaya jaya Krishna hare.
> (Praise to Lord Krishna who leads people out of suffering)

While teaching at the university and taking trips to see Maharaj in Detroit and Chicago, Ralph learns the song. We sing it together when he is ready, and Maharaj is very pleased.

In July, we hear that Guru Purnima will be celebrated at a resort in the Poconos. Ralph is on summer break, and we go to the Poconos and spend

Ralph and I with Maharaj. U.S.A., 1998

the day with Maharaj. Many devotees are present, and we attend the ceremony. After the ceremony is over, we all queue up to pay our respects to Maharaj. When it is my turn, I kneel and place my forehead on Maharaj's soft feet. When I lift up my head to receive the black dot of sacred ashes on my forehead, I am blinded by a light that startles me. It seems as though Maharaj's whole form is glowing with luminosity. I move away and wonder what I have seen.

From the Poconos, we go to Boston because Mother is arriving. Bonie and her husband Jim were in India when my father passed in June of 1998, and my sister has decided to bring Mother back with her. Perhaps a change of place will help assuage the pain Mother is experiencing due to Father's death. Ralph and I pick up Mother and Bonie from the airport, and later go to Connecticut to see Maharaj. The first evening we are told that Maharaj will not come down from his room to see anyone because he is resting. Mother tells the host to tell Maharaj that she has come all the way from Calcutta to see him. The minute Maharaj hears my mother's name, he comes down. He can barely look at her face, he feels her pain so intensely. He can see that she has lost the love of her life. We learn that our guru will be at another house the following day. So we drive again from Boston to spend more time with him. I see how Mother changes in his presence. When she had disembarked from the plane, I could barely recognize her. She had looked ravaged by pain. Her complexion had looked darker than usual as though darkness had settled on her. Two visits to Maharaj and Mother's skin is glowing. I know she has found the ground under her feet.

Bonie (at Maharaj's feet) and Jim (next to her) with Maharaj. Boston, 1996

Chapter 23: The End of an Era

It is July of 1999, and Ralph and I learn that Maharaj is in McMinnville, Tennessee. We want to go visit him, but I have heard that Maharaj is not well. So we decide to see him before Guru Purnima, an auspicious day when many disciples may be visiting him. We are able to spend a few days with Maharaj before returning to Michigan.

In the third week of August, my phone is ringing off the hook with news that Maharaj is getting ready to leave the body. My fingers go numb from punching numbers, calling people, hoping to hear that the news is not true. But the news is sad. In between bouts of uncontrolled anguish, I pack while Ralph books a hotel. Eleven hours later, we are in Tennessee with our hearts in our throat, not knowing whether we will be able to see Maharaj or not. In the dead of night, we knock at the hospital door only to be denied admission by the receptionist.

Next morning, we are not alone. Many have flocked to the hospital from all directions. Some have flown thousands of miles to get a last glimpse of their beloved guru. We sit and wait in the waiting room. For decades, Maharaj has visited the sick in hospitals. Today, we are here to see him. I see blood-shot eyes, streaming tears, sorrowful faces. I listen and hear words of woe, cries for help, and tales of death as the disciples await their turn to enter the room where Maharaj lies. I want to flee, but our turn has come.

Walking softly, we enter the hallowed room. I cannot bear to see Maharaj surrounded by tubes and medical equipment, doctors and nurses. Ralph and I go down on our knees. Our foreheads touch the cold floor of the hospital room. As I raise my head, the light shines on the spot where Maharaj lies. Once again, I see radiance, brilliant and dazzling. Perhaps it is a window, perhaps it is the angle of the sun, perhaps it is a fluorescent light in the ceiling. I do not know what the source of the light is, but that is all I see. Perhaps even at this moment, Maharaj is shielding me.

A few days later, on August 29, 1999, phones ring across the world announcing Maharaj's passing away. To us and to all his devotees, it is as though darkness has swept the face of the world, and the sky has fallen on our heads. Tears drip from our red eyes, while desolation seizes and empties our hearts. I sit in my living room and wonder if all who have left this earth before us are rejoicing. Perhaps joyous bells are pealing in that world beyond this. Perhaps fireworks are lighting up the sky and voices ringing with glee are announcing his arrival. Perhaps happy souls are laughing joyously as ecstasy seizes hold of them. Perhaps.

Ralph has gone to work, and I sit and think of Maharaj. Memories flood me and I am unaware of the passage of time. Whenever we went to see Maharaj, we felt that we were in his home regardless of who actually owned the house we were in. On seeing us, his face would light up like that of a father whose child has come back home after a long absence. When we told him our success stories, his eyes would shine like that of a teacher whose star pupil had won an award. He filled our laps with juicy fruits and fed us all day like an anxious mother whose beloved child has come home for the holidays. He sang devotional songs that filled our hearts and taught us how to love God. He drenched our heads with holy water, peace and rest. And now that he is gone, we have nowhere to go; we are all alone, with no one to turn to.

I think of how Maharaj labored and toiled, roaming the globe for more than six decades on this planet. I think of how he listened to us, to all our prayers and all our woes. I think of all he did for us and wonder what we had done to deserve such a guru.

I call Mother, who is in Calcutta, and she says Maharaj was 95 years old. I am surprised to hear that because to me he always looked like an angel who had just arrived from the kingdom of light. Not a wrinkle creased those soft baby feet, not a line marked the smile that had lit up the lives of many people who had come across land and sea to lay their sorrows at his feet. The older he grew, the more it seemed to me that his beauty shone with a new radiance. Those who attended the last rites marveled at Maharaj's divine beauty. He looked like a fresh lotus, they said. Even sickness had failed to make a dent on this great yogi.

As summer draws to a close in Michigan, the air is tinged with the first chill of fall. It is the day Maharaj's ashes are leaving the little hamlet nestling in the mountains of Tennessee. I go for a walk and sense the nip in the air. Looking up, I see the intense blue of the sky, the puffy white of the clouds and think of Deoghar. In yester-years, this was when the ashram bustled to celebrate not just the coming of the goddess Durga, but also Maharaj. Today, the ashram stands silent, waiting--waiting for the final homecoming. On this crisp autumn day, my heart breaks. As the century crawls to its end, I feel that our world, which had centered around Maharaj, has come to an end, too.

From left to right: Bonie, Maharaj, I, and Mother. Barkakana, 1989

119

Chapter 24: My Eternal Companion

The days seem endlessly bleak. I call my mother, who is in Calcutta, and tell her that the world feels empty without Maharaj. She tells me to listen to the tapes I have of his kirtan. Unable to imagine that anything can bring me solace, I reluctantly start playing the tapes just so I can tell Mother that I did what she asked me to do. At first, even hearing that mellifluous voice brings a stabbing pain to my heart. We will never sit at his feet again and listen to him singing for hours; we will never again listen to the sound of the small cymbals in his hands which he used to accent the rhythm of each song; there will be no showering of candy and fruits, no more sprinkling of peace water, no more filling hearts with the joy beyond compare. But as the tape plays song after song, I find a mellow peace creeping into my heart and suffusing my entire being. The songs soothe the pain in my heart. I listen to the words that echo my sentiments. The devotee is singing to Krishna and asking:

> O Beloved Krishna! Won't you come again?
> Won't we, once again, hear the melody of your flute?
> Won't you run after the cows on the banks of the Yamuna,
> And steal the butter from the milkmaids of Vrindavan?
> Are we never to see such scenes again as those of
> Mother Yashoda trying to tie you up,
> Or your beloved Radha dancing with you under the Kadamba tree?
> Won't you illuminate the darkness of this heart, O Compassionate One?
> I implore you to please come once more.

I have heard this song many times since I recorded Maharaj singing it in Burnpur in the 1970s, but never has the emotion embedded in the lyrics pierced my heart with such clarity as it does on this dark afternoon in Michigan. For the first time I understand the pain of the devotee longing for God, the heartache of Radha and the *gopis* separated from Krishna, the darkness that enshrouds our existence when we cannot connect with the Beloved.

I am surprised to find that the first song that catches my attention is one which seems to echo my sentiments. Then I remember how at each kirtan, I would always hear someone say, "I had a question and Maharaj sang a song that answered my question. He is an *Antarjami*, One who knows what is in each heart." Or someone would say, "I had come with a heavy heart, but the wisdom I found in the songs he sang has shown me the way out of my predicament." Each devotee felt that Maharaj had sung a particular song just for her or him. On this fall day, as the leaves in Michigan turn yellow and scarlet, I have the same experience. I feel Maharaj's palm reaching out and blessing me on the head and reassuring me that he is there with me to see me through my bereavement. My compassionate guru is here with me to enlighten me, chase the shadows away, and lighten the burden of my heavy heart.

Other songs follow, and I listen with deep attention to the lyrics. The words "Even though I may have left, I am still with you./Your love is a garland around my neck" are especially poignant in this context and I receive them as a reassurance from my guru. My heart's reply comes in the next song in which the devotee sings, "You may not be visible to these physical eyes/ But that does not mean you are not in my heart." Embedded in the kirtans of Maharaj I find myself listening to a conversation between him and us. There are songs that give voice to our love for him and our yearning for his presence, and there are songs that shower us with his wisdom and show us the way out of suffering.

Maharaj's kirtans supply an endless repertoire of songs composed by some of the greatest composers of India. There are songs by Bengal's renowned composers, such as Rabindranath Tagore and Ramprasad; there are songs by great saints such as Mirabai, Kabir, Surdas and Tulsidas; there are songs that have been sung by kirtan singers for centuries in Bengal; there are Sanskrit chants from the scriptures which Maharaj often translated into Bengali so that the meaning was accessible to those of us who do not know Sanskrit; there are chants that contain the recitation of the various names of God; and there are songs that Maharaj himself composed.

Through his kirtans Maharaj taught us not to attach to the world whose nature is transitory; he showed us the importance of focusing on our goal in life, which is to realize our Divine Self; he made us aware of all the different ways in which we can love God so we can choose the path that best suits us; he presented the renowned compositions of our saints and chanted from our ancient scriptures so that we could be aware of our great spiritual heritage; he made us proud of our country by singing the glories of our Motherland lest we forget the sacrifices made by those who freed us from the shackles of foreign rule; he sang about the marvelous contributions of the women of India, especially mothers who not only raised us but kept families together for generations. Almost every song is rooted in the reality of worldly life even as it points to a world beyond this world of momentary joys and endless sorrows. He reminds us, again and again, that we are not the limited beings we think we are. We are not caged birds. We are much more than that. We are the Divine that we seek.

Emphasizing the transience of this world, there are songs that remind us that our days are coming to an end, and wasting this life will also affect our next life. Our Life-bird in the Body-cage will not linger much longer. We don't really own anything or anybody, so it is futile to harp on the concepts of "I and mine." We have come to this world alone, and we shall go out alone because no one can go with us. Being aware of the bondage of repetitive lives and deaths, we must recite God's name to find a way out of suffering.

Day after day, I listen to Maharaj's songs and all separation dissolves as I feel His presence in my heart, in my home, in my life. I am grateful that Mother had given me the precious job of taping the kirtans. At that time, in the late 1970s, I had not known how these songs would become my lifelong companions and the source of much of my spiritual knowledge. The songs assure me that my guru will always be with me and guide me and keep me focused on my goal of liberation from the cycle of birth and death.

More than two decades have passed since Maharaj left his body, but it would be no exaggeration to say that he has become more embedded in my life than ever before. With each day, I appreciate more and more all the blessings He has showered on me. In a thousand ways, some subtle and some quite prominent, He lets me know that He is with me. Most of my spiritual wishes are instantly fulfilled; many of the questions I have are answered in meditation or through dreams or through his songs. I listen to his songs each morning and, as I age, I go deeper and deeper into the multi-layered meanings of each song. It is hard to describe the power of Maharaj's kirtans because providing the reader with the lyrics is not enough and the English translations do not convey the depth of meaning of each song. Kirtan is an experience. One must be present and participate to feel the vibrations seep through one's being. Even if one does not know the languages in which the kirtans are sung, the philosophy embedded in the songs enters the heart by a process akin to osmosis. This experience cannot be conveyed in words.

When I was initiated at the age of twelve, Maharaj had told me to focus on Krishna when I meditated. Through the years, I have always tried but failed to focus on Krishna. Instead, my focus alights on my guru. This had never bothered me until Maharaj left the body and I began to meditate for several hours each day. Struggling to stay focused on Krishna and failing almost every day, I felt I was unable to meditate the way I was supposed to. One night, I dreamed that Maharaj was standing in front of me and I was bowing by placing my forehead on his feet. His blue robe with a broad golden border covered his feet and I lifted the robe so I could touch his feet. What was my surprise to find a pair of blue feet crossed in the manner in which only Krishna's feet are crossed! When I woke up, I realized the significance of the dream. Maharaj was indeed my guru and my God. I have no words to express the depths of my gratitude to Maharaj for taking me under his wing. May he continue to guide and bless both my worldly and spiritual lives so I can one day find a place at his lotus feet.

Maharaj. Dehradun, 1971

123

Part II: My Mother and the Sages She Met

Chapter 25: My Mother and Her Stories

Like the ants, who sniffed out every sweet my grandmother made, my mother sniffed out holy sages, seekers of liberation, enlightened ones. In a hut by the Ganges, or in a crag of the Himalayas, in a holy place for pilgrims, or a forest full of silence, she sought and always found what she had been seeking. Whether they lived in solitude or were surrounded by multitudes, whether they lived the Hindu way or followed the Buddha's Path, whether they came from far off lands or were natives of the Indian plains, without fail the holy ones treated my mother like a kindred spirit. When they met, it seemed as though two halves had joined to become a whole.

Mother was an unconventional Bengali mother in more ways than one. For instance, while other mothers told their children fairy tales, my mother told us spiritual stories of gods and sages. The intention was never to indoctrinate us. It was just that those were the stories she liked to share. I grew up with some favorites.

The Story of the Old Man who went on a Pilgrimage

A favorite tale of my mother's was that of an old man who made a very long journey by foot to Badrinath. It took him days and days and much hardship to trek up the Himalayan mountains. He did not have a lot of resources and had to depend on the generosity of other pilgrims to provide him with food and shelter on the way. Many a night he had to sleep under a tree and go hungry. As he climbed up the mountain, his old bones ached, his lungs pumped furiously as he gasped for breath, and the cold bit into him like a shark's teeth. Sometimes it rained, but he walked on reciting God's name, pleading with the deity at the Badrinath temple to make his journey fruitful. As he climbed higher and higher, snow began to fall. Many pilgrims were coming down the mountain after having paid their respects to Badrinathji. They looked surprised to see the old man, but he failed to notice the looks they were giving him. He was focused on each step that brought him closer and closer to his God. Finally, he was there! He had arrived at Badrinath and could see the temple shining in the last rays of the setting sun. The place was quite empty and as he approached the temple, he found himself face to face with a priestly figure and a small crowd of people. The old man stopped in his tracks and bowed to the priest who looked at him in surprise.

"Have you just arrived?" asked the priest.

"Yes," replied the old man and he told the priest of his hard and challenging climb.

The priest's face crumpled up with compassion. He said, "I am so sorry, but we just locked the temple for the winter and are heading down to the plains. No one lives here in the winter because of the cold. You will have to return in the summer when I shall come back to open the temple."

The priest and his entourage left the old man standing at the steps of the temple and began their descent to the plains.

At first, the old man could not believe his ears. The fact that he had come all this way and borne so many hardships only to be denied a glimpse of his Lord was too much for him. His legs gave way and he slumped down on the steps of the temple and began sobbing.

"Oh Lord!" he cried. "How could you do this to me? Just one day, just one day, just a few hours ... if only I had arrived this morning, I would have seen you. How could you be so cruel? Why didn't you bring me here on time? Why couldn't you wait one more day for me? You know I cannot come again next year. All right then. I am not going back. I will sit here and freeze to death, but I am not going back." With these words the old man cried his heart out.

Suddenly, he felt a soft touch on his shoulder and heard a gentle voice ask, "Why are you crying, dear friend?"

He looked and saw through the mist of his tears a young boy around ten or eleven years old. He was dark skinned and had dark curly hair. His eyes were luminous and darted here and there like lightning. His face was so beautiful that the old man forgot all his woes and began to wipe his tears away so he could look at this child of unearthly beauty.

"Who are you, my child?" he asked.

"I am a cowherd," said the child. "But you did not tell me why you were crying."

The old man told him his story and the child laughed. "You must be mistaken," he said. "The priest will open the temple tomorrow morning. You must have misunderstood. Come with me and I will find you a place to stay tonight. Tomorrow morning you will visit the temple. You were tired and did not understand that the priest was just saying that he had closed the temple for the day and would be back tomorrow to conduct his duties."

The old man was so exhausted from the trials and tribulations of the day that he decided to trust what the child was telling him. The child led him to a cave and there they spent the night playing a game of chess to entertain themselves. In the morning, the child said, "Go and bathe in the river and meet me at the temple. I will be waiting for you. Today you will see Badrinathji." The old man did as he was told and arrived at the steps of the temple after a bath. As he stood there waiting for the child, he saw a group of people coming towards him. They were led by the same priest he had seen the day before. The old man bowed to the priest, but the priest stood there with a bewildered look on his face.

"How did you arrive before us?" asked the priest.

"We met yesterday," said the old man, "and then you all left. I misunderstood your words and thought you were gone for the whole winter. I was crying when a young boy came and told me I was wrong. He took me to a cave and spent the night with me. In the morning he told me to take a bath and come here. He said he, too, would be here but I don't see him. I see now that I was mistaken and he was right because here you are. He told me you would come and open the temple doors so I could see my Lord."

As he spoke, tears began to well up in the priest's eyes. In a quivering voice he asked, "What did the boy look like?"

"His face was the color of a rain cloud. His eyes sparkled like flashes of lightning. His curly hair cascaded down his shoulders. And when he laughed, the world stood still. Such a beautiful child. You will see for yourself. He will be here any minute."

"No," cried the priest falling at the feet of the old man. "He will not come for us. He came for you because of your devotion. It was the Lord Himself who came to you. You have spent the whole winter here. We are returning after five months. No one can survive in the wintery conditions in these places. Yet you are here. The Lord took care of you. You spent the winter with Him."

And the priest cried and the old man cried and my mother cried and we cried. These were tears filled with joy, compassion, wonder, and yearning. Perhaps we all experienced a deep yearning for the ever-elusive Krishna who had played chess with his devotee but was so hard to catch, so hard to find.

The Story of Krishna Stealing Kheer

Among all the stories I heard, the one that fascinated me the most was the story of a great devotee of Krishna named Madhavendra Puri.

Madhavendra Puri lived in Vrindavan and worshipped Gopal, a statue of baby Krishna. One night he dreamed that Gopal wanted him to go to Orissa to get some sandalwood for him. By smearing sandalwood paste on Gopal, one could bring him some relief from the heat. On waking up, Madhavendra Puri began his long journey on foot.

After many months, Madhavendra Puri came to a place called Remuna where there was a temple of Krishna. This deity of Krishna was called Gopinath. Madhavendra Puri heard that twelve pots of a special dessert of condensed milk called *kheer* were offered to Gopinath in the temple. The great devotee thought, "If only I could taste the *kheer*, I could make it for my Gopal when I returned to Vrindavan."

Later, that night, the priest of the temple saw Gopinath in a dream. Lord Gopinath told the priest that He had taken and hidden one of the pots of *kheer* for his devotee, Madhavendra Puri. The priest knew that each night, all the pots of *kheer* were moved out of the shrine room after they had been offered to the Lord. But when the priest went to the temple, he found a pot of *kheer* in the shrine room which the Lord Himself had stolen.

The priest took the pot and went looking for the Lord's devotee as instructed. He found Madhavendra Puri on the outskirts of the town and told him of his great fortune. The great Gopinath, the Lord Himself, had stolen a pot of *kheer* for his disciple so that Madhavendra Puri's wish could be fulfilled. From that day onwards, Gopinath acquired a new title and was known as Kheerchora Gopinath or the Gopinath who stole the *kheer*.

The Story of Madhusudan Dada

And then there was the popular story of the little boy, Jatila, and Madhusudan *dada*. Jatila lived with his widowed mother at the edge of a forest. They were very poor and had to live on whatever she could provide. However, Jatila went to school even though the school was quite far and he had to walk through the dense forest each day.

"I am scared of walking through the forest, Mother," said Jatila.

"Do not worry, my son," said his mother. "Madhusudan (another name for Krishna) *dada* (elder brother) is always with you. He will take care of you and ensure your safe passage through the forest."

Happy to hear this, Jatila left for school. As he entered the forest, he stopped and called out, "Madhusudan *dada*! Madhusudan *dada*! Where are you?"

A beautiful young boy with an enchanting smile came and stood before Jatila. "My name is Madhusudan and I will take you to school."

The two of them walked along, chatting happily, until they came to the edge of the forest when Madhusudan said, "There is your school, Jatila. I won't go any further, but I will be waiting for you when school is over and we will walk back home."

Bidding his new friend goodbye, Jatila ran along happily and immersed himself in his studies until school ended. With his bag on his shoulder, the little boy ran back enthusiastically because he knew that he would have a companion on his way home. Sure enough, there was Madhusudan waiting for him as promised. Thus began a wonderful friendship with Madhusudan walking Jatila to school each day.

One day, the headmaster announced that a picnic would be held in which all the students and teachers would participate. Each student was required to bring a dish, and everyone had to sign up and indicate what they would bring. The rich boys said they would be responsible for mutton and fish and the best desserts that could be bought in the village. Others said they would bring their chefs to cook hot food. As each boy volunteered, Jatila did not know what to say. What could his poor mother provide that would feed the school?

When he went home and told his mother, she said, "Tell Madhusudan *dada* and he will provide something." So, the next day, Jatila told his friend his problem and Madhusudan told him not to worry.

The day of the picnic arrived, and Jatila looked around nervously for his friend. But true to his word, Madhusudan emerged from the forest with a small pot of yogurt. Happy that he had something to share, Jatila went to the feast without any apprehensions. There he saw huge cauldrons of rice and lentils boiling with chefs fussing over the preparation of the feast. Finally, everyone was seated to eat, and the headmaster was naming each item brought by each student. Suddenly, his glance fell on Jatila.

"What did you bring, you poor boy?" asked the Master tauntingly.

All the boys were looking at Jatila as he hesitantly held up the small pot of yogurt. Everyone burst out laughing. The headmaster said, "Look! Just look at the size of the pot! It may provide just one serving!" And they laughed and jeered and taunted Jatila who hung his head in shame.

But soon everyone focused on the food because they were hungry and longed to taste the sumptuous feast that had been prepared for them. After the rice and lentils and vegetables and fish and mutton and chutney had been eaten, the headmaster asked the chef to bring the yogurt. Huge pots of yogurt had been supplied by the rich boys and the chef was about to bring one such pot when the headmaster said, "Wait, wait. Let's start with Jatila's pot." This gave rise to a round of elated laughter.

The headmaster emptied the pot of yogurt, and it was a full serving as he had predicted. Mocking Jatila, the headmaster said to the teacher sitting next to him, "I will pass it on to you now. See if you can squeeze a drop out of it." And they all laughed again. Jatila wished he could just vanish into thin air. But suddenly, the laughter died away as everyone watched a full serving of yogurt slipping out of the pot onto the plate of the teacher sitting next to the headmaster. And so it went. Each time the pot was emptied, it filled up again. In perfect silence the teachers and students and all who were eating emptied the pot on their plates and saw it filling up. The taste was heavenly. No human being could have made yogurt that was so delicious. This one dish was better than everything they had eaten so far.

When the meal was over, the headmaster called Jatila and asked him where he had bought the pot of yogurt. "Madhusudan *dada* gave it to me," said Jatila.

"Is he your elder brother?" asked the headmaster. "I mean, you called him *dada* and that is why I ask."

"No, he is my friend and he walks me to school every day."

"Can we see him?"

"Of course! He is waiting to take me home. Come with me and I will introduce you to him."

Jatila ran to the edge of the forest with the whole school following him. But no matter how hard he called, his friend did not come. Finally, they heard a voice say gently, "Dear Jatila, I reveal myself only to the pure hearted like you."

The headmaster hung his head in shame and went back to the school. Jatila walked into the forest and soon Madhusudan was right beside him. "How was the feast?" he asked, and Jatila walked home happily with stories of all he had eaten and the stunning impact his magical pot of yogurt had had on everybody.

Stories such as these, and so many more, were the bribes Mother offered to make me eat. She mixed the food on a plate, as most Indian mothers do, and made little balls of rice and lentils or rice and vegetables and put them in my mouth. The ball sat in my mouth, and I refused to chew or swallow until she started a story. Each meal was a delight. We did not get stories at bedtime, but we never swallowed a morsel without a story.

And then there were the stories of the *sadhus* Mother had seen—great sages, holy men and women. Some sages remained in my imagination because I had never seen them, but there were others whom Bonie and I had the great fortune to visit as Mother took us along with her when she went to visit them.

Mother. Boston, 20017

Chapter 26: The Loving Sage-- Premananda Swamiji

One sage I did not have the fortune to see was Srimat Premananda Tirthaswami. Nevertheless, I have many childhood memories associated with him, and in our home he was known as Swamiji.

One of my earliest memories is that of a portrait of Swamiji which used to hang on the dining room wall of my grandmother's house in Calcutta. White hair, white moustache, and a white beard framed a benign face with two tenderly compassionate eyes and a gentle radiant smile. The saffron robes of a monk were draped around the shoulders of the figure in the painting. As I grew older, I heard that my mother had given a picture of Swamiji to a painter and he had painted the portrait for our family.

Premananda Swamiji

Another early memory connected with Swamiji is that of our shrine room in Jhansi. It is 1965 and I am sitting on my father's lap with my mother sitting next to us. We are in the *puja* (shrine) room and all three of us are chanting Swamiji's Puja Mantra. I am barely six years old, but I know the chant by heart. Every evening, my parents chant the Sanskrit *slokas* (verses) selected from Hindu scriptures by Swamiji, and I have somehow managed to memorize the *slokas* even though I do not understand them. That particular evening I am chanting and wondering why tears are falling from my mother's eyes as we sit before the shrine on which Swamiji's photograph is placed. The next day, my father, who is in the Indian Army, moves with his men to the front as war breaks out between India and Pakistan. Left behind in Jhansi with her two children, Mother has nothing to give her hope, strength, and courage except the strong faith that Swamiji is always with us to protect us. These are two vivid memories from my childhood that I have carried with me through my life.

My family met Swamiji after my grandfather built a house on Keyatala Road in 1955. Diagonally across from my grandfather's house was the house of Mr. Narayan Dasgupta, and it was in Mr. Dasgupta's house that my family met Swamiji. Life is full of ups and downs for those of us who are not enlightened, and our family had faced its share of unhappy experiences in the 1940s. My grandfather had lost a beautiful eight-year-old son to typhoid and had witnessed the smile vanish from the lips of his angelic daughter, Dolly, after yet another tragedy had struck the family. It is often said that we do not turn to God when we are happy but we do seek Him in times of adversity. In trying to cope with life's blows, our family turned to God. Grandfather started to read various books based on Hindu philosophy and also encouraged his daughters to gain comfort from the wisdom of our eminent Indian sages. When my family met Swamiji, they no longer needed to seek wisdom from books because now they were in the shining presence of a truly enlightened soul who was a fountain of unending bliss and love and a source of great peace and happiness to humanity.

Describing to me the first time she saw Swamiji, Aunt Dolly said, "Swamiji used to visit Mr. Dasgupta's house. In 1955, one day I saw a *sadhu* on the terrace of their second floor. The color of his complexion was like that of heated copper—bright and radiant. He had a beard and wore saffron-colored robes. I liked him the minute I saw him. He stayed for a couple of hours and then left by car. Later, I went to Mr. Dasgupta's house and asked who had visited them. I was told that Swamiji had paid them a visit. I learned that he was staying for a few days in the house of Dr. Chuni Sanyal, who revered Swamiji as his own guru even though Swamiji did not initiate anyone. I also learned that whenever Swamiji visited Dr. Sanyal, he also tried to visit his other devotees in Calcutta.

"Later, on 24th January 1957, Swamiji had come to the Dasgupta household and I said to my father, 'Let's go and meet Swamiji.' Father agreed and we both went to see him.

"Upstairs, in the Dasgupta house, there was a room and bathroom for Swamiji, and he was sitting in his room. Many people were present; the men sat on one side and the women sat on the other side. There was no room for more people inside, so I sat on the terrace just outside the door. Soon Swamiji looked at me and beckoned with his hand asking me to go to him. He made me sit right next to him, put his arm around me and embraced me as though I were a little child. I burst into tears and my tears kept flowing. He blessed me and said, 'Ma, you sit here.' I experienced such peace in my heart that I cannot find the words to describe it. From that day onwards I felt a strong attraction to him. I do not know why he was so kind to me. Soon he established a relationship with all members of my family through me. Because he called me Ma (Mother), he called my father *Dadu* (Grandfather), my mother *Didima* (Grandmother), my sister *Mashi* (Aunty), and my brother *Mamu* (Uncle)."

When I reflect on my Aunt Dolly's words, more than half a century later, I am amazed at how with this simple gesture Swamiji, a *sanyasi* who had left home and entered the spiritual life, made our family his own. It wasn't that our family was in any way special or that Swamiji heaped special favors on us. He treated us the way he treated all who came to Him. Great sages have told us to love God by establishing a relationship with Him. He can be our child, friend, spouse, parent, or lover. However, my heart wells up with gratitude at the thought that in this case Swamiji did not wait for us to establish a relationship with him; he himself made us his own. In this way, this great enlightened being made himself accessible to us as a son, a grandchild, and a nephew.

After meeting Swamiji, Aunt Dolly and my grandfather became regular visitors to the Dasgupta house whenever he was visiting. If for some reason my aunt could not go, he always asked my grandfather why she had not come. At this point in his life, Swamiji was suffering from heart problems and was extremely ill on most days. In Aunt Dolly's words, "We would go and hear that he had been lying in bed all day and had barely touched any food. However, the minute I entered, he would sit up and talk about many things. Even his voice would become strong, and it was hard to see that he was so sick. I did not know much about the spiritual path. I had read a few books and had started developing some devotion; however, I was in no way a special person. There was nothing about me that deserved Swamiji's compassion, yet he was so kind to me. I could not remember much of the content of his spiritual discourses once his talks were over, but I could understand what he said while he was speaking. Although I was young and inexperienced, I knew that I was in the presence of a great soul. For instance, I knew Swamiji was an *antarjami* because he always knew what was in my heart.

"There was a photograph of Swamiji in Mr. Dasgupta's house that I really liked. I wished I had a copy of the photo, but I was too shy to ask anyone. One day I went to see Swamiji with my father. He usually stayed in a devotee's home for two or three days and he never met a woman alone. The woman could be an eight-year-old girl or an eighty-year-old elderly woman, he would only see her in the presence of a guardian or chaperone. He met people in the evenings and rarely met anyone in the morning. After visiting him, we were about to leave when Swamiji said to me, 'Come and see me tomorrow morning with your father.' Next morning when we went, he gave me an envelope and said with a big smile, 'Ma, see what I have for you.' His face was full of affection. I looked inside the envelope and saw many pictures of Swamiji but not the one I wanted. I went through the whole pile of photos and at the bottom of the pile was the photo I wanted. I took the photo and Swamiji said, 'I know you really liked that photo, so I ordered it for you.'"

After a pause, Aunt Dolly continued, "I remember another incident that convinced me that Swamiji knew what was on my mind. It was the festival of the goddess Saraswati and I was helping my mother make the arrangements for the *puja*. Swamiji used to visit us from time to time, and that day I found myself thinking how wonderful it would be if Swamiji suddenly dropped by and visited us. There was little possibility of my wish being fulfilled because he had left for a devotee's house and would not be back at the Dasgupta household until evening. However, at 11:30 a.m. the doorbell rang. I was making the *khichuri* which was to be offered to the deity. I ran and opened the door and there stood Swamiji. He walked right in and went straight to the kitchen. He said, 'Ma, you were thinking of me and here I am. Send me some *khichuri* in the evening after the *puja* is over.' I was thrilled to have my wish fulfilled in this miraculous way. In the evening, I went with some *khichuri* and *payesh* (rice pudding) to Mrs. Dasgupta and told her to offer the *bhog* (food offered to the deity) to Swamiji. At that time, a *Brahmachari* (monk) was with Swamiji. His name was Sadananda and we called him Sadanandada. Next day, Sadanandada came and said, 'Yesterday, the *bhog* we ate was excellent.' We all agreed because we had had the same experience. *Bhog* is always tasty, but that day the food tasted like nectar. We all knew that the food tasted so special because Swamiji had come to our kitchen and his glance had alighted on the food as it was being prepared."

While growing up in Calcutta in my grandparents' house, I heard many such stories about Swamiji. Even though he had left his body, I felt his presence because my mother and Aunt Dolly often talked about him. While other children listened to stories of Cinderella and Snow White, I begged my mother and aunt to tell me stories of Swamiji. Often, I would listen to these stories as I was being fed. Aunt Dolly would roll some rice and mashed potatoes into a ball and place it in my mouth and start a story: "Swamiji loved to feed people. This is a common trait of most great sages. They become like our mothers and constantly wish to feed us. One day, Swamiji sent word and asked my brother, Sankar, and me to visit him. We went and found him sitting with a big smile on his face and looking very delighted to see us. He said, 'I have something for you.' He asked someone to give him a container inside which were some sweets (*pantuas*). Swamiji said, 'Someone brought these for me yesterday and I have saved some for you.' He sat there and watched us eat and it gave him great happiness to see us relish the juicy sweets.

"Another day a couple invited everyone to their place for a celebration. Swamiji asked me if I had been invited and I said, 'I don't think so.' He said, 'You must attend the festivities and if anyone says anything just tell them I told you to come.' I obeyed his request and went to the celebration. The food was wonderful. I still remember the *halva*. It was delicious. I do not think I have ever eaten such wonderful *halva*.

"I remember going in the evening to see Swamiji on *Janamashtami*, the day we celebrate Krishna's birthday. His devotees had brought many sweets and fruits and various delicacies. He made me sit next to him and asked someone to bring an old newspaper. On this newspaper he put a little bit of every kind of food that had been offered. Finally, he packed up the food and gave it to me and said, 'Give this to everyone at home and then eat some.' He knew that whenever I went home after seeing him, I always first shared with everyone the *batasha* (sugar candy) he had given me and then ate the *prasad* (blessed food). Even such little details were not hidden from him despite the fact that he had no way of knowing that I never ate *prasad* without first sharing it with my family members.

"One day, Swamiji said, 'Ma, come tomorrow morning with your father. I wish to feed you." We went the next day around noon. Only the family members of the Dasgupta household were present. Swamiji was offered *bhog*. He first mixed some food on his plate and put a little bit of food in the mouth of each person who was present. This was something he usually did. Then he began to mix each item and I remember that he squeezed a lot of lemon juice into his food as he mixed the various items with rice. When the food was mixed properly, he started eating. As he ate, he put some food in his mouth and then put some food in my mouth. In this way he fed me not only on that day but also on another day. I still do not know what I had done to deserve such kindness, but I am immensely grateful for all the love and compassion he showered on me at a time when I was going through a very difficult phase of my life. I am convinced that it is due to his blessings that I could overcome my unhappiness and live such a long and happy life."

As I listened to these stories, I often forgot to chew the ball of rice and potatoes in my mouth as I kept visualizing the scenes depicted in the tales. No fairy tale about handsome princes and beautiful princesses could rival these stories of Swamiji feeding his devotees and filling their lives with his loving presence.

Aunt Dolly told me that many famous people used to come to see Swamiji. They were not only his devoted followers but also quite well established in society. These spiritual seekers came and listened to his spiritual discourses, participated in the chanting of the Puja Mantra, and sang beautiful devotional songs. These were indeed happy evenings that my grandfather and aunt spent in Swamiji's room, which throbbed with the spiritual energy of his enlightened presence. He brought great solace and bliss to many a distressed heart. While there were some stories that Aunt Dolly shared with me, there was much that she never talked about. I was relentless in pestering her for more stories, but she was very careful about what she told me. One of the stories that she finally shared a few years before her death was a story that I do not remember hearing when I was a child.

Aunt Dolly said, "One evening when father and I had gone to see Swamiji, we found that he was very sick. The room was full of people. Mrs. Dasgupta came and offered Swamiji a drink made with lemon juice, sugar, and water (*lebur shorbot*). Swamiji asked me to take a sip of the drink. I was stunned and did not know what to do. He said, 'Do what I am telling you to do.' Since he was so insistent, I had no other option but to obey him. I took the glass in my hands, lifted it high above my lips, and was about to pour a little bit of the drink in my mouth when I heard his voice. He said, 'What are you doing? Drink properly. Put your lips to the glass and drink.' My head was swimming with confusion. He was such a great sage. How could I drink first and then let him drink what was left? Trembling, I put the glass to my lips and took a sip. After that, Swamiji drank what was left in the glass."

The story seemed strange even to me when I heard it. I knew that in our Bengali culture we never give someone food or drink that has touched our lips because such food or drink is considered unclean or tainted. There is however one exception. Food left over on the plate of a great sage is treated as blessed and it is perfectly acceptable for the sage's devotees to eat this food. But for a devotee to first eat the food and then offer it to a sage is unheard of. However, evidently it was not uncommon for Swamiji to do this. No one knows why he did such things, but all I do know is that when I am sad and I turn to him for comfort, he "drinks up" all my pain and leaves me filled with peace.

I also used to plead with my aunt to tell me her spiritual experiences about which she was very tight-lipped. After much nagging, one day she told me the following story: "I had heard that sometimes one can see God in great sages. One day I went with Mr. and Mrs. Dasgupta to see Swamiji at Dr. Anil Bose's home in Chowringhee. When we arrived, Swamiji had not yet come so we waited. After some time, Swamiji arrived, and I clearly saw Ramakrishna Paramhansa in Swamiji. He was wearing saffron robes, but it was Ramakrishna that I saw."

There were probably many such stories that my aunt never shared with anyone because she was a very humble person and did not like to say anything that would bring her into prominence. However, in December 1997, I begged her to tell me her stories and allow me to tape them. Very reluctantly she agreed, and I am writing them down more than a decade after she passed away.

In 2010, I was in Calcutta for three months because my mother was very sick. Worried that the stories of all her wonderful spiritual experiences would be lost after she left us, I switched on my voice recorder and taped several stories. Like her sister, my aunt Dolly, Mother too was very reluctant to share most of these stories. However, by then I had become an expert nag. I had heard some of these stories as a child, but it was nice to have recordings of them. Of all the stories associated with Swamiji told by my mother, my favorite story is the one that focuses on my birth.

Some details of this story I have heard from Mrs. Dasgupta, whom I often visited with Aunt Dolly many years after Swamiji had left us. Mrs. Dasgupta told me how before I was born, Swamiji was very sick and the doctor had forbidden him to leave his bed. But one night when she and her husband were downstairs getting ready for bed, they suddenly heard the unmistakable sound of Swamiji's wooden sandals and walking stick as he descended the stairs. They looked at the clock and it was almost midnight. Thinking that he needed something, they rushed to his assistance. When they realized that he was going to go to my family's home across the street, they tried to stop him but he brushed aside their concerns and said, "Let me go. I have received a divine intimation and must go (*Amake jete dao. Ami opor theke adesh peyechi.*)." Saying this he left the house, crossed the street, and came to our house.

From Mother I learned the rest of the story. After she and Father were married in 1958, they went to live in a beautiful little hill station near Simla called Dagshai where my father's battalion was stationed. At the start of 1959, when Ma was pregnant with me, the doctors at the military hospital said the pregnancy was complicated. There was a great possibility of losing either the mother or the child. When Swamiji, who was in Calcutta, heard this he sent a message asking my mother to be brought to Calcutta. She was flown into Calcutta and arrived late at night. It was almost midnight when suddenly the doorbell rang. Mother said, "I knew at once that it was Swamiji, and we hurried to open the door. When we opened the door, we saw the radiant figure of Swamiji and a very worried looking Mrs. Dasgupta standing behind him."

Swamiji came and sat in my parents' bedroom and talked about many things for almost an hour. He left after blessing everyone, and all the anxieties that had plagued my family regarding my mother's health vanished into thin air.

After my mother settled down in Calcutta she found that she was unable to keep down whatever she ate. Aunt Dolly mentioned this problem to Swamiji and he gave her a *batasha* for my mother. After my mother ate the *batasha* the vomiting stopped, and she could eat once again.

One day my mother heard that Swamiji was soon going to leave the Dasgupta home and she went with my grandfather to pay her respects to

Swamiji and say goodbye. They both met Swamiji downstairs and sat on the front porch of the house. Mrs. Dasgupta came and offered Swamiji a glass of fruit juice *(beler shorbot)*. After she had left, Swamiji asked my mother to take a sip from his glass. My mother drank some of the juice and then he drank the rest of what was left in the glass. As my mother touched his feet and said goodbye to him, he said, "When I hear that all has gone well with you, I will leave. Just as a bird that finds the window of its cage open flies away, I too will fly away *(Jokhon shunbo je tomar shob bhalo bhabe hoye giyeche, pakhi jemon tar khanchar janala khola pele ure jaye, ami o ei deho chere chole jabo.).*"

In April of 1959, Mother gave birth to me. The delivery was so smooth and painless that the nurses at Presidency Nursing Home said to my mother, "You must never scold this little girl. Always remember that she did not give you any trouble during her birth." Both Mother and I survived, and what was to have been a very complicated case turned out to be an easy delivery. True to his words, shortly after I entered this world, Swamiji opened the "window of his cage" and left us on May 2, 1959.

Although the Great Soul left his earthly body in 1959, his devotees continued to feel his presence in their lives. In 1960, Mother was on a train coming back from Dagshai with me when her mind was very disturbed with worries and anxieties about my father, who was at the Indo-China border. There were rumors about trouble brewing between India and China, so Mother was naturally extremely anxious. Two Christian nuns who were also travelling on the train asked her why she looked so worried. She talked to them, and they comforted her and invited her to visit their Church once she arrived in Calcutta. After the nuns had fallen asleep, Mother sat on her berth worrying about her husband and her own future if something were to happen to him. Suddenly, she had a vision of Swamiji in the first-class compartment of the train in which she was traveling. He smiled at her and raised his hand to bless her and said, "Why are you scared? I am there *(Bhoi ki? Ami acchi.).*"

In 1961, Mother, who was an extremely brave woman, left the safety of my grandparents' home in Calcutta to go with me to Shillong. She decided to stay there because she would be closer to my father and would be able to get news of him from time to time. After arriving in Shillong, Mother rented a house. Right next to our house was the house of our landlord. She had hardly settled down when she heard that the elderly gentleman next door, who was her landlord's father, was on his death bed. Soon the gentleman died, and Mother felt obligated to go over next door and convey her condolences. Not knowing that the relatives of the deceased were washing his dead body in the courtyard, Mother arrived at an inopportune moment and witnessed the ritual. The scene disturbed her, and she left quickly. All alone with her little child, Mother had no one to turn to for comfort and spent the day with an uneasy sense of disquiet as the image of the deceased man kept flashing in her mind.

Finally, night descended and Mother went to bed. Tired after her long day, she switched off the light and went to sleep. Suddenly, in the middle of the night she woke up with the uneasy feeling that someone was in the room. As she opened her eyes in the dark bedroom, she was aware of something near the little crib in which I was sleeping. Instinctively she knew that there was a spirit in the room, and it was circling my crib. She froze with fear as the realization dawned on her that the spirit was that of the landlord's dead father, who had been cremated that evening. Even though her motherly instincts wished to protect me, she found that she could not move an inch. She felt paralyzed and could not breathe. She stayed in this position for what seemed to her an eternity when suddenly she remembered Swamiji. She had his photograph on the mantel over the fireplace. With all her strength she jumped out of bed and ran to the mantel and snatched the photograph saying, "You are there. Why should I be scared (*Tumi thakte amar bhoy kisher*)?" At once she felt the spirit disappear and then she turned on the lights. My mother said that after that incident she was never again afraid of anything.

A similar incident was experienced by Mother in 1965 after the end of the war between India and Pakistan when we moved to Kashmir. Father was stationed in Uri, which was close to the border between India and Pakistan. Mother lived in a huge bungalow in Srinagar with me, my newborn baby sister, and a young boy called Dhanraj who was supposed to look after me but was really too young to do so. Dhanraj was probably fourteen years old and I was six. As Mother took care of baby Bonie, Dhanraj and I played together and ran around all over the neighborhood exploring the fruit orchards and other places of interest. One day we ran into a beautiful garden behind our house. It was huge and had a wall surrounding it. We entered through a gate and to my delight I found acres and acres of narcissus. Dhanraj and I began to play in the garden, and when we were tired we sat on smooth flat slabs of stone that the garden seemed to be full of. After spending a whole afternoon playing, we finally decided to go home with a bunch of flowers for Mother. When she saw me come in with my arms full of narcissus, she asked where I had been. When she heard what we had been doing, she threw away the flowers and in a scolding voice told us never to go back to that garden again. What Dhanraj and I did not know was the fact that the garden was a cemetery. Mother knew about it and was already looking for another house to move to, but she had never dreamt that Dhanraj and I would go there.

That night, we were all asleep when suddenly my mother woke up because she heard me crying. While narrating the story, Mother said to me, "I woke up and found you standing on your bed, shaking with fear and crying. You were saying, 'Mother, look—those people have come.' You kept repeating the same sentence, and no matter how hard I tried I could not stop you from crying. The baby woke up and started crying, too. I had no time for the baby because I was trying to hold you in my arms and comfort you. At this point I realized that there was a terrible storm raging outside. The wind was howling, and I could hear the poplars thrashing in the gale. It seemed almost as if someone was knocking on the front door, but I knew it was only the wind. Our bedroom was at the back of the house and there were huge glass windows through which the moonlight was pouring in. With a sudden start I realized that the poplars in the backyard were not moving. I ran to the windows and saw the moon shining in the sky, the backyard flooded with moonlight, and the poplars standing still. Not a leaf moved. With horror I realized that the storm that was threatening to break down the front door was only in the front of the house and not in the back. I looked at you and you were looking towards the front of the house and shaking with fear. It was obvious to me that you could see something that I could not."

In the midst of all this terror and confusion, my mother suddenly recalled that Dhanraj and I had spent the afternoon in the cemetery. Once again, she ran to Swamiji's picture, grabbed the photo, and sat with the baby and me in her lap. She kept calling Swamiji for help and gradually the "storm" in the front of the house died down, I stopped shaking, and Bonie stopped crying. Everything was calm and we all finally went to bed.

While Mother and Aunt Dolly had many stories of Swamiji, my uncle, Sankar Chakrabarti, who was fourteen years old when my family met Swamiji, had one story. Uncle Sankar used to suffer from a terrible colic pain that would keep him up all night. Swamiji's devotees had told my grandmother and aunt to tell Swamiji about my uncle's ailment because Swamiji knew how to concoct different types of medicines that could cure certain illnesses. Several times my grandmother and aunt went to see Swamiji to tell him about my uncle, but each time Swamiji was so sick that they did not wish to trouble him. One evening, as they were leaving Swamiji's room, he said, "Wait. I know you want to tell me something. What is it?" Grandmother told him about my uncle's colic pain and next day Swamiji came to our house. Uncle was in a lot of pain at that time and Swamiji came and told everyone to get off his bed. Then Swamiji lay down next to my uncle and stroked his forehead and stomach. After doing this, Swamiji got up and washed his hands at the basin. Before leaving, Swamiji said, "He will be fine. Come and get the medicine from me and give it to him." From that day onwards, my uncle never experienced that pain again.

Even though the members of my family knew Swamiji for a very short period of time, he filled their lives with his blessings because his generosity knew no bounds. As a little girl, I looked forward to visiting Mr. Dasgupta's house with my aunt. We would first go upstairs and prostrate in Swamiji's room where his bed and some other belongings still remained and were meticulously taken care of by Mrs. Dasgupta. I loved looking at the bed and imagining Swamiji sitting on it and speaking affectionately to his devotees. His devotees sometimes gathered in the evenings to chant the Puja Mantra and I happily joined them. On some occasions the sessions were led by Sadanandada. Even though I did not know Sanskrit, I could feel the intense vibrations throbbing through the congregation. Sometimes I felt that the room would explode.

In the late sixties, Sadanandada visited us in Roorkee and one evening we gathered to chant the Puja Mantra. Sadanandada was thrilled to see that I knew all the verses and could join in the chanting. Whenever I saw Sadanandada I experienced Swamiji's love and affection through him.

My mother had another story of Swamiji that I loved to hear as a child. In the early nineteen forties, my mother and her family were in Kushtia when they saw an amazing picture of a beautiful Indian sage and a tiger in a magazine. The sage was leaning against the tiger and they seemed to be good friends. Years later, when my mother met Swamiji, she asked him if he was the sage with the tiger and he said he was. Swamiji had named the tiger Mastoram.

Swamiji's picture now hangs on the wall next to my computer desk. I look up and see his smiling face looking down at me. May His blessings always be with us and all who seek the spiritual path, and may we learn to love and cherish all beings as Swamiji did.

Chapter 27: Phalahari Baba (The Fruit-Eating Sage)

In 1964, Father was transferred from Mhow to Dehradun. Mother was going through a difficult time because the doctors had found some problem with Father's heart, and he was not allowed to go to the battlefield. Even though he felt fine, the doctors said he should not climb any hills or mountains. This was a setback in my father's career. He was a true soldier and was upset that he would not be able to join his battalion if war broke out. Moreover, there was not much of a chance of any further promotions with health being an important criterion in the military. Being of a cheerful nature, Father accepted his fate and did not let his situation depress him. But Mother loved my father and could not come to terms with the doctors' diagnosis.

While all this was happening, some friends of my parents came over and stayed with us for a few days. They were going on pilgrimage to Kedarnath and Badrinath. Mother had lost faith in God and Father could see she was depressed. He said, "Why don't you go with them? Perhaps you will regain your faith in God." Thus, urged by my father, Mother decided to join her friends and make the trip to these sacred places. They went by bus up to a certain point, and then had to choose between going on horseback or walking. Mother saved the money my father had given her to ride on a horse because she wanted to give the money to the *sadhus* (sages)she would see in Badrinath. She and her friends decided to walk. It was a long and arduous journey through rough terrain. All day they walked until they came to a place where they could stop and rest for the night. Here they ate and rested until the next day. It took several days to reach Kedarnath. Sometimes they bathed in a spring or washed their clothes in the water. At Gauri Kund, they bathed in the hot springs. Sometimes they walked through heavy rain, sometimes the climb was very steep, and sometimes they did not see anybody for several hours in these remote sparsely populated areas of the Himalayas.

At one point during the journey, Mother began to lag and fell behind the rest of the group because her left foot was hurting. She had blisters from days of walking and was in pain. Worried that she was delaying the other pilgrims, she told her friends to go ahead and she would catch up with them. Soon she was all alone. Having always been fearless and adventurous,

Mother did not worry and walked at her own pace. Suddenly, she could feel a presence behind her. She felt an invisible form that seemed to be gently pushing her forward. The form had four arms and long hair. Mother could sense the hair blowing in the wind and brushing against her shoulders. This did not frighten her and she kept moving. She was not tempted to look back. It felt as though she was being carried forward. After she had walked for quite a long time, she came across a raised slab of stone on the side of the road and sat down to rest a bit. As she sat there, she noticed a group of pilgrims climbing up the winding road. As the group neared her, she was stunned to find her friends. They looked at her in shock. How could she have overtaken them? If she had overtaken them, they would have seen her pass by. Yet here she was. Mother had no answer to explain this strange incident. Her friends became quiet as they resumed their journey.

Mother (behind the lady in the sari) on her way to Kedarnath. 1964

When they arrived at the temple of Kedarnath, a priest named Bhardwaj took them to the temple where they paid their respects to the Shiva Lingam. After performing *puja*, Mother's friends went to relax in the rest house where they were going to spend the night. Mother stayed back and asked Bhardwaj whether there were any holy men or women she could meet.

Mother (with her head covered) and Phalahari Baba (with the gray hair and beard). Kedarnath, 1969

Bhardwaj said, "Yes, there is a great *sadhu* named Phalahari Baba who lives here through the year. We come to the temple in May when the temple is opened for pilgrims. But in October the temple is closed for the winter and we go down to the plains. However, Phalahari Baba stays here. As the winter gets severe, his hut is buried under the snow. We do not know how he survives, but each summer we find him under the snow and often have to dig him out. At this time, when the place is flooded with pilgrims, he climbs up to the higher peaks of the Himalayas where the Brahma Kamal blooms. Unfortunately, he is not here now." Mother looked at the snowcapped peaks Bhardwaj was pointing at and felt sad that she was going to miss the opportunity of seeing this great sage.

As she turned to go to the rest house, she heard a gentle voice behind her say, "My child, were you looking for me?"

She turned around and saw a *sadhu* of slight build who introduced himself as Phalahari Baba. Mother bowed and told him she was hoping to see him. He took her to his hut and started talking about spiritual matters. Mother had hoped to pray for my father's health at the temple but had been unable to ask for anything as she stood before the Shiva Lingam. Now was her chance to ask the sage for his blessings but, once again, she couldn't ask for anything. Finally, she said, "Baba (Father), tell me something that I will remember all my life."

The sage touched her forehead between the eyebrows and asked, "Do you sense His presence here?" Mother nodded. "Always remember Him," the sage continued. "If the world says you are wrong, but your conscience says you are right, listen to your conscience. And when you go to bed each night, think of your day and notice what you did wrong. Do not do it again." Having given her this simple and profound advice, he placed his palm on her head in a blessing and wished her well by saying, "All will be well with you, my daughter (*Beti, tera bhala hoga*)."

After returning from her pilgrimage, Mother found that her meeting with Phalahari Baba had been extremely fruitful. She had regained her faith in God. She asked my father to take leave and we went to Calcutta to my grandmother's house. Mother took my father to meet some renowned doctors who were heart specialists. They conducted various tests and concluded that my father was fine and could resume a normal life. Father took the reports to the military doctors and after they had examined him, they declared that he was fit for military service.

Mother sent money to Bhardwaj each year with instructions to provide Phalahari Baba with all he needed to survive the winters. In 1969, Father was once again posted to Dehradun. After we were settled there, Mother went to Kedarnath again. This time she travelled with Major Diptimoy Banerjee, the military doctor stationed at 39 Gorkha Training Center, and his wife, Bandana Banerjee. At Kedarnath, Mother met Bhardwaj and asked if she could meet Phalahari Baba. Luckily, the sage was in his hut and was very happy to see her. Many devotees came with fruits for him. He asked my mother to distribute the fruits among the people who came to see him. Since Phalahari Baba only ate fruits, Mother was touched to see how he did not hesitate to generously give all his fruits away instead of saving a few for himself.

Some years later, Bhardwaj wrote to tell her that Phalahari Baba had left the body and there was no need for Mother to send more money. Our family always felt indebted to this great sage because we believed that it was due to his blessings that the setback in my father's health and career was reversed.

The temple of Kedarnath against the backdrop of the snowcapped Himalayan peaks.
1969

Chapter 28: Sitaramdas Omkarnath

In 1965, we moved to Jhansi after the birth of my sister. Later that year, war broke out between India and Pakistan and Father's battalion moved to the battlefront. I remember going to the station and seeing a whole train full of soldiers. The band was playing, wives were crying, the officers were laughing, the soldiers were chatting with each other, and the children were playing. I could sense that underneath her dignified appearance, Mother was tense and apprehensive. But I was still too young to understand the significance of the event.

All alone in Jhansi with two children and an orderly named Chitra Bahadur, Mother waited every day for news of her husband. The military cantonment where Father's battalion had been stationed was almost empty. The wives of all the officers had gathered their children and gone to stay with their parents. But the families of the Gorkha soldiers could not go back to Nepal. They too were waiting for news of their husbands.

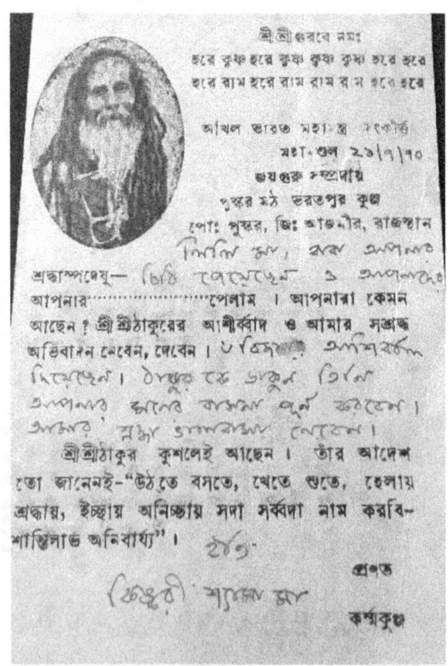

Letter to Mother from Sitaramdas Baba's ashram

As news started trickling in of casualties, Mother's fears worsened. She had heard of a great sage named Sitaramdas Omkarnath. She began to write to him. She told him that her husband was on the battlefield and asked the sage to protect my father. She also expressed her wish to be initiated by him. Sitaramdas Baba wrote back to my mother and said, "Don't worry. Your husband will be fine. As for your request to be initiated, I am not your guru. I will give you a mantra to repeat, but later you will find a *satguru* or enlightened guru."

Another night, while in Jhansi, Mother had a vision of Sri Sri Mohanananda Brahmachari (Maharaj). He said, "Do not worry. He is well. I am there for you." The very next morning, Mother received a letter from Aunt Dolly. My aunt wrote that she had gone to see Maharaj and he had asked, "How is your sister?" Maharaj did not know Mother very well at this time even though she had met him and paid her respects to him the evening before Bonie's birth. Aunt Dolly told Maharaj that my father had gone to war and Mother was all alone with two children. Maharaj said, "He is fine. He will be fine." In her letter to my mother, my aunt had written, "Maharaj's words can never be false."

With the help of Mother's daily prayers and the blessings of these great sages, Father came home from war and our family was together again.

During the second half of the sixties, Aunt Dolly began to visit Maharaj whenever she had an opportunity to do so, and when we visited Calcutta during our vacations, we all went and paid our respects to Maharaj. The first person in our family who was initiated by Maharaj was Mother. This took place during one of our visits to Calcutta in 1969. At this time, Father was posted in Dehradun. Maharaj told Mother that since she lived in Dehradun, she had access to many great sages. He encouraged her to spend time with Anandamayi Ma, who had an ashram in Dehradun, and Sitaramdas Baba, who had an ashram in Rishikesh which is close to Dehradun. Maharaj also told Mother to go to the Himalayas where she would find many sages and hermits. He said, "Since you cannot always be with me, try to spend time with sages whenever you can."

Father was in Dehradun from 1969 to 1971. One day, he came home from work and told Mother that the guru of the Sub Area Commander's wife was going to visit her and she had invited Mother to be present during the visit. Mother did not know this lady or her guru, but she was only too glad to oblige because she was eager to meet a sage. What was Mother's surprise when she found that the sage who was about to arrive was none other than Sitaramdas Baba! Mother was helping with the arrangements for a ceremony the sage was going to perform when suddenly, some young men rushed in to announce the arrival of the sage and everyone hurried out to welcome him. Mother watched the sage as he got out of the car. His head was full of dreadlocks, and he had a beautiful smile. Mother was standing in one corner of the front yard when the Sub Area Commander said, "Mrs. Bagchi, Baba is calling you." Mother was taken aback since she had never met him even though she had corresponded with him while she was in Jhansi.

After he entered the house and sat down, Sitaramdas Baba beckoned to Mother to come and sit at his feet. He asked her, "Who is your guru?" His face lit up when Mother mentioned Maharaj's name as he was very fond of Maharaj. He placed his hand on Mother's head and kept it there for a long time. At this point, my father arrived with Bonie and me. We paid our respects to the sage and he blessed us all. He touched Bonie's forehead between her eyebrows and asked, "Whose child is this?" Mother said Bonie was her daughter and he kept silent. Then he turned to Mother and said, "Your guru is a great sage. If you do not take into account the sages who live in the Himalayas, there is no sage greater than your guru (*Himalayar niche tor gurur moton boro sadhu nei*). You must visit our ashram in Rishikesh."

Thus began a beautiful relationship between Sitaramdas Baba and Mother. Almost every weekend, she would plead with my father to take us to Rishikesh. Father was always supportive of my mother's spiritual practice and would take us whenever he could even though he was not very interested in sages. Sitaramdas Baba was very happy to see us each time we visited him. Even in a big crowd, he would wave at my mother and some of his disciples would usher us in. He blessed us all, but he was especially fond of Mother. He also made sure that we ate a meal before returning to Dehradun.

One day, we were sitting next to a foreigner who was wearing a diamond. My father asked him, "Why do you come here? What have you found?"

The man said, "I come for the real diamond: Baba."

Another day, Mother was talking to a Sikh disciple's wife who told her an interesting story. When her husband became a disciple of Sitaramdas Baba, her mother-in-law was upset that her son had been initiated by a Hindu sage. When he heard this, Sitaramdas Baba said to his disciple, "Take me to your mother. I hear that she is upset with you." The disciple brought his guru and mother face to face, and she saw Guru Nanak, a saint who is revered by the Sikhs, in her son's guru. After that, the mother and son were reconciled.

The ashram was always crowded because Sitaramdas Baba had thousands of followers. Among his disciples were many renowned men and women who held high positions in the government and the Defense Forces.

Standing: Sitaramdas Baba at his ashram in Rishikesh
Seated (from left to right): Father, Bonie, I, Uncle Sankar. 1970

One day, the sage noticed that my father was sweating profusely as he was eating his meal. He called his disciples and told them to get a hand fan and fan my father. The disciple who began fanning my father was a high ranking official in the Army. Father, who recognized the bigwig, was most embarrassed and quickly gulped down his food. We all laughed when my father told us the story on our way home.

On one occasion, Mother returned from a pilgrimage to Gomukh and went to the ashram in Rishikesh with a bottle of sacred water from Gomukh for Sitaramdas Baba. A special ceremony was being performed and hundreds of devotees were attending. The disciples told Mother that she would not be able to meet the sage that day and if she gave them the bottle of Ganges water they would give it to him. Mother hesitated and was pondering what to do when suddenly she heard, "What did you bring for me? Give me. (*Ki*

153

enechish amar jonne? De)" And there was Sitaramdas Baba with his arm outstretched. Mother was delighted and ran to give him the bottle. He sprinkled some water on his head and then sprinkled us all with the sacred water.

We usually went on a Saturday because Father would take us, and he had to work during the week. On one of those Saturdays, Sitaramdas Baba placed his hand on Mother's head and something happened to her. She did not say anything to us, and we came home after our visit. But Mother found that she could not function normally. She was unable to do the chores. For instance, she would be in the kitchen trying to cook and the spatula would fall from her hands. She experienced a strong sense of aloofness towards worldly life. Finally, she realized that she could not wait until the next Saturday to see the sage. She told my father to take a day off and take her to Rishikesh. The minute she was before the sage, he touched her head and immediately she became normal.

Many years later, when she told me this story, I asked her what had happened. She said sages have tremendous power in their beings which they keep under control. Sometimes just a touch of theirs can unleash a similar power within us. If we are unable to handle the power, life can become difficult. If Mother could have just stayed quietly and meditated, she may have gradually stabilized. But to have to run a household and attend to all the worldly details of life while in a state like that was very disorienting. Hence, she went to the sage to regain her balance.

Sitaramdas Baba's words provided Mother with many deep insights into the spiritual world. He said, "You have my blessings. You will meet many sages but none will be a fake *sadhu*." When she asked him how one can tell if a sage is genuine or fake, he said, "When you see your mantra arising automatically to your lips in the presence of a sage, you will know he is a true sage." With his blessings, my mother was never afraid of meeting a sage because she knew that she would always gain wisdom from these holy men and women who had left their homes in search of God.

Chapter 29: Anandamayi Ma

My mother was a little girl when she first saw the great saint, Anandamayi Ma. "I went with my grandfather to see her," said my mother. "I remember seeing a radiant being who was stunningly beautiful. Her beauty had an ethereal quality to it, and she looked as though nothing on this earth could touch her. Later, in the 1950s, when we had moved to our house on Keyatala Road, Anandamayi Ma visited one of our neighbors and we all went to pay our respects to her. I remember being fascinated by the kirtan her devotees were singing."

In 1970, while we were living in Dehradun, Mother got a letter from Aunt Dolly telling her that Anandamayi Ma was going to visit her ashram in Dehradun and Mother should contact her. My aunt's letter was followed by a letter from Maharaj, Mother's guru. He wrote, "Since you do not have the opportunity to spend much time with me, you should try and spend time with Anandamayi Ma." Mother gathered the necessary information and started visiting Anandamayi Ma at her ashram. On most occasions, Bonie and I went along because Mother did not like leaving us alone at home.

"The first day I met her," said my mother to Bonie and me while recalling her visit to the Dehradun ashram, "the room was full of people. Ma beckoned to me to come close to her and asked, 'Who is your guru?' I mentioned Maharaj's name and her face lit up as she said, 'You are Mohan Baba's disciple? Come, sit close to me.' I placed my forehead on her bed, and she blessed me by placing both her hands on my head. She asked her disciples for sweets and flowers and gave them to me. Afterwards, I sat at her feet for a long time.

"I tried my best to go to her each evening. One day she called me inside and I was led to a room where I was alone with Ma. In the room was a life size photo of Ma by the seashore. I was mesmerized by the photo. I had never seen any woman as beautiful as Ma. She made me sit close to her and asked, 'How is my Mohan Baba?' She was very fond of Maharaj and treated him as though he were her child. I told her that he had asked me to visit her, and she told me to come every day. She spoke of some spiritual experiences, and I was struck by the fact that she always said 'this body' while referring to herself instead of using the word 'I.'

"In 1971, I went to see Ma during Durga Puja. Her disciples first worshipped Ma and then the image of Goddess Durga. We were all looking at Ma and there were lots of people. A disciple came and told me Ma was calling me. I followed the disciple and paid my respects to Ma. She gave me a small Gita and blessed me by touching my head. Later, she found out from someone that my husband was on the battlefield in the Bangladesh War of 1971. Once again, she showered me with many blessings to comfort me.

"One night I lay in bed and was thinking how wonderful it would be if I could be alone with Ma and my family. The phone rang and someone told me that Ma was arriving the next morning by Doon Express enroute to her ashram. I took the two of you and went to the station. The train arrived and the platform was empty. I helped Ma descend from the train. Her disciple was taking care of the luggage while the three of us stood on the platform alone with Ma. As she was leaving for her ashram, she turned to me and asked in a low tone, 'Was your wish fulfilled?'"

As I listened to my mother's stories, I remembered that on one occasion Mother had taken a couple of her friends to see Ma, and Bonie and I had tagged along. When we arrived at the ashram, everyone seemed to be very busy and something important was taking place. We were told that Ma was feeding *sadhus* or holy men that day. Such an event is called *Sadhu Bhandara*. Many *sadhus* had assembled on this auspicious occasion, and they were sitting on the veranda. Ma came with food for them. Her glance fell on my mother, and she looked pleased and asked, "When did you come?" My mother told her we had just arrived, and Ma told us to wait. After she had fed the *sadhus*, she came to where we were standing. She asked a disciple to bring food and she asked us to open our mouths. We obeyed and Anandamayi Ma fed us with her own hands. Everyone was looking at us and I knew what we were experiencing was special.

Even after we left Dehradun at the end of 1971 and went to Calcutta, Mother met Anandamayi Ma several times. In 1974, Mother decided to go to the Kumbha Mela which was being held in Allahabad. Millions of pilgrims attend this festival and take a holy dip in the waters of the Ganges and Yamuna rivers. Mother had decided to go on this pilgrimage all of a sudden and had made no arrangements. After she arrived, she asked to be directed to Anandamayi Ma's tent. Ma was sitting on a slightly elevated seat and was surrounded by *sadhus*. She recognized my mother and asked, "When did you come? Who is with you? Has Mohan Baba come?" Mother told her that she was alone. Anandamayi Ma told one of her disciples to arrange for my mother to stay with Ma's followers.

Mother spent her time at the festival roaming around seeing innumerable holy men and women. There were millions of people and many arrangements that had to be made to take care of the pilgrims. Anandamayi Ma was giving robes and the Gita to the *sadhus*. All night long people were singing kirtan. It was a deeply spiritual experience. Early in the morning, Mother took her dip in the holy waters. She said the Ganges was ochre colored and the Yamuna was blue. Later, Anandamayi Ma's followers invited my mother to eat lunch. After eating, Mother went to bid goodbye to Ma who gave her a piece of crystallized sugar (*misri*) before placing her hands on my mother's head and blessing her.

One year, Mother saw Anandamayi Ma in our ashram at Deoghar. She ran to Ma and welcomed her. Then she went to Maharaj and told him that Anandamayi Ma had come. Maharaj hurried out to greet Ma. He first took her to the *Yagna Mandap* and then took her to the building called Mohan Mandir. Here he made her sit on a higher seat while he sat on a lower seat to show his respect for Ma. Mother was standing near the door and Ma called her and told her to sit close to her. Maharaj looked like a little boy and was humble and shy. Ma told him to give sweets to everyone. It was obvious to everyone how fond she was of our guru.

Another year, Mother and Aunt Dolly were in Benares with Maharaj when he went to visit Anandamayi Ma. Ma was very happy to see him. She kept referring to him as "My Gopal" (*Amar Gopal! Amar Gopal!*) as she gave him sweets.

The last time Mother saw Ma was during one of her visits to Dehradun. Ma had invited a monk from the Ramakrishna Mission to discuss mantras. She was delighted to see my mother and once again asked, "How is Mohan Baba? How is my Gopal?"

Mother always had a picture of Anandamayi Ma on her dressing table. She would often tell us stories of her visits to Ma. After Ma left the body, disciples of Ma would come to our house to hear stories of their guru. As a result, even though I had not seen her since I was twelve, I was aware of Ma's presence in my life as I grew up. I did not know then that she would continue to play a role in my life even after I came to the United States.

Chapter 30: The Swamiji of Tapkeshwar

In 1969, we moved from Roorkee to Dehradun. After we had settled in, we went to visit the temple of Tapkeshwar. As we parked the jeep, we could hear the roar of the raging Tons River that flows right next to the temple. We walked down many steps and saw a *sadhu* standing on the veranda. He turned to us with a big smile and said in Bengali, "Come. I was waiting for you."

We entered a cave and saw a Shiva Lingam. The *sadhu* pointed to the ceiling of the cave and said, "See how water drops from the ceiling onto the Lingam. This happens all the time. But when the world is going through a bad time, the water stops dripping." We saw that drops were seeping out of the ceiling and dropping on the Lingam. After paying our respects and making a donation, we moved to the adjoining space where the *sadhu* lived. When we were comfortably seated, and he had given us fruits, Mother asked, "How did you come here?"

The *sadhu* replied, "I was an anarchist during the British rule. When the British began imprisoning us, I escaped and came here."

Mother addressed him as Swamiji and thus began yet another close relationship between our family and a sage. My parents used to visit him often, and sometimes Bonie and I went with them. Swamiji also came to our home on more than one occasion. He had a handsome face with beautiful soulful eyes and always wore a cheerful smile. His hair was white and came down to his shoulders in waves, and he dressed in saffron robes. He would make tea for my parents and tell amazing stories of all he had witnessed and experienced through the years he had been in Tapkeshwar. I heard some of these stories from Mother.

"At the back of the temple," said Swamiji, "there are stairs that lead down to the river. There is also a cave in that area. Many years ago, a *sadhu* came and said, 'I wish to meditate in that cave. Do not disturb me. Block the mouth of the cave with a rock and do not move the rock until I call you.' Fifteen days went by and his followers became worried. They opened the cave and saw him seated in meditation. He opened his eyes and said, 'Why did you open the cave?' Having said these words, he passed away."

Mother said, "Swamiji, I don't understand. What happened?"

Swamiji explained, "If someone is in *nirvikalpa samadhi* and you suddenly pull him out of that state, he could pass away. *Nirvikalpa samadhi* is the highest state where a practitioner has become one with God. If one were to see such a person in this state, one might conclude that the man was dead because there may be no evidence of his vital signs. The practitioner must come out of this state before he can function in the world. But when his followers opened the cave before he had come out of his state of deep absorption, he left the body."

Near the temple was a cremation ground and Swamiji had a story about this area. "One day, I had gone to the market," said Swamiji, "and when I came home, I saw an Aghori on the cremation ground. Aghoris are *sadhus* who belong to a particular sect of devotees of Shiva. This Aghori was eating something from a half-burnt dead body. I was repulsed by the sight and was ready to move away when he called out to me and said, 'Wait. Come here.' I was terrified but forced myself to go close to him. His eyes were like balls of fire. The food he was eating was stinking and made me want to run. 'You are revolted by what you see, right?' he asked. And without waiting for me to answer, in a commanding voice he said, 'Lower your shawl.' I did what I was told, and he dropped some of that repulsive meat into my shawl. 'Go eat,' he said, 'and do not be repulsed by it.'

"I came to my room and was shaking from the encounter. Suddenly, I realized that my room was filled with a beautiful fragrance. I looked at the contents in my shawl and instead of decaying human flesh I saw sumptuous sweets. Then I realized that I had just met someone who was not an ordinary *sadhu*. I ran out to meet him, but he was gone. I ate the sweets and I can tell you that I have never eaten sweets that were more delicious than the ones I ate that day."

Swamiji affectionately called Mother "Mrs. Colonel Bagchi." Father was a Colonel in the Indian Army and Swamiji liked to insert the word "Colonel" when he addressed my mother. He was also good friends with my father, who enjoyed Swamiji's company because the sage told us interesting stories. Once while visiting us, Swamiji said to Mother, "Here is a mantra for you. I have written it on a piece of paper. If you recite it and feed the fish in a river with pellets of dough for seven days, you will be able to understand what the birds and animals are saying." Mother did not perform this ritual but later heard that there were sages who could understand the language of animals.

Even though we left Dehradun at the end of 1971, we often went back during our vacations. Naturally, we always visited Swamiji. The last time Mother saw him, he was very sick and was living in a different ashram. He was very happy to see her and told her it was the last time he was going to see her. Soon after that, he passed away.

In 1997, I visited Dehradun with my parents, and we went to Tapkeshwar. It was no longer the quiet place of solitude where Swamiji had spent hours and hours looking at the rushing Tons and reciting his mantra. The place was bustling with pilgrims, shops, and vendors. Mother used to say that she never found out who Swamiji's guru was. In fact, we never learned his name. We always called him the Swamiji of Tapkeshwar (*Tapkeshwarer Swamiji*).

Chapter 31: The Sages of Uttarkashi

In 1970, while we were still in Dehradun, Mother decided she wanted to go to Uttarkashi. Father could not accompany her but he made all the arrangements for her trip. My uncle, Sankar, was visiting us in Dehradun and he would accompany Mother. Bonie and I were included in the trip. A young officer, whom I called Uncle Bose, joined us on the trip and we all left for Uttarkashi. The place is a haven for *sadhus* who go there to further their spiritual progress by meditating and listening to the advice of advanced practitioners. Mother always looked forward to spending time with people on the spiritual path, and Uttarkashi was a place which provided her a good chance of meeting one or two highly evolved *sadhus*.

We travelled by road and arrived in the evening. We checked into a guest house overlooking the raging Ganges River as it rushed downwards towards the plains. We learned that higher up was the glacier of Gomukh from which the Ganges descended. I looked at the river and was stunned by its beauty. As the river hurtled downwards, the waters dashed against huge boulders. Everything seemed startlingly white. The roar of the Ganges was such that we had to shout at each other to be heard.

Around 7:00 p.m., we went to the Officers' Mess for dinner. Father's friend was in charge of the Mountaineering Institute at Uttarkashi and we were his guests. After dinner, while other guests were mingling with each other, Mother asked the waiter, whose name was Bahadur, "Do you know of any *sadhus* nearby?"

This was a strange question in this setting, but Bahadur told Mother that there was a *sadhu* who lived close to where we were. Mother asked, "Can you take us to him?" Bahadur agreed.

Uncle Sankar and I were embarrassed with Mother for focusing on *sadhus* at a dinner party, but she never worried about what people might think of her. Soon we bid our host and other guests farewell. No one realized that we were headed out into the darkness to see a *sadhu*.

Bahadur led us down a mountain trail which was quite steep. It was pitch dark and we had two flashlights: Mother carried one and Bahadur the other. As we descended, the roar of the Ganges grew deafening. I realized we were heading towards the river and descending into the gorge. Halfway down, Bahadur turned left, and we walked towards what seemed like a shack. I tried to dissuade Mother from this expedition by telling her it was too late to call on anyone and we could come next morning. But my mother was undeterred. She said, "If we see that the hut is dark, then we won't knock."

It was cold and dark when we knocked on the door of the *sadhu's* hut after Mother saw that there was a light on within. A voice asked in English, "Who is it?"

Mother answered, "Strangers."

From left to right: Reverend Cole, Mother, Abhishiktananda. Dehradun, 1970

The door opened and there stood a radiant being with a smile that warmed our hearts and lit our souls. "Come in," he said. We entered what

162

was a small room. Taking the blanket from off his shoulders, the *sadhu* spread it out on the floor for us to sit on. Then he introduced himself as Abhishiktananda and asked us our names. One could see that Mother and the sage had already formed a strong bond. They talked for hours while the rest of us sat and listened. He was French and had lived in India for decades. He spent six hours of his day doing chores, eating, and sleeping. The other eighteen hours were devoted to his spiritual practice.

When I think of Abhishiktananda, I see white. White skin, white hair, the white snows of the Himalayas. I see the tiny hut he built on the banks of the Ganges, which came prancing down from the white glaciers before dashing onto the boulders and foaming white, matching the brilliance of the *sadhu's* smile.

Standing (from left to right): Reverend Cole, Father, Mother, Abhishiktananda
Seated: Friend, Bonie, I, Friend. Dehradun, 1970

Later, Abhishiktananda came to visit us in Dehradun and stayed with us. He was on his way to Delhi to renew his visa. After spending the night in our home, he left the next day. I remember going with my parents to the station where the sage was boarding a train. He had the same blanket with him that he had spread on the floor. It looked like it had seen its day, and Father had brought a brand-new blanket as a gift. We stood on the platform and my eleven-year-old mind could not understand why the sage refused my father's gift and clung to his tattered old blanket. That was my first experience of renunciation. Finally, Mother took the blanket and offered it. It seemed as though he could not turn down Mother's request. He looked at Mother and accepted the gift.

Mother met him several times after we left Dehradun for Calcutta. He asked her how her spiritual practice had been impacted by the hustle and bustle that is part of a huge metropolis such as Calcutta. My mother, who was a child of Nature, felt suffocated in a city. She told him she was miserable. He said, "It is difficult to meditate for long hours in such an environment. Read the Gita every day." Mother told him she did not know Sanskrit. He said, "Do not worry about that. If you read the Gita, you will always be in good company and your mind will be focused on the verses." Mother followed his advice and read the whole Gita every day for twenty-four years. At first it took her five hours each day, but later it took her only two hours.

One year Mother went to Dehradun and she found out that Swami Abhishiktananda had passed away. We always marveled at how a French Benedictine monk came to India, became a Hindu sage and renunciate in Uttarkashi, and there met a Colonel's wife who became deeply indebted to him for his spiritual guidance. Such connections are hard to fathom. Today there are many books on him. But on that dark night when a small group of strangers knocked on his door, the world did not know much about Swami Abhishiktananda.

After meeting Abhishiktananda, Mother took us to a place called Ujali where we met a sage named Gangananda. He was ninety years old and told us that he had left home and come to Uttarkashi when he was seven years old. As always, the sage focused on Mother. The rest of our group sat and watched. The sage placed his hand on my mother's back and looked surprised. He said, "These have all opened."

Mother did not understand. He explained to her that all her *chakras* in her spine had opened. He asked her what type of yoga she practiced. Mother said all she did was recite the mantra her guru had given her. Once again, the two of them talked for a long time. My mother asked when Uncle Bose and Uncle Sankar would be initiated, and the sage said they would be initiated soon. This prediction was fulfilled when in 1971 both became disciples of Maharaj.

We next went to meet a sage named Ramananda Avadut. He was a big hulk of a man, sitting in the cold air without any clothes. His attendant told us that the sage was 175 years old. He had gone to Kailash seven times and had stood in the Ganges for a year and a half and meditated. He did not accept any money from us. The attendant said the sage rarely ate anything. He and his attendant managed to survive with whatever the local people gave. The sage sat quietly looking at us with compassion pouring from his eyes. Our minds were stilled, and we felt enveloped in peace. Mother was not going to leave without hearing some words of advice, and she pleaded with the sage to say something. He turned to her and said, "What happened is good. What is happening is good. What will happen is good. My child, recite God's name."

Ramananda Avadut and Father. Uttarkashi, 1970. (This photo was taken by Mother when she visited the sage on her way to Gomukh.)

Chapter 32: Of Priests and Sages

Father Charles

When I first met Father Charles, I was ten years old. This is what Santa Claus must look like, I thought, as I looked at his smiling face. Full of vitality, he was an Italian priest who was in charge of the Roman Catholic church in Roorkee, a place in India where my father's battalion was stationed in 1968. I was admitted to school at St. Anne's Convent and Mother became friends with the nuns. They introduced her to Father Charles whose joyous laughter was soon booming in our home where he was a frequent visitor. Speaking with his heavily accented English, he exchanged recipes with my mother. She taught him how to cook some Indian dishes and he taught her how to make wine the Italian way. But their main interest was philosophy, and he learned a lot about the essence of Hinduism from Mother.

At midnight mass, on Christmas Eve, we witnessed baby Jesus come alive at the stroke of twelve. The doll in the crib was my doll and I felt very proud that Father Charles had to depend on me for the most important figure in the Nativity scene. I sat with my parents in the front pew of the church as we attended midnight Mass. When the service ended, we got up to leave. Suddenly my mother almost collapsed. Everyone began to fuss over her. I heard her say she was okay but her voice was barely audible. After some time, she slowly got to her feet and we came home. My father asked her what had happened, and she said it was nothing. Years later I found out that she had experienced a vision of Christ.

At Easter, we mourned the crucifixion of the sad figure on the cross. Our drooping spirits were uplifted when Father Charles presented us with beautiful Easter eggs, covered with rich icing, that had come all the way from distant Italy.

Sometimes his friend Revered Cole, a priest at a church in Dehradun, would visit him and they would both come over to our house. Reverend Cole was a gentle and peaceful man and provided somewhat of a contrast to Father Charles' benignly jovial personality. Later, when we met the French *sadhu* Swami Abhishiktananda we found that he also knew Reverend Cole. After a year in Roorkee, my father was posted to Dehradun where Mother continued her friendship with Reverend Cole, and Father Charles continued to send us gifts whenever anyone he knew was making a trip to Dehradun. One year, my parents were in a scooter accident. Mother got off lightly, but

Father broke a couple of ribs and was in pain. Hearing this news, Father Charles rushed over to see us. Mother was really touched by his affection for our family.

After we left for Calcutta in 1971, Mother stayed in touch with Reverend Cole and met him each time we visited Dehradun during our summer vacations. It was from him that she got news of both Father Charles and Swami Abhishiktananda. These friendships were very dear to my mother and taught me to be open to all religious and spiritual beliefs.

The Sage of Barharwa

In December 1970, our family decided to visit my grandmother and aunt in Calcutta. Bonie and I had a long winter break, and Father was on his annual leave. After spending some time in Grandmother's home, we went to visit Uncle Sankar who was posted in Sahibganj. At my uncle's we had just spent a couple of days when Mother said she wanted to visit the famous place of pilgrimage called Tarapith. My parents left us with my uncle and made the journey to Tarapith.

After spending several hours at Tarapith, my parents came to the station to take the train back to Sahibganj. Father was hungry and wished to stop for lunch, but Mother did not want to miss the train. So, even though my father was grumbling, they boarded the train. One of the stops on the way back was the Barharwa Railway Junction. Mother had heard that a great sage named Pau Hari Baba resided nearby. She asked a porter about the sage, and he said the sage was in town. On hearing this, my parents got off the train. Hailing a rickshaw, they headed for the temple where the sage lived. Everyone seemed to know him and the rickshaw driver dropped them off at the door of the temple. On climbing the stairs to a veranda, my parents saw the sage sitting there as though waiting for them. He was an imposing figure.

Later, recalling her visit to the sage, Mother said, "We bowed to him. He put his hand on my back and said, 'Ma.' His voice sounded to me like a peal of thunder. I felt a flash of lightning on my back and my whole body vibrated. He was a disciple of the great yogi, Shyamacharan Lahiri Mahasaya. He wanted us to go and eat first because he knew we were hungry. So, we went to the kitchen where a devotee gave us food to eat. The devotee said, 'We finished eating lunch at 1:00 p.m. and then Baba called me and told me that two people were coming after visiting Tarapith. He said they were going to eat lunch here. So, I cooked again.' We ate and then went and sat with the sage. He said, 'The Path is tough. Not everyone can follow it or even be called to it.' Around 4:00 p.m. your father said we should leave. The sage told us the train was late and we could sit with him for a little longer, but your father was worried we would miss the train. We paid our respects to the sage and to a large statue of Shyamacharan Lahiri Mahasaya. We took a rickshaw and came to the station only to find that the train was late."

The story always enthralled me because my parents had no plans of visiting the sage. They had gone to Tarapith. On the way back, they suddenly detrained and went to the sage. How did the sage know they were coming? Perhaps such events that will always remain a mystery to us are not mysteries to these great yogis.

Pashupatinath Baba

In 1975, after retiring from the Indian Army, my father got a job as the Chief Security and Vigilance Officer at the Indian Iron and Steel Company in Burnpur. My parents moved there with Bonie while I stayed back in Calcutta with my grandmother. Bonie was admitted to Loreto House in Asansol, a renowned school. But I had gained admission to Bethune College, Calcutta, and it was thought wise to let me stay with my grandmother and aunt in our Keyatala home.

One day, after they had moved to Burnpur, someone who was aware of Mother's interest in sages told her that a *sadhu* had come from Ayodhya and was visiting his follower in Asansol. Mother immediately arranged to visit the holy man and went to Asansol, which was a short drive away from Burnpur. She entered and saw a few male devotees sitting on the floor; the sage was lying on a mat on the floor. Mother asked, "Can I touch your feet?" The sage sat up and allowed her to pay her respects to him. Treating Mother as though she were a long-lost friend, he said, "In your past lives, you used to come to me." Thus began a friendship that would last for many years.

Bonie and I were fortunate to visit Pashupati Baba, as we called him. He was very tall and had light skin. I remember him as being extremely affectionate, childlike, always smiling and laughing. He had white hair and looked saintly. He was so simple and humble that it was hard to believe that he was someone to be revered as a great saint. But once we were in his presence, all we experienced was joy. He spoke Hindi and was surprised to hear Bonie and me speaking in Hindi. He said, "Goodness! They speak better Hindi than I do!" We all laughed at his childlike joy.

When Mother first met him in the 1970s, his followers told her he was at least 170 years old. Apparently, his guru came and took him away from his family when he was eight years old. In those days, if a holy man came to someone's house and asked for something, one could not refuse. People had many children and giving one to a sage was not seen as something bad. After all, the holy life was revered by all.

Pashupatinath Baba

Like most holy men, Pashupati Baba had roamed all over India and been to many places. He was a good storyteller and charmed his audience with stories of his travels. He said when he went to Tibet to visit Kailash, he did not know it would be so cold. He almost froze to death. However, a sage came and took him to a cave. The sage gave Pashupati Baba something to eat and Baba's physical needs disappeared. He did not feel cold. He was neither hungry nor thirsty. The sage who rescued him had been there for 300 years but looked 50 years old.

Baba also related a story of a time when he decided to stay in a ruined temple at Gopi Talav. This is a place in Gujarat. Legend has it that the *gopis* (milkmaids) of Vrindavan who loved Krishna came to see him there one last time after He moved to Dwarka. Unable to live without Krishna, they gave up their bodies at this place. The sandalwood-colored soil is considered sacred and used as Gopi Chandan (sandalwood). Baba was staying in the abandoned temple and did not have any resources. But soon after his arrival, a man came to him with wood and fruits. Baba was surprised since he did not know a soul in that area. The gentleman said that while he was saying his morning prayers that day, he heard a voice telling him to go look for a sage at the ruined temple and to provide for him.

On one occasion, when Mother went to visit Pashupati Baba in Burnpur, she was surprised to see that the door to the house he was staying in was open. Baba's followers laughed and told her that Baba had said, "Keep the door open. My devotee is coming." When Mother sat down and listened to Baba that day, he said, "Keep reciting God's name until the name automatically rises to your lips."

On another occasion, Mother found that Baba had a high fever when she went to see him. He sat up and welcomed her. She could see his legs were shaking from the chills caused by the fever. With his cheerful smile, he said, "I have pushed the fever down to the legs so I can talk to you. Stay on the Path, my child. Remember that you are always supported."

We also met him in Calcutta where he had devotees. During one visit, he said, "When you are serving a sage, you must make sure that your heart is pure. I used to go to the house of one of my devotees. It was a large house and my devotee lived with many relatives. One day, I had been invited to lunch. The woman in charge of cooking resented my presence and cooked with reluctance. I sat down to eat and found all the food was so salty that I could not eat anything. In fact, no one could eat that day. Her negativity had tainted the food."

Mother's last visit to Baba was at his ashram in Gushkara. He had lost his vision and was ill. He was lying down but blessed Mother profusely. He knew at once who she was. Mother suggested that she could arrange for his eye surgery, but he said, "No. This is better. I have no contact with the outside world. I see Him inside all the time."

Barfani Maharaj

In 1982, my father retired from his job at Burnpur and the family moved back to Calcutta. Grandmother no longer wished to rent the apartment upstairs and wanted Father to live there with us. In 1983, Mother heard of a sage named Barfani Maharaj whose ashram was in Haridwar. He was visiting a disciple near Park Circus in Calcutta. She took me with her, and we went to pay our respects to the sage. I was able to go only once, but Mother went every day during his stay in Calcutta.

The sage's followers, whose ancestors had been the sage's disciples for centuries, told Mother that he was 300 years old. Mother said Barfani Maharaj was always performing yogic asanas even as he sat and talked to his visitors. He had lived in Tibet for several years where he performed many austerities while living in subzero temperatures with his body covered with snow; and that was why he was called Barfani Maharaj (*baraf* is the Hindi word for snow or ice).

Mother said the sage, like all sages, seemed to be filled with joy whenever she saw him. He said, "It is hard to recite God's name all the time and very difficult to get out of *samsara*." *Samsara* represents the cycle of birth, death, and rebirth that human beings are trapped in according to Hinduism. He said, "Do not get involved in *samsara*." The word *samsara* is also used to represent worldly life with its joys and sorrows. He said, "You can get out of God's bondage because God does not hold you back, but it is hard to get out of the bondage of *samsara*."

Devraha Baba

In the late 1980s, my parents were visiting Varanasi and Mother expressed a wish to see a great saint named Devraha Baba. When they arrived at the place where the sage lived, they saw a huge crowd of people. Mother saw that the sage lived on a wooden platform called a *machan* which was on a tree. The crowd stood on the ground looking up at him as he talked to people. My parents stood in the crowd and watched. A gentleman standing next to them said, "The sage is 300 years old. My ancestors have been coming for decades. My wife is supposed to have an operation and I have come to ask for his blessings." Soon, his name was announced and he hurried towards the tree.

Mother said she was trying to make sense of all this when suddenly she heard an announcement on the loudspeaker: "We are calling the Colonel of

the Gorkha battalion and his wife to come and meet Baba." My parents were
stunned. No one knew them. How could such an announcement be made?
There was no time to think, and they made their way towards the sage.

The sage blessed my parents by placing his feet on their heads. He asked,
"Do you want anything?"

Mother said she forgot everything and mumbled, "Bless me so I may
continue to stay on the spiritual path."

The sage said, "Yes, yes, of course you will. I have seen you before this."

Having paid their respects to the sage, my parents moved away from the
crowd. They were puzzled by his remark. It was the first time they were
seeing him. Yet he told Mother he had seen her before. As they were waiting
at the station for the train that would take them back to Varanasi, Mother
thought perhaps he had met her in a past life.

Later she asked another sage about how some sages lived for hundreds
of years. The sage told her that there were yogic processes where one could
leave the old body and take on a new body.

Chinmayananda Saraswati

Chinmayananda Saraswati, who inspired the formation of the Chinmaya
Mission, was renowned for his lectures on the Gita. Occasionally, he would
come to Triangular Park in Calcutta for a seven-day retreat during which he
lectured on the Gita each day. The Park was within walking distance of our
house, and my mother and aunt attended regularly. Mother said his talks were
profound and accessible. One day, she and Aunt Dolly went up to him and
paid their respects. He blessed them and said, "Everything is Brahman
(Supreme Being). When you do household chores, think of each task as a
yagna or fire sacrifice. If you are cooking, think that you are Brahman, the
fire is Brahman, the utensils are Brahman, the food is Brahman. You cannot
think of anything that is not Brahman. In this way you will always be
connected to Brahman and your mind will be focused on Brahman." Mother
carried this wisdom with her in her heart and encouraged me to read
Chinmayanandaji's Gita.

Chapter 33: Mother in Vrindavan

In the early 1970s, Mother decided to go to Vrindavan. She was not in good health, and we were worried about her going on a pilgrimage. But she was determined. On Shiva Ratri, the day when the festival of Lord Shiva is held, my mother went to see Maharaj and said, "I really want to go to Vrindavan. Should I go?"

Maharaj blessed her and said, "Yes."

She said, "I hope to get something."

Maharaj said, "You will."

We were all together and had gone to pay our respects to Maharaj on this auspicious day. When we came home, I asked Mother what she meant. She said, "It's nothing." Much later I realized that she wanted to experience the deep spiritual nature of Vrindavan, which is the place we associate with Krishna and his childhood.

My grandfather's brother, Pranesh Chakrabarti, and his wife, Nilima, decided to accompany my mother on this pilgrimage. That year, the famous Kumbha Mela was to be held at Haridwar. One month before that event, Kumbha Mela would be held in Vrindavan. Mother and her relatives arrived during the Mela and found accommodation at the ashram of Swami Sureshwarananda. When they arrived at the dimly lit ashram, it seemed as though Swamiji had been expecting them even though he did not know them. The ashram was situated close to the Yamuna River and after checking in their luggage, they first went and saw the Yamuna.

Mother felt very happy at the ashram, which was packed with people who had come for the Kumbha Mela. There were no rooms available, so Mother and her relatives slept in the Radha Krishna temple. At 4:30 a.m., they were woken up by Swamiji who said he needed to perform Mangal Arati. Most priests at Hindu temples perform the ritual of Mangal Arati before sunrise. Mother watched while Swamiji performed the ceremony before the statues of Lord Krishna and his consort, Radha. Suddenly, he turned to my mother and said, "Give me some sweets."

Mother was perplexed by this strange request at this unearthly hour and said, "Sweets? I don't have any."

Swamiji said, "Look in your bag."

Mother said, "You cannot offer those sweets to the deities. We ate some of those sweets on the train."

"Just give them to me," said Swamiji.

Reluctantly, Mother handed over the box of sweets and saw Swamiji offering them to the deities. Anything that has already been used by human beings cannot be offered to God. If we buy sweets, we first offer them to God and then eat them. Mother had bought a box of sweets with her, and during their journey to Vrindavan she and her relatives had each eaten a sweet from the box. But Swamiji did not seem to be bothered by these details and my mother realized that he was so evolved that he had transcended the man-made boundaries between God and human beings. Later, while discussing this incident with her relatives, Mother was struck by the fact that Swamiji knew the sweets were in her bag. How could he have known, she wondered. This convinced her that even though he looked quite simple and ordinary, there was something special about this *sadhu*.

That morning, after Mother had bathed and said her prayers, she met a Bengali *sadhu* who had come to the ashram. He saw my mother and asked, "When did you come?" It seemed as though he had known her for a long time. He introduced himself as Radhika Das. Mother learned that he was an artist and had graduated from Madras School of Art. He had lived in the Ramakrishna Mission in Deoghar and knew Maharaj, our guru. He was a great storyteller and sang beautifully. He also had a wonderful sense of humor and was deeply devoted. He had been living in Vrindavan for quite some time and Mother was delighted to find someone who could guide her to the right places and people.

"I want to see a truly evolved sage," she said. She addressed him as Radhikada, which meant elder brother. He promised her he would introduce her to such a sage.

One afternoon, Radhikada invited Mother to his home. She went and saw a sage wearing tattered clothes. She bowed to him, and he blessed her saying, "Jai Radhe! Jai Radhe!" And then he started saying something. At first, Mother did not understand him. Then she began to listen to him with keen attention. Suddenly she realized that he was describing Radha, Krishna, and the *gopis* (milkmaids)of Vrindavan bathing in the Yamuna. It was all clearly happening before his eyes. He was immersed in his trance and describing every detail. Then he came out of the trance and told Mother that he had *prasad* for her. Radhikada gave her some food that had been offered to the sage, and she learned that the sage's name was Gopal Baba.

A young woman came and sat next to my mother. Her name was Radha. Pointing at my mother, the sage said to her, "Radha, she is your *sakhi* (friend)." The stories of Krishna's childhood abound in tales of Radha and her *sakhis*. It was clear to my mother that Gopal Baba kept drifting in and out of this world of the cowherds and milkmaids of Vrindavan. Rarely was he in this world of mundane realities. Suddenly, he said he was hungry. Radhikada provided some puffed rice (muri), and people were feeding Gopal Baba, but he asked for my mother and told her to feed him. As Mother began to feed him, he said, "You are feeding Radharani." Mother watched him closely: at times he seemed to be radiating light, at times tears would be streaming down his cheeks, and at times his face turned red. My mother wondered what he saw with his inner vision. Perhaps he saw little Gopal (baby Krishna) stealing yogurt from the milkmaids of Vrindavan; perhaps he saw Krishna teasing the cowherdesses as they ran to do their chores; perhaps he saw Gopal playing with his friends as they kept an eye on the cows grazing in the fields; perhaps he saw Radha and Krishna dancing under the full moon.

Untitled painting by Radhika Das which he sent to Mother (Vrindavan with Krishna's beloved trees, cows and peacocks)

The next day was the night before the spring festival of Holi or the festival of colors. Back in the ashram where Mother was staying, Swamiji said he wanted to cook a big meal for the deities and then feed people. Mother's name was Lily, but Swamiji used to call her "Lilu." With a childlike simplicity, he said, "Lilu, give me some money." Sensing that he wanted money to buy groceries, my mother asked him what he was going to cook. He mentioned several items.

Then Mother asked, "How many people will you feed?" She was alarmed to find he had invited at least forty people. She gave him what she could afford and then went and started asking the other guests at the ashram to give what they could. Once she had counted all the money she had collected, she knew that it would be impossible to carry out Swamiji's plans.

When she shared her concerns with Swamiji, he nonchalantly said, "It will all work out." As Mother was beginning to get anxious, the postman arrived with a money order. Someone from Calcutta had sent a large sum to Swamiji. He took the money and happily went to the market. After he came back with vegetables and other ingredients, everyone helped with the cooking. Many *sadhus* came and were fed with great love and care. Swamiji was beaming with joy while Mother was still in a state of mild shock as she pondered the day's events.

Swamiji had also announced that there would be *ashta prahar naam gaan*, which involves the constant recitation of God's name for twenty-four hours. All through the day, lots of people joined in the devotional chanting. However, at night, most people went to sleep. In the middle of the night, Mother woke up and sensed that the singing was waning. She did not want the recitation to break off, so she went and joined the two people who were still carrying on with the chanting. One was singing and the other man was playing an instrument. Mother began to sing songs Maharaj sang. Soon other guests woke up and joined in. In this manner, Swamiji's wishes were fulfilled.

The next day, Mother went to see how the people of Vrindavan celebrate the festival of colors. Legend has it that Krishna and Radha played Holi, so this is an important festival. Mother went to the famous temple of Lord Banke Bihari. The priests there were dressed in regal attire. People were playing with colors and had huge water guns (*pichkaris*) with which they squirted water on the crowds. The statue of Banke Bihari is one of the oldest statues of Krishna in Vrindavan. The temples of Vrindavan were attacked and plundered on more than one occasion by invaders, and many statues of Krishna were moved from Vrindavan to Rajasthan to keep them safe. That day Banke Bihariji looked beautiful. In her rush, Mother had forgotten to bring her purse to buy food, and she was wondering if she could get some *prasad* (food offered to the deity) when two boys came and gave her *laddoos* (sweets). Watching huge crowds playing with colors, Mother gradually made her way back to the ashram.

In the next few days, Mother met many *sadhus*. She also participated in the Kumbha Mela by taking a dip in the Yamuna river. One day, she visited Ramdas Kathia Baba's ashram and was invited to eat there the next day. When she told Swamiji that she had been invited for lunch, he was very pleased and said, "Bring some food back for us." My mother did not think too much about Swamiji's request because she had grown used to his childish ways. She arrived at Kathia Baba's ashram and sat with many *sadhus* and ate a delicious meal that was served by the *Mahant* or Abbot of the ashram and his disciples. They fed everyone with great care. When Mother went to wash her hands, she found that the person pouring water on her hands was none other than the Abbot. When she looked embarrassed that such a great man like him was helping her wash her hands, he smiled and said, "*Atithi Narayan* (The Guest is God)." Later, Mother talked to the Abbot who told her stories of Ramdas Kathia Baba and his famous disciple Santadas Babaji.

After she had paid her respects to the Abbot and thanked him for his generosity and hospitality, Mother got ready to leave. She had forgotten about taking some food for the ashram for Swamiji, but she had scarcely taken a few steps when the Abbot called her. She turned to find him standing with a packet of *jalebis* (a delicious sweet) in his hands. The Abbot said, "Take this for the ashram you are staying in. And next time you come, come and stay with us in our guest house." That's when Mother remembered Swamiji's innocent request to bring something for the ashram. Without her asking for anything, his wish had been fulfilled. When she gave the packet to him, Swamiji was delighted and shared the sweets with everyone.

When Mother decided to visit Barsana, the place where Radharani had lived, Radhikada told her to visit a great sage named Sachinandan Das. Mother and her aunt arrived in the evening at Barsana. A man was standing at the bus stop at which they alighted. When Mother asked him if he knew where the sage Sachinandan Das lived, the man said he would lead them to the sage. He stopped in front of a small room in a house that was in ruins. When he opened the door, Mother and her aunt were greeted by such a foul odor that Mother's aunt backed off and refused to enter. The man who had led them to this place said, "He is very sick, and the room is cleaned once a day." While hesitating at the threshold, it suddenly occurred to my mother that sages often test us. Determined to meet this sage, she braced herself and

Untitled painting by Radhika Das which he sent to Mother (perhaps a portrait of the bereaved Radharani yearning for the absent Krishna)

entered. The minute she entered, she noticed that the offensive smell instead of intensifying had vanished.

Lying on a tattered mat was an old man. He said, "Jai Radhe! Jai Radhe!" This is a common way of greeting people in Vrindavan. His vision had failed. Mother touched him gently and he asked, "Who are you?"

Mother replied, "I am Lily."

He said, "No. You are not Lily. You are from Vrindavan. You are Radharani's *sakhi* (friend)." He told Mother to help him sit up. She did. And then he talked to her for a long time. He asked her to feed him. Mother called the man who had brought her to the sage and told him to buy some *rabri*, which is a famous sweet of Vrindavan. When the *rabri* arrived, the sage told my mother to first offer it to a picture of Krishna that hung on the wall. "Now feed me," he said, and Mother began feeding him. He ate a little and then told her to share the sweet with others who were standing outside the room. He showered many blessings on Mother and told her that she had Radharani's blessings (*Tomar opor Radharanir daya ache*). Mother's heart was filled with bliss.

Mother and her aunt stayed that night in a hotel. The next day, they visited some other places before going back to Vrindavan. They went to Nanda Gram where Krishna's foster father had lived. Then they walked back to Barsana. On the way, they visited Prem Sarovar. A local boy came and asked them if they wanted to bathe in the pond. Mother agreed but her aunt was hesitant. The boy helped my mother bathe by holding her hand. Then he led them to a nearby temple where they ate lunch.

Thanking the devotees who had provided them with lunch, Mother and her aunt walked along until they came to a field where peas were being grown. An elderly woman came and held Mother's hand and made her sit down. Shelling the peas in her lap, she began to feed my mother as though she were feeding her child. Since Barsana is regarded as Radharani's kingdom, Mother felt that all these incidents were Radharani's blessings. It was here that Mother found a peacock feather on the ground. Since Krishna wears a peacock feather in his crown, she saw this as an auspicious sign. People say Krishna and Radha could appear in disguise to anyone. Was the beautiful young boy who helped her bathe Krishna? Was this woman feeding her peas Radha? Mother's heart raced with excitement as she forgot the rest of the world and became immersed in Radharani's world of Krishna and the *gopis*.

When we later heard some of these stories, we were glad Mother's aunt had been with her. She coaxed my mother to stop daydreaming and walk on to the next place they were going to see. Radhikada had mentioned a place called Mayur Kutir where legend has it that Krishna danced as a peacock. Radhikada had said that in this place there was a sage who did not meet anyone. He lived in a hut made of leaves. Once a day, he would come out, chew a couple of leaves, get a drink of water from the well and go in again.

In Mayur Kutir Mother met a woman who invited her to visit where she lived in a hut on the hillside. She said her son lived on top of the hill. Evidently he had returned home after getting his doctoral degree in music from Allahabad University. Then, one day, he had gone missing, and he was finally found on top of this hill. He had left the world at a young age and become a *sadhu*. The woman said, "I live here in a hut so that I can see my son once a day." She told Mother to go and see him. Mother and her aunt visited the woman's son who was living the life of a young ascetic. There was a beautiful picture of Chaitanya in his small temple. He asked my mother to sing, so she sang a song that Maharaj used to sing. Then she told him to sing, and he sang a song about the *gopis*. After leaving his temple, Mother went to say goodbye to his mother. As they were leaving, Mother looked up and saw the sage Radhikada had mentioned, the one who lived in solitude. He came out of his hut, went to the pond and drank water. He stood there for some time. Mother and her aunt bowed to him from a distance. He raised his hand to bless them from far and then entered his hut.

This may have been her first trip to Vrindavan but it was not Mother's last trip. She said she had never experienced elsewhere the joy she felt when she was in Vrindavan. When there, she would go to the famous sacred forest called Nidhivan with Radhikada. The gates to Nidhivan are locked at night and no human beings are allowed to stay there at night. Even the monkeys and other animals leave after dusk. The locals believe that Krishna dances there all night with Radha and the *gopis*. Mother would go each day to Nidhivan and sit there and meditate. The monkeys, who often disturb tourists and pilgrims, left her alone.

Mother stayed in touch with Radhikada and wrote letters to him. She often sent money to provide for the sages and the ashram she had stayed in. Radhikada would write to Mother and even sent her some of his paintings. Even though Mother spent the rest of her life in Calcutta and the U.S., her heart was always in Vrindavan. She firmly believed that she had lived there in her past lives and that is why she felt completely at home in the land of Radharani.

Chapter 34: The Old Woman of Nimta

After we moved to Calcutta in 1971, Mother became quite close to her uncle and aunt, the couple with whom she went to Vrindavan for the first time. One day, her aunt took her to a place called Nimta where they met an old woman who belonged to a community of fishermen. People referred to her as Buri, which means old woman.

Buri was eating lunch when Mother and her aunt arrived. Two women were sitting in the courtyard. Mother and her aunt, too, sat down. Buri's house was a tiny mud hut, and one could tell she was very poor. When she had finished her lunch, she sat on the threshold of her hut and asked if anyone had any questions. One of the ladies said, "My grandchild cries constantly. I don't know what to do." Buri asked for a ten paise coin and began to spin it on the floor of the courtyard. She seemed to be mumbling something. Finally, she told them to go to a temple, light a lamp, get some holy water and sprinkle it in their house. The ladies left looking satisfied.

On hearing that Buri never asked for money for her services, my mother asked her why she did not accept any money. Buri said, "We were fisherwomen. One day a stone got trapped in the fishing net. That night I had a strange dream. The stone said, 'I am Lord Jagannath. Put me back in the river. I will give you a gift with which you can help people.' The next day, I put the stone back in the river. Ever since that day, I have this ability to help people in my own humble way. But this is God's gift. I cannot make it a business."

Mother used to visit Buri from time to time, and she made predictions to my mother that were fulfilled. My mother told Buri that she had heard that my father's family had a beautiful statue of Krishna that had been worshipped in our ancestral home in a place called Faridpur (which, after the Partition of India, was assigned to Bangladesh). Mother had a strong desire to worship the statue. She told Buri about her desire and the woman spun a ten paise coin and told my mother that the statue would come to her one day. This prediction was made in 1974 and was fulfilled in 1993. On another occasion, Mother told Buri that Maharaj was going on a pilgrimage to Amarnath. Mother wanted to go on this pilgrimage but Buri told her not to. She mentioned one word, "Snowstorm." As it turned out, there was indeed a severe snowstorm, and many pilgrims were lost. However, all the people who went with Maharaj were safe.

Buri could provide solutions to problems, foretell the future, and see the past. In Mother's interactions with her, not once was she wrong. After I took my final exams in high school, Mother took me to Buri. I saw the hovel in which she lived and was wondering what we were doing there when I saw her. With her face creased with a thousand wrinkles, she peered at me from behind her thick glasses as she sat on the threshold to her hut. She seemed so old to my young eyes that I thought she would just crumble away and turn into dust before my very eyes. Mother told her I had taken my exams and asked if I would do well. The woman asked for a ten paise coin and began to spin it as she mumbled some words. After some time, she said, "Yes. She will do very well." Naturally, I did not believe her. But when the results were announced, I found that I had passed my Senior Cambridge in the first division, which was what we all wanted.

I am not interested in horoscopes or palm reading or tarot cards, but I often think of this woman's lack of greed. She could have used her extraordinary powers to make money but chose not to abuse the gift given to her by God.

Chapter 35: Bijoly Ma

While living in Burnpur in the 1970s, Mother was introduced to a young woman in her teens whose name was Bijoly Ma. Even at that early age, Bijoly Ma had followers and they told mother that Ma worshipped Goddess Kali. A sweet relationship began to bud between my mother and Ma. My mother loved her as a daughter and Bijoly Ma was very fond of my mother. She also adored my father whom she called her son. She had an ashram in a place called Ariadaha which was close to Calcutta.

After our family moved to Calcutta in 1982, Mother sometimes visited Bijoly Ma at her ashram. The rest of our family members also met her on a couple of occasions. When I first saw her, I was struck by her beauty. She reminded me of the images of Goddess Durga we see in Calcutta during Durga Puja. After 2000, whenever I went back from the U.S. to visit my family, Bijoly Ma would invite us to her ashram. She would cook lunch for us and feed us with great love and warmth. The ashram was small and some of the people there were Ma's relatives. Even though Ma was a *sadhu,* she appeared to me like a mother who runs her household, cooks, gives instructions, takes care of her loved ones and her guests, and listens to everyone's problems. There was a sweetness in her behavior that was endearing.

As the years went by, Bijoly Ma became a great source of comfort and love for our family. She was always there for us through thick and thin. As our elders began to pass away, Bijoly Ma never failed to arrive on the scene, accompany mourning family members to the cremation ground, and provide support for those of us who were devastated by the loss of a loved one.

In 2011, I was in the U.S. when I developed a blood clot and was hospitalized for ten days. My condition was serious and there was little hope of survival. Uncle Sankar was the only member of the family who was still alive in Kolkata. I had to tell him that I was sick, and he was traumatized by the news. He contacted Bijoly Ma and she promised to pray for me. She assured him that I would get well. My uncle was very grateful for her support at a time when he was all by himself and had no one to turn to.

Even after all these years, Ma still stays in touch with me and I cherish her affection and concern for me and my loved ones.

Chapter 36: Govinda

After marrying my father in 1958, my mother heard that the Bagchi family had an ancestral deity, a statue of Krishna, named Govinda. When the Bagchis were *zamindars* or feudal landowners of a place called Bhakla in Faridpur which is in Bangladesh, the deity was worshipped by the family of a gentleman named Jagannath Bagchi. Govinda, the deity, had his own temple and priest and great care was taken to worship him according to the rules and regulations of the Hindu scriptures. In 1947, India was partitioned and the Bagchi ancestral home was now in East Pakistan. My grandfather and some other members of my father's family then moved from East Pakistan to India. Govinda remained in East Pakistan until the Bangladesh war of 1971 when the remaining members moved to India and brought Govinda with them.

During the Partition of India, many homes, families, and people were uprooted. Most people who moved from India to Pakistan or from Pakistan to India lost everything. Millions died as riots broke out between Hindus and Muslims. People considered themselves lucky if they found they were alive after they had crossed over. Who has time to think of deities when one is fleeing from death? In some cases, images of ancestral deities may have been brought to India but then the owners were faced with the dilemma of how to take care of the statues. People had lost their homes, possessions, jobs, and money. Many were in refugee camps. They barely had room for themselves, leave alone providing their deities with respectable accommodation. Moreover, people are afraid that they will accrue bad karma if their deities are not treated as required by the scriptures. But there was no money with which to hire priests who knew the appropriate mantras and there was no money to provide food for the deities. Afraid that they might invite God's wrath on themselves, the owners gave their deities away to temples. Abandoned by their owners, these images crowded the temples and waited for the priest's attention.

Mother was intrigued by the story of Govinda and wanted to see the statue. In 1973, she went with my father to Jagannath Bagchi's home in Santipur. Here she saw the beautiful image of Govinda and was mesmerized. She spoke to Jagannath Bagchi's mother and said, "If you ever decide to give Govinda to a temple, please let me know. I would like to take him."

For twenty years, Mother never forgot Govinda as she waited for him. She used to send money and clothes for him from time to time but never heard back from anybody. In the 1980s, she made a trip to Govinda's home and found that Govinda had been given away to a temple. She took the address of the temple and went to it. An elderly woman opened the temple for her and pointed at Govinda. The statue looked dull and unattractive. He looked so different from the statue she had seen in 1973 that Mother was not quite sure if this was indeed the right statue.

In 1993, my father went to his sister's grandson's wedding and met a lady whom he called Haripadada's wife. While chatting with my father, she mentioned that Govinda had been moved to another temple. She was sad about Govinda's fate. Father told her that my mother had always wanted to take Govinda. She was delighted to hear this and said, "Tell Lily to contact me if she is still interested."

After attending the wedding, my father came home and casually mentioned this conversation to Mother. Next morning, Mother left home with nothing but the name "Haripadada's wife" on her lips. Father had not asked for her address, so neither he nor Mother knew where she lived. But Mother went to the house where the wedding had taken place, and there she procured the address. Then she went to a place called Salkia and found the house. Haripadada's wife was very happy to see Mother. She told her that she would take her to Santipur the next day.

So the next morning, Mother met Haripadada's wife and they took a train to Santipur. They went to the house where Mother had first seen Govinda and found the address of the temple where Govinda presently resided. It was a small temple. The woman who welcomed Mother said, "I am surprised. People come to give away their deities. No one comes to take them back." Mother put Govinda in her bag. Along with him came an equally beautiful statue of Lakshmi. Her heart filled with bliss, my mother brought back our ancestral deity to our home on December 3, 1993. The statues which at first looked as though they were made of mud were shining like gold after they had been cleaned. Govinda and Lakshmi stayed with us until my mother's death in 2010 when they were handed over to a member of the Bagchi family.

Shortly before she passed away, Mother said, "Govinda is very powerful (*khub jagroto*). His presence fills the house. I also feel Maharaj's presence in this house. After Govinda came to me, my spirituality developed a lot. Money has not been a problem because of Lakshmi. You have to love Govinda like you love your loved ones." Those of us who knew her can verify that Mother spent seventeen years of her life loving Govinda with all her heart and soul.

Govinda (left) and Lakshmi (right) in Mother's shrine room. Kolkata, 2010

Part III: Buddhism

Chapter 37: Mother and the Buddha

In the early 1960s my parents had gone to Varanasi to visit my father's mother and his sister. One day, the family decided to go on a picnic to Sarnath. They took a bus and carried cooked food with them. When they had found a pleasant place where they could eat lunch, my mother arranged food on a plate and turned to walk to the spot where my grandmother was sitting so she could offer her mother-in-law lunch. But as she turned, everything disappeared before her eyes. There was no one. A radiant *sadhu* sat in front of five *sadhus* who seemed to be listening to him. The light emanating from the teacher was almost blinding. Suddenly, Mother heard voices. People were asking, "What happened? Are you okay?" When she came to her senses, she saw the plate lying at her feet and the food scattered. She mumbled something about suddenly feeling dizzy and sat down. She did not tell anyone what she had seen. After they returned from the picnic, she woke up early next morning and went to see Sadanandada (Swami Premananda's disciple), who was also in Benares at that time. She told him what she had seen, and he looked at her in amazement. He asked her to repeat the details and said, "You are indeed blessed. Swamiji (Swami Premananda) saw exactly what you saw. You had a vision of the Buddha delivering his first sermon."

Even though Mother had always been attracted to the Buddha from the time she was a little girl and had seen a statue of the Buddha in her grandfather's house, she knew very little about him. All she knew was the story of the Buddha eating the rice pudding offered by Sujata and the fact that he had become enlightened in Bodh Gaya. So, when she had the vision of the First Sermon of the Buddha, she did not realize what she was seeing until she talked to Sadanandada.

Many years later Mother had another vision when she went to Kushinagar. While sitting at the stupa that marks the area where the Buddha was cremated, Mother had a vision of the Buddha lying on his right side. Great kings were bowing before him and laying shimmering robes of gold on the Buddha. However, the light emanating from the Buddha was even more brilliant than the radiance of the robes. Mother said the light was stunning, blinding, dazzling. Later, she went and saw the Parinirvana Stupa which houses the statue of the reclining Buddha. Here she went into deep meditation. "Such places have strong vibrations and one can feel them," she said. She shared her experience with Sadanandada when she met him later, and he confirmed that Swamiji had had the same vision and she was not imagining what she had seen.

In the 1970s, two golden Buddha statues were brought to our house in Dehradun: one large and one small. They were made of papier-mâché and were sculpted by Tibetan lamas. The big one was for us and the small one was for my uncle. Mother's Buddha statue always occupied a central space in our living room, and she never forgot to light candles and incense sticks in front of the statue each day. Towards the end of her life, she wanted to make sure that the statue was sent to either Bonie or me. During one of her visits to India, Bonie ordered a special box to be made for the statue and brought Buddha to her Boston home.

Behind my grandmother's home in Calcutta is the Dhakuria Lake which is also known as the Rabindra Sarobar. We often went for walks around the Lake in the early hours of the morning, and Mother loved to stop and pay her respects to the statue of the Buddha at the Japanese Buddhist temple located at the southern end of the Lake. Each year, on Buddha Purnima, we visited the Japanese temple. Buddha Purnima is the day of the full moon in May when the birth, enlightenment, and passing away of the Buddha are honored in India.

Mother's deep respect for the Buddha and her interest in Buddhism had a major impact on my life after my father passed away in 1998. Ralph and I were living on campus at the University Village while Ralph was teaching at Michigan State University. Father's sudden death in June 1998 was hard for all of us. I could not imagine how Mother would overcome her grief. However, Mother appeared calm when she arrived in Michigan in August 1998, and I realized that years of spiritual practice and the blessings of our guru, Maharaj, had given her the strength she needed.

Being a prolific reader, Mother told me she would like to read certain books on Tibetan Buddhism that were out of print in India. I took her to the Michigan State University Library, and we came home with bags full of books. I had never heard of *The Tibetan Book of the Dead* or *The Hundred Thousand Songs of Milarepa* but Mother was familiar with these titles and had looked for them all her life. Each night when Ralph and I went to bed, she was still reading, and each morning when we woke up we found her still reading. I don't know when she slept. She stayed with us for two months that year and we often discussed Buddhism. She would read all day and then share with us what she had read when Ralph came home from work. Ralph, a sociology professor, is very interested in religious studies and he listened enthusiastically. Mother was a gifted speaker and had a remarkable capacity to read something and then share the main concepts in a manner that held us spellbound. When she left to visit Bonie in October of 1998, the seeds of Buddhism had been planted in our hearts even though Ralph and I were not aware of it.

Mother's Buddha statue that has been in our family for more than fifty years

Chapter 38: Ajahn Khemasanto

It was a cold February morning in 1999, and Ralph had gone to do our laundry at the University Village laundry facility. On the bulletin board, he saw a flyer informing university students and staff that there was going to be a talk on Buddhism that afternoon at the Union building. Having listened to Mother speak of Buddhism for two months while she was with us the preceding year, both Ralph and I decided to attend the talk. The room at the Union was packed when we arrived, and we barely managed to find a couple of empty chairs at the back. Those who arrived after us had to stand. I saw the speaker who had a shaved head and was wearing ochre-colored robes. I presumed he was a Buddhist monk. Everyone sat quietly and soon the talk began. Ralph and I listened, mesmerized. After the talk was over, we heard that the monk was coming to Michigan State University as a Visiting Professor and was going to live at University Village. I was delighted and took the contact information of a Thai woman who seemed to be one of the organizers. Later, I contacted her and found that the Thais addressed their monks as Ajahn, the word Ajahn meaning teacher and deriving from the Sanskrit word for teacher which is Acharya. This monk's name was Ajahn Khemasanto.

On March 6, 1999, Ajahn Khemasanto moved to University Village to an apartment that was so close to ours that it took me only five minutes to walk there. From the first day Ralph and I met Ajahn, a strong bond was established between us. I was not working at that time and so could visit him every day. I learned that in Thailand, Sri Lanka, Burma and some other countries the Theravada tradition flourished. Gradually I began to learn some of the rules one had to follow in Theravada Buddhism. Women could not touch the monk or be alone with him; monks in this tradition ate one meal at noon and could not save leftovers for the next day; they did not handle money or cook for themselves and were dependent on the lay people for their meal; they did not drive cars; they did not till the land and grow vegetables; the lay community made merit by donating all that was needed for the survival of the monks, and in return the monks gave Dhamma (Pali: Dhamma; Sanskrit: Dharma) talks and taught the lay people how to meditate. There were some surprises, too. I had presumed that Buddhist monks were vegetarians because the Buddha taught non-violence, but Thai monks are not vegetarian. They must eat whatever they are offered and cannot indulge in preferences. They have few possessions: three robes, a bowl, an umbrella with a mosquito net, and medicine.

From left to right: Ajahn Khemasanto, Ajahn Maha, and Ajahn Nattakul at Dhammasala Forest Monastery. Michigan, 2004

Ajahn was a wonderful storyteller and we spent long hours listening not only to what the Buddha taught but also to stories of his life as a monk in Thailand. Born in a Catholic family, he had grown up in Midland, Michigan. When he was a little boy, he was sick with a high fever and delirious. While in this state, he saw a strange unfamiliar figure telling him silently to come to him. Ajahn was muttering in his delirious state, and from his description of the man who was calling him his mother thought he was seeing St. Francis of Assisi. Later, when he was older, he went to the public library and borrowed a number of books on world religions. When he read a book on Buddhism, he knew without a doubt that this was his path. After high school, at the age of 18, he left home and embarked on a journey that led him to Thailand. When he saw Buddhist monks in Thailand, he recognized the figure he had seen when he was sick. He realized he had seen a Buddhist monk. Eventually, Ajahn ordained as a monk in Thailand.

Monks on alms round at Dhammasala Forest Monastery. Michigan

Both Ralph and I were drawn to Ajahn and the words of the Buddha. A small number of Thai, Taiwanese, and Chinese families living in the Greater Lansing area where we live were responsible for inviting Ajahn to Lansing, and they came each morning to offer him his meal for the day. Even though I am not a good cook, each morning I cooked a few dishes and took them to Ajahn. If I was early, I had to wait outside until someone else showed up to offer food. After the food offering was done, people ate and chatted mostly in Thai which I couldn't understand. I did not mind just sitting there because my heart was flooded with peace.

In the evenings we went to listen to Dhamma talks. After a talk, we meditated. Ajahn had told us that if we were already using a meditation technique, we should just stay with that. Since Ralph and I were initiated and had been meditating for a while, we just stayed with what our guru had taught us. Each day was filled with bliss as my life was immersed in the Buddha's teachings. Ajahn had translated from Thai into English the biography of Ajahn Mun, a famous Thai meditation teacher. One day, when I had gone for food offering, Ajahn asked me if I would like to proofread the manuscript. I was delighted to be given this job and spent many a happy hour reading about Ajahn Mun.

In this way, Buddhism entered our lives and soon became an integral part of who we were. The group continued to grow in numbers and Ajahn moved out of the small university apartment to rented houses until, in 2000, the community found a beautiful piece of property in Perry, Michigan, where on 32 acres of land the Dhammasala Forest Monastery was established along with the Lansing Buddhist Association. Ajahn was the abbot of the Thai monastery, and the Taiwanese and Chinese members formed the Lansing Buddhist Association (LBA); later, the members of LBA built their temple called the Great Hall where they practiced. By then Ralph and I knew the founding members of both organizations and participated in all events. Apart from meditation and Dhamma talks, Ajahn started a class on Buddhism which was attended by Thai members of Dhammasala, members of LBA, and Americans. There was a library from which we could borrow books, and I spent most of my hours reading Dhamma books, listening to Dhamma talks, and meditating. When my mother visited us in 2000 and 2002, she was delighted to meet Ajahn and wanted to spend all her time listening to him. Ajahn, too, was very fond of my mother and always happy to see her.

We spent four fruitful and happy years with Ajahn Khemasanto studying Buddhism and learning from him. His teachings were authentic, and I have never read anything on Theravada Buddhism that contradicted what I learned from him. Our time with him was well spent and helped form a solid base on which we relied heavily as we continued our spiritual practice. In 2004, I went back to work and gradually our visits to Dhammasala became infrequent. But what Ajahn had taught us remains in our hearts and has played an important role in making us who we are today.

Chapter 39: Sister Medhanandi

In May of 1999, two months after Ajahn Khemasanto had moved close to us, Ralph and I went for a week to Fort Lauderdale, Florida, to join Bonie and her husband, Jim, for a short vacation. Of course, all we talked about was Buddhism as we enjoyed time together on the beach and ate sumptuous meals at restaurants. Very early one morning, Ralph woke me up and said, "Get up! I want to show you something." Thinking that Ralph wanted to show me the sunrise, I walked to the balcony and looked at what he was pointing at. Our apartment had a beautiful view of the beach and the sea, and on following Ralph's pointing finger I was stunned to see a Buddhist monk sitting under a palm tree meditating! People go to Florida to swim in the sea and bathe in the sun. One expects tourists on the beach, not a monastic. Reacting impulsively, I ran to the bathroom, brushed my teeth and washed my face, dressed quickly and ran down the stairs of our apartment.

"What are you doing?" asked Ralph.

"I am going to talk to the monk," I replied and ran faster because I could see that the robed figure had finished meditating and was getting ready to leave.

"Aloka!" said Ralph. "You can't do that!"

But I just kept moving. The robed figure saw me from far and moved away from me. I adjusted my direction accordingly. As I was moving, thoughts were racing through my mind: what if he did not know English, what if he were too young to teach me anything. But my feet kept moving and suddenly I stopped as I realized I had been wrong the whole time. This was not a monk. It was a nun!

Seeing me so close to her, the nun stopped and asked, "Do you wish to talk to me?"

I smiled with relief to hear English words and bowed and asked the obvious: "Are you a Buddhist nun?"

This was how I met Sister Medhanandi.

Not knowing what his wife was going to do, Ralph had followed close behind me and soon we were both chatting with Sister. We told her about Ajahn Khemasanto and our recent interest in Buddhism. She said her father lived in one of the high rises behind our hotel and she was visiting him. She generally came early in the morning, before the tourists were up, and meditated on the beach. Apparently she usually walked down the beach, away from where our hotel was, and meditated. But on this day, she had chosen this spot. She took our telephone number and said she would meet us later. We were thrilled by this chance encounter and were still talking about it when Bonie and Jim woke up.

From left to right: Sister Medhanandi, I, Bonie, Ralph. Florida, 1999

For the rest of our week in Florida, I woke up early each morning and went and sat behind Sister and meditated on the beach. She used to call me her "shadow." We visited Sister at her father's home twice that week. During our first visit, she told us that she lived in England at a monastery called Amaravati. When she was quite young, she had gone to India where she had lived in a village and met a spiritual teacher from whom she had learned a lot. She knew Hindi and we sang a couple of chants together. Later she had come back to the U.S. to finish her studies and then had gone back to work in Nepal. Finally, she had become a nun at Amaravati. On our second visit, we met her father and ate lunch together. After lunch, Ralph and I sat with Sister and we shared stories. When we were leaving, she gave us a book and a cassette saying, "These are by my teacher." We thanked her and left, not knowing what a profound impact this meeting would have on our lives.

Inscription on the first page of one of the books Sister Medhanandi sent us through Richard Smith.

197

Chapter 40: Ajahn Sumedho

After returning from our vacation, Ralph and I read the book Sister had given us. The title was *Mindfulness: The Path to the Deathless* and it contained the talks by a monk named Ajahn Sumedho. The tape contained a talk which was also by Ajahn Sumedho and the title of the talk was *Accepting the Demons*. Both the book and the talk made a deep impact on Ralph and me with regard to our understanding of Buddhism. That summer we read Ajahn Sumedho's book again and again and listened repeatedly to his talk. We introduced all our friends, who were interested in Buddhism, to Ajahn Sumedho by photocopying the book and making copies of the tape.

In July 1999, I received a call from Richard Smith, a follower of Ajahn Sumedho who told me that he had just returned from England and had mailed a parcel to me. I was surprised by this information but was told that Sister Medhanandi had gone back to Amaravati and had shared the story of how we had met her on the beach in Florida. When Richard arrived at Amaravati, she shared the story with him because he lived in Michigan. Through him she was sending us books and tapes, a small golden coin with the Buddha's image embossed on it, and a small image of the Buddha. I thanked Richard for his kindness and waited for the package to arrive. Once it did, we found that it contained more books and tapes with teachings by Ajahn Sumedho. Thus began our association with Ajahn Sumedho that was to last a lifetime even though he was in England and we were in the U.S.

In the next decade, more books became available and we also became familiar with the teachings of Ajahn Chah, a famous Thai meditation teacher under whom Ajahn Sumedho had trained. As we listened to Ajahn Sumedho, we realized that he was teaching us to accept life just the way it was. The talks were straightforward, the examples were simple, the stories were delightful, the humor was always at his own expense, and everything seemed doable until we tried to do it. That's when we realized how profound the talks were. For example in one talk Ajahn Sumedho points out that even though we may not like everybody, we must love everybody. I did not understand this at first. I thought it should be the opposite: I may not love everyone but I could try and like everyone. It took several years for me to see what the teacher was trying to say. That's when I truly understood the practice of *metta*, which is often translated as loving kindness.

My Buddhist friends made it possible for me to attend many talks given by various monks who were invited by Richard Smith and members of the Thai community in Detroit. Ralph and I had the opportunity to listen to talks by Ajahn Pasanno, Ajahn Sucitto, Sister Thanasanti, Ajahn Sundara, and Ajahn Amaro. These monks and nuns were followers of Ajahn Sumedho and considered him their teacher. Our spiritual life remained very active as we attended sanghas where we meditated with our Buddhist friends, drove to Richard's home to listen to monastics giving talks, made food offerings to monks and nuns whenever possible, and continued a steady practice at home.

My mother visited us from time to time and she was deeply absorbed in Ajahn Sumedho's talks. She would say, "You and Ralph must go to England and see this great monk." I did have a strong desire to see Ajahn Sumedho but I did not know if that would be possible.

In 2007, Ajahn Amaro was visiting Richard Smith, and the Lansing Buddhist Association invited Ajahn Amaro to hold a one-day retreat at the Great Hall that was still under construction. Almost a hundred people attended the retreat. After a wonderful day spent listening to Dhamma talks, meditating, offering food to Ajahn Amaro and then sharing a meal with the other attendees, we ended the retreat with a visit to Ajahn Khemasanto.

When the two Ajahns went for a walk, a group of us chatted with Richard and I asked him if he had ever invited Ajahn Sumedho to come and visit him. He said he had not. Since Richard was soon going to England, we pleaded with him to invite Ajahn Sumedho. When Richard came back from England, he said that Ajahn Sumedho had suddenly asked him if there was a non-stop flight from Detroit to Seattle. Apparently, Ajahn Sumedho's sister lived in Vancouver and whenever he came to the U.S., he tried to visit her. We were delighted to hear this and clung on to the hope that one day Ajahn Sumedho would stop by and visit Michigan on his way to see his sister.

I have noticed that a Dhamma wish is usually easily fulfilled, and sure enough Richard informed us that Ajahn Sumedho was going to spend a week at Richard's home in Michigan in May 2010. So, finally, Ralph and I were able to see the teacher we had followed since 1999. We spent seven wonderful days listening to the Dhamma pouring from Ajahn's lips. Even though Richard's home is almost two hours from where we live, and both Ralph and I were teaching that summer, we drove every evening to meditate with Ajahn and to hear the Dhamma. All I had wanted was just to see him and pay my respects to him. My wishes were fulfilled in a manner that was beyond anything I could have possibly anticipated.

Over the years Ajahn Sumedho became a part of our lives. Often, when in a particular situation that required the wisdom of the Dhamma, we would say, "Now what would Ajahn Sumedho say?" instead of saying, "Now what would the Dhamma say?" The wise teachings of this monk saved us from many a pitfall, both in our private and public lives. His presence filled our home, and soon we felt as though this wonderful channel of the Dhamma truly lived with us.

Ajahn Sumedho (left) and Ajahn Viradhammo (right) in Sri Lanka, 2017 (Photo courtesy of Maureen Bodenbach)

Ajahn Sumedho's teachings make one realize that the Dhamma is simple. Even though he has a brilliant and questioning mind, he never gets trapped in a net of intellectual complexities. He speaks directly and clearly. This does not mean that he simplifies the Dhamma. All the subtle nuances of the Dhamma are embedded in his talks, yet they do not confuse us. It is amazing to see how captivatingly brilliant his analyses can be. However, one never gets the sense that he is trying to be brilliant. He has a brilliant mind but has also practiced everything he teaches. Perhaps that is why his presentation of the Dhamma is so easy to understand.

A strategy used by all teachers is to use specific and concrete examples to support their statements. Ajahn Sumedho's talks are peppered with stories of himself which most of the time depict him as an erring human. He has an infectious sense of humor and is quite adept at making jokes at his own expense. So, he regales us with funny stories that highlight his weaknesses and then goes on to show us how one can gradually overcome such weaknesses or at least learn to be aware of them. As we listen to these stories, we get carried away by Ajahn's humility and begin to relate to his inability to be the most perfect human being on earth. The more he makes fun of his frustrations, the more we find ourselves warming up to him. "Yes," we say to ourselves, "I know exactly what he is talking about. That's how I feel." Without even realizing it, we begin to believe that we are indeed like Ajahn. However, through it all we are aware that Ajahn has reached a high level of spirituality, and soon we begin to say, "Well, if Ajahn Sumedho can do it, then so can I." That is perhaps one of the greatest gifts Ajahn has given us: The assurance that we can do it! We begin to be convinced that liberation from suffering is possible.

Liberation, as we listen to Ajahn Sumedho, is not something that is far away; it is not some distant possibility that we may realize in some distant future. Freedom from suffering is here and now, in the present moment. "Here and now," or "the present moment"—these are terms used so often by Buddhist teachers and students that sometimes they seem almost bereft of any meaning. However, that is not the case with Ajahn Sumedho. As he teaches us to watch the mind, as he teaches us mindfulness, as we begin to watch the mind, as we begin to become aware, we realize that the freedom we are seeking is possible. We watch as the mind threatens to traipse down its habitual path of greed, hatred, and delusion, and we watch as our *watching*, our mindfulness, provides the mind with the option of choosing the path the Buddha pointed out to us—the way out of suffering. In those rare mindful moments in our lives when we choose to follow in the Buddha's footsteps, we experience liberation, release, freedom. The realization that the key to liberation is right here, within our control, fills us with awe. The realization that what we have been seeking in books, talks, retreats, and teachers is right here within us can be breathtaking. As these deep insights rush through us, we understand what Ajahn is trying to tell us: That life is just the way it is.

Of course, such moments are rare in our lives and most of the time we forget to use the tools Buddhism has given us as we deal with all the trials and tribulations that life puts us through. We would then like to blame ourselves, hate ourselves, punish ourselves for failing in our practice, but when we listen to Ajahn Sumedho we realize that there is a much better way of dealing with the mind that went astray or the defilements that surfaced and made us falter on the path to freedom. We look at our "demons" and learn to accept them because that is what Ajahn Sumedho has done and has taught us to do. So, once again, we watch the mind and say, "Okay, you can go on a guilt trip or you can travel with *metta* (loving kindness) and *karuna* (compassion)." Once again, the options are before us. Self-hatred and guilt have been our companions throughout many lifetimes; however, we can now make friends with *metta* and *karuna*.

With this new wisdom we try to see how it feels to embrace our demons (defilements) with loving kindness, we try to see how it feels to embrace our failures (our inability to be mindful) with compassion, and to our utter surprise we realize that replacing aversion with acceptance can set us free. We do not run away from our mistakes and weaknesses, we do not turn the other way and ignore our faults, we do not beat ourselves over the head with a stick about our failures; we simply embrace them all. We see the defilements for what they are and let them be without feeling guilty or giving up. Even as such a thought arises and we find ourselves doubting whether it is right to not feel guilty, we think of Ajahn Sumedho. He does not encourage us to water the seeds of our defilements; he simply tells us to look at our defilements and recognize them for what they are. Perhaps seeing the defilements will help us gradually shed them. If that happens, good; however, if we make the same mistakes again and again, that is acceptable too as long as we are able to see what we are doing and reflect on the experience. As Ajahn Sumedho teaches, guilt and self-hatred do not help rectify a problem we have created; *metta* and *karuna* help us realize that after all we are only human, and we will err from time to time. This realization that we are human does not make us complacent; it simply strengthens our understanding of the all-inclusive nature of the Dhamma.

Ajahn Sumedho's words exude loving kindness and compassion which endear him to us. Many of his stories reveal that he is a gentle and sensitive person. He often talks about how we, human beings, are very sensitive and vulnerable creatures. We have the world constantly impinging on us as it rushes in through our senses. Not only are we physically impacted by the world, but our mind too can play havoc with us. All this pressure can be too much for such a frail creature as the human being. Hence, we all suffer and it is no surprise that the Buddha's first noble truth states that life is *dukkha* (suffering). However, as Ajahn Sumedho reminds us, the Buddha did not stop there; he went on to investigate the cause of suffering and the way out of suffering. The cause of suffering is desire: this is what we learn from the second noble truth. Ajahn encourages us to trace our own suffering to its root, to the realization that our suffering is being caused by a desire—something we want or even something we do not want. As we investigate further, we realize that all desire is rooted in the ego, in our sense of the "I" and "Mine," in our sense of self.

As we listen to Ajahn, we train to become detectives of the mind. We learn to investigate each case thoroughly until we solve our personal Who-done-it mysteries. Usually when *dukkha* strikes, we at once blame others. That is our habitual tendency and the mystery is solved in a second and the case is closed, or so we think. However, from time to time someone or something threatens to open that "closed" case, and we experience a sense of dis-ease. We turn to Ajahn Sumedho and start applying all the skills he has taught us. We open our eyes and begin to trace the *dukkha* back to its roots, to desire. Now we dig deeper and deeper and find the culprit, our old friend, our self. The more we practice, the more adept we become at tracing everything back to the ego, to self-view. We see, we recognize, we realize the source of *dukkha*. Sometimes we let go and are free; sometimes we cling on and continue to experience dukkha *but* with the awareness of its source. Whatever be the case, as Ajahn would say, *it is just the way it is.*

As we gradually become familiar with our self, we realize how strong our social and cultural conditioning is. We listen to Ajahn Sumedho and begin to see all that influences what we call our sense of self or identity, and we realize that this self is nothing but a social and cultural construct. As we start to explore the self from this perspective, we see how our attachments to views and opinions, right and wrong, justice and injustice, joy and sorrow, have bound us to *dukkha*. We see how we have become so set in our ways that we never realize that while our innumerable ties to our society and culture provide us with a place in society, they also suffocate us because they are a source of bondage. As we investigate further we realize that while it is easy to give up what we think is "bad" or "evil," it is much more difficult to give up what we think is "good" and "just." We argue with ourselves and try to convince ourselves that our anger over the injustices of the world is right; however, by now Ajahn's words have made it impossible for us to close our eyes to the fact that righteous or not, anger is a source of discomfort. Now we start letting go, bit by bit, of all that conditions us socially and culturally. Of course, that is difficult and often we fail to let go. We keep going round and round in our habitual cycles even though, as we spin, we know how to stop the wheel. On some rare occasions we do stop and breathe the heavenly fragrance of awareness, of consciousness, which helps us let go. We sigh with relief as we lift our wings and soar up into the blue sky of freedom. However, we know this is just a short reprieve and we will again get on the merry-go-round of *dukkha* and spin.

As we go through life and keep hopping on and off the merry-go-round of our habitual tendencies, we are often afflicted with doubt. We doubt ourselves, we doubt the Dhamma, we doubt our practice, and we even doubt our teachers. We wonder about Ajahn Sumedho. Who is he? He makes it all sound so easy and so effortless but why does it all turn out to be so difficult? Why did it all sound so easy to do when Ajahn talked, and why do we see ourselves falling flat on our noses as we find life hurling its wrenches at us? However, by now it is too late; there can be no going back; Ajahn Sumedho has a firm grasp on us and we pick up one of his books or turn on one of his tapes and his words fill us with the melody of assurance.

Gradually doubt dissipates and conviction arises. Everything he says makes sense; it all ties up together; there is nothing that does not gel. The Dhamma flows from Ajahn's heart. It is this effortless powerful ever-flowing stream that pours out of his heart into ours. Soon there is no sense of self; we forget who we think we are and we no longer think of Ajahn as a person. He is simply a great channel through which the Dhamma enters our hearts that seem to open their receptive petals one by one as the Buddha's gems of wisdom penetrate us. We are convinced that we are on the path of the Buddha, that we are on our way out of suffering, that we know for sure that suffering will cease. Here is someone like us who has suffered and erred and spun around in circles, and if he has made it so can we. Listening to Ajahn makes us believe in ourselves, believe in the Dhamma, believe in our practice because we believe in this great monk. We laugh at our doubts and hug our precious treasure which is the knowledge, the complete certainty that the Dhamma works.

Indeed, there are so many reasons for us to be grateful to this teacher who has dedicated his life to finding freedom and sharing his reflections with us. Trying to put down in words all the innumerable gifts we have received from Ajahn Sumedho is like trying to pour the ocean into a bottle. He has taught us how to love ourselves, how to spend time with ourselves, how to sit quietly and listen to the sound of silence, how to feel the resounding peace in our hearts, how to experience the mellow joy that fills our being, how to watch the mind and be mindful, how to develop the *Brahma Viharas* (loving kindness, compassion, sympathetic joy, and equanimity), how to accept and embrace our "demons," how to "love" everyone even though we may not "like" everyone, and how to find within ourselves *that* which we are seeking. His presence fills the room and his smile fills our hearts. We listen to him and know he has done it. We listen to him and know we can do it. And that, indeed, *is just the way it is.*

Chapter 41: Lansing Buddhist Association

Even though our Thai, Taiwanese, and Chinese Buddhist friends in Michigan had joined hands together in buying the property in Perry, their practice was affiliated with different schools of Buddhism. The Thai community established the Dhammasala Forest Monastery and supported Ajhan Khemasanto who belonged to the Thai Forest tradition. The Taiwanese and the Chinese, led by Lina and Chen, established the Lansing Buddhist Association and followed the Pure Land school of Buddhism. Initially, we would all meet in the main house on the property to listen to Ajahn's Dhamma talks and meditate with him. There was a small house, which we called the "Yellow House" because it was painted yellow, and this is where the members of LBA practiced for several years.

Venerable Tashi with some members of the Lansing Buddhist Association. Michigan

Finally members of LBA built their temple, the Great Hall, a huge building for holding Buddhist services and retreats; they also bought a house across the street to accommodate the teachers who visited from time to time to hold retreats. They invited Buddhist teachers from all traditions, and we were able to practice with both monastic and lay teachers. Venerable Chi Chern belonged to the Chan tradition and held an annual retreat for years. Venerable Tashi came twice with his group of Tibetan monks. Two nuns belonging to the Burmese tradition, Sister Dipankara and Sister Susila came and taught meditation and the Abhidhamma. Monks from Amaravati, the monastery founded by Ajahn Sumedho in England, came for one-day retreats, and we were able to practice with Ajahn Sucitto and Ajahn Amaro. They would come to visit Richard Smith in Troy and offer Dhamma talks and guided meditation at various venues in Detroit, apart from Richard's house. We would plan ahead of time and invite them to come and hold a one-day retreat hosted by the Lansing Buddhist Association. Lina and Chen, Lisa and Peter Kong, Nancy and Jim Jean worked tirelessly with other members of LBA to host these retreats. Feeding hundreds of retreatants and housing out-of-towners involved a lot of work but the members took care of everything with equanimity.

Ralph and I with members of LBA at our house blessing ceremony. Michigan, 2004

The LBA members wished to reach out to the American community and, inspired by Anna Kong, formed a group called Buddhism at Peace and started holding meetings. Many of us attended these meetings which were first held at the residence of Peter and Lisa Kong and later at the Spartan Village Community Center. These meetings were delightful. Peter Kong led us in Tai Chi which was followed by a short period of meditation. Then one of us would make a presentation on a topic of Buddhist interest and the audience would discuss the Dharma. Delicious food was provided by members of LBA and we came home with hearts filled with peace and joy.

Much later, after 2016, we began to meet at a studio called LotusVoice where we read several Buddhist texts and discussed the teachings of the Buddha. In this way I remained connected with the members of LBA.

My debt to them is immense. Because they opened their doors to many teachers of Buddhism, I was able to practice with several great monks and nuns from various parts of the world. In members of LBA, I saw dedicated practitioners. I had been a beneficiary of their generosity and goodness for two decades and could not turn down Lina's request to help with the Dhamma group when Covid struck in 2020 and the group could only meet via Zoom. Lina asked me if I could help with their group which attracted English-speaking practitioners interested in Buddhism. I agreed to facilitate and we started in January of 2021 by reading Christina Feldman's book *Boundless Heart* which focused on the Brahma Viharas or Divine Abodes.

Chapter 42: Bishop Road Mindfulness Center

In August of 2002, our friends Bill Rittenberg and Marina Levine invited Ralph and me to attend a group led by a woman named Carolyn White. It was called the Bishop Road Mindfulness Center and was housed in a Vietnamese temple, the Van Hanh temple of Lansing. The group, whose members were mostly English-speaking Americans, met on Tuesdays. It was at this group that I met one of my dearest Dharma friends, Anna Fisher. Carolyn White focused on the teachings of the renowned Vietnamese teacher Thich Nhat Hanh whose teachings are well-known throughout the world and are very popular because of their accessible nature. Deep profound truths are to be found in his talks and books, but they are expressed with such simplicity and honesty that they leave behind an indelible impression on the mind of the practitioner. I looked forward each week to my time with this group and experienced great peace while meditating with them and listening to the teachings.

In November of 2002, Jack Lawlor, a lay Dharma teacher in the tradition of Thich Nhat Hanh, came to Lansing and held a day-long retreat. By then, I had become familiar with the teachings of Thich Nhat Hanh and felt comfortable participating in sitting and walking meditations at the retreat and listening to the Dharma talks of Jack Lawlor. There was a break for lunch, and I understood we were to participate in eating mindfully in silence. I am not sure I ate much, but the fact that even such an act as eating can be an experience in meditation became clear to me that day. It was then that I understood what Thich Nhat Hanh meant when he encouraged us in his teachings to meditate not just on the cushion but all through the day by practicing mindfulness.

On August 23, 2003, I had the great fortune of seeing Thich Nhat Hanh in person. Four of us from Carolyn's group drove to Chicago where a crowd of 5000 people listened to the gentle teachings of this famous teacher. Such was the presence of this petite figure that even though we were sitting very far from him, we experienced an indescribable peace. After listening to his talk, I carried this peace in my heart for more than a week.

That year my friend Anna Fisher went to a retreat with Thich Nhat Hanh and came back with beautiful stories of her experiences. It was from her that

I heard about Sister Chan Kong and her melodious chanting. Anna taught these chants to many of us who were attending the LBA group Buddhism at Peace. Being an activist, Anna was attracted to Thich Nhat Hanh's teachings on Engaged Buddhism. We learned from him that one must stand up for justice, but one can and must do it with a peaceful and loving heart. While attending Carolyn's group, I benefitted greatly from the teachings, poetry, and songs of this gentle and compassionate Vietnamese teacher.

Chapter 43: Quan Am Temple

In April 2004, I saw an article in the university newspaper about the serious problems that had arisen in a Vietnamese temple called the Quan Am Temple. This was not the Vietnamese temple that was situated on Bishop Road. In fact, I was surprised to hear that there were two Vietnamese Buddhist temples in our area. According to the article, the city had ordered that the Vietnamese nun in charge of the temple be evicted on grounds that the temple had violated city ordinances. They were given a week to move out. I shared the story with Anna, and she shared it with some of her friends. Soon a group of us went and visited the nun, who asked us to address her as Suco. A monk named Sakya Minh Quang was present and we were told to call him Thay (which means "teacher"). He had come over from Grand Rapids to help Suco communicate with us because her English was weak. Thus began yet another beautiful relationship with a Buddhist sangha.

House blessing ceremony at Anna Fisher's home.
From left to right: Thay, Mieken Van de Waerden, Anna, and Suco.
Looking up at Anna is her dog, Dumar. Michigan, 2004

Anna and her friends were able to get a year's extension for Suco, and within a few months Suco had found a property in Mason, set in a rural setting in the country, and moved her temple there. On the property, apart from a nice house, there was a big barn. This barn was converted into a beautiful temple by the Vietnamese congregation. They met on Sundays to pray and on special days to celebrate their festivals.

On Thursday evenings, Thay led our group of mostly English-speaking American practitioners in walking and sitting meditation which was followed by a talk. He was studying at the Grand Rapids Community College when we met him in 2004. After completing his degree there, Thay moved to Lansing and started taking courses at Michigan State University. There were two semesters when Thay took a Sociology course taught by Ralph. On many a Thursday afternoon, I walked from my building (where I taught English) to the parking lot where Ralph had parked our car, and on the way, I would see Thay and we would wave at each other. He was on his way to the temple after finishing his class with Ralph. Ralph and I would come home, eat something, freshen up and rush to the temple where I would witness a role reversal. Now Thay was the teacher and Ralph the student. This was something that made all of us laugh. Of course, Thay was an excellent student and got good grades in the classes he took. We also heard from our friends that he could be seen in the library until late hours of the night. His sincerity and dedication touched our hearts and we felt blessed to have him as our teacher.

When we first met Thay, we found it hard to understand his English because of his pronunciation and accent. But he was an eager student and learned quickly. Soon he could speak fluently and we looked forward each week to his talks. Thay was very knowledgeable and his talks were full of wisdom. He would often use stories, anecdotes, and parables to make the Dharma accessible to us. Sometimes, he would share a koan and we would chew on that and look to him for help. He would smile and provide us with insights that would help us make some sense of the koan.

Thay's generosity knew no bounds. When people asked if they needed to donate money for these sessions, Thay would say, "You are already donating your time. You are busy people and have made time to listen to the Dharma. That is enough."

I also found that Thay's practical nature impressed me. One evening, someone mentioned the Heart Sutra. Thay pointed at his chest and said, "You do not have to go to books to read the Heart Sutra. Your Heart Sutra

Sakya Minh Quang (Thay) and Ralph at the Quan Am Temple. Michigan.

is here. Read your own hearts." As I listened, I thought of how true his words were. I need to know who I am, what goes on in my mind and heart.

Thay's humility was quite extraordinary. He never said he was the teacher and we were his students. He always said, "We are all teachers here and all students. I learn from you and you learn from me." He was very friendly and kind, but always knew how to set boundaries between himself and the lay people. He did not meet us outside the temple. He kept himself busy with his studies and I never saw him sitting and idly chatting.

One day we were discussing the concept of *metta* or loving kindness and Thay told us a story to prove how powerful the practice of *metta* can be. Before getting his visa to come to the U.S., Thay had heard many stories of how other monks' visas had been rejected. Most of the people in our group were Americans, but I could relate to Thay's story. All immigrants suffer great anxiety when they go to the U.S. Embassy in their country for a visa. One never knows if one's request will be granted or denied. Thay, however, was not worried about whether he would get the visa because he was not attached to acceptance or rejection. As he watched other candidates leaving with dejected faces, he remained calm and practiced loving kindness meditation. The authorities asked him three questions and Thay got his visa. We were all relieved that the story ended on a happy note, and we had Thay before us as our teacher.

From 2004 to 2010, we were very lucky to have Thay with us as he finished his degrees at Michigan State University, spent several months in Japan on a scholarship, and finally went to pursue his doctoral degree at the University of Illinois Urbana-Champagne in Illinois. We were devastated when we realized that we were going to lose Thay. Someone said, "But what will happen to us?"

Thay immediately answered, "I am not taking the Dharma with me. You will continue to meet and teach each other." His quick reply made me realize that here was a truly wise monk who practiced what he taught. Thay left and the sangha continued successfully under the guidance of Anna Fisher. We continued to practice walking and sitting meditation and read and discussed many valuable books for the next ten years. Finally, in 2020, the Thursday Evening Meditation Group at Quan Am Temple stopped meeting due to Covid.

Part IV: Paramhansa Yogananda

Chapter 44: The Book

In April of 2003 I was in Boston with my sister, Bonie, and her family. Mother was visiting us and we were all having a good time together. One day, Mother and I were sitting on the deck in the tepid warmth of an early spring when she asked me what I had been reading. I rattled off a list of books on spiritual themes and suddenly she said, "You know what? There is a book I want you to read. I read it when I came here last year. It is Yoganandaji's *Sayings of Yogananda*, and I loved the book. There are these short sayings, and it is very simple but very profound. We must remember to get hold of that book before you leave."

Bonie was about to have a baby, and she and her family had just moved from an apartment to their own house. Only the essentials had been unpacked and much needed to be done before life could be lived in an orderly fashion without the chaos of packed, unpacked, and half-unpacked boxes that seemed to be strewn all over the place. To motivate ourselves, Bonie and I decided to start with the books.

The lovely new house had innumerable shelves and we had innumerable books. Box after box was unpacked and book after book was lovingly put away on the glowing wooden shelves. Shakespeare and Marlowe, Austen and Bronte, Wordsworth and Coleridge, Dickens and Hardy, Whitman and Emerson and many more—old trusted friends with whom we had spent many a day in full-throated laughter and heart-rending tears. As we two sisters worked, Mother hovered over us--her sharp eyes not missing a single book--looking for something. We finally asked her what she was doing, and she said she was looking for Yoganandaji's book. We assured her that we would get it for her the minute it turned up.

When Mother was resting after lunch, I asked my sister, "What is this book Mother keeps talking about?"

Bonie said, "I don't know. I haven't read it. I found it on a bookshelf at my boss' house when I was there for a party. I saw the name "Yogananda" and recognized it. Remember Mother used to have his *Autobiography of a Yogi* in our house in India? Well, I asked my boss what the book was doing on his shelf. He immediately gave it to me and said I could keep it. I guess I must have put it on one of our bookshelves. Mother found it there and read it and was deeply impressed. You know her—she is always reading."

Every box was unpacked that week, and the whole house was made ready for the new baby, but Yoganandaji refused to show up. Mother was quite upset and finally I said to her, "Stop fretting. I know someone back in Michigan who knows some followers of Yoganandaji. I will go to their group, and I am sure they will have the book. I promise you that I will buy it and read it. Okay?" Reluctantly, my mother relaxed.

After spending three months helping with the new baby and listening to my mother's heart-warming spiritual stories and discussions, I came home to Michigan and immediately contacted my friend, Anna Fisher, and asked her how soon she could take me to this group she had earlier mentioned. She told me the group held service on Sundays and we could go as soon as I wanted. So, I chose the very next Sunday and was ready in the morning to be picked up by Anna.

We went to a little apartment where there was a small group of people. We sat quietly until the service started and then I simply followed what the others were doing. A man seemed to be leading the group, and he sang some songs and gave a sermon and soon the service was over. My mind was not receptive because I had only come to buy the book. I did not pay much attention to the congregation or the service, and I was ready to go. After the service was over, Anna introduced me to the man who had led the group. He was very nice and warm towards me, and I learned that his name was Lorne Dekun. I asked him who the sages on the altar were. I had recognized the pictures of Jesus, Yoganandaji, and Lahiri Mahasaya, but did not know who the other two sages were. Lorne told me that the sage next to Lahiri Mahasaya was his guru Babaji Maharaj, and the sage next to Yogananda was his guru Sri Yukteswara.

I went straight to the point and told Lorne why I was there. He looked quite surprised and said, "How did your mother find that book? That is an old book and I am afraid we do not have it. But we do have something similar." He handed me a book which also contained sayings by Yogananda. I opened it and saw that the sayings were short, and the format of the book resembled that of the book Mother had mentioned. I bought the book, put my name on the group's email list out of politeness, declined the group members' hospitality and their suggestion that we stay back for pancakes, and left with Anna.

The minute I came home, I called Mother. Before I could say a word, she said, "You went to Yoganandaji's group today, didn't you?"

I was stunned and asked, "How did you know?"

She laughed and said, "The book turned up this morning."

I sat down and blurted out, "You've got to be kidding!"

My mother laughed and asked me to tell her about my visit. I gave her all the details and as I was trying to remember the gurus on the altar and struggling with the names, she said, "Don't you remember Lahiri Mahasaya?"

I said, "Yes, I do. In fact, when I came to the U.S. you gave me a tiny picture of him which I still have. But that is the only reason I knew who he was. I don't know anything about these gurus. All I know is that Yoganandaji wrote *Autobiography of a Yogi* and the book used to be on your shelf."

"But don't you remember the story of Lahiri Mahasaya going to the mountains and finding a cave and then meeting his guru?" asked Mother.

As she uttered these words, I was overcome by a strange sensation. I could scarcely breathe.

"Mother," I said with chills running up my spine, "I just remembered that I had this dream last night. I was high up in the Himalayas and was taking leave of a *sadhu*. He sat on a mat, outside a cave, and was dressed in saffron robes as most ascetics are. He had dreadlocks and was looking up at me as I stood up. It seemed as though we had spent quite some time together and it was getting late, and I had to leave.

"In the dream, I pressed my palms together and bowed and said, 'I feel so blessed to have found you. I came upon you by chance, and it was wonderful spending time with you. I feel reluctant to leave but I must. I don't know if we will ever meet again.'

"At this, the holy man looked at me. He did not speak with his lips, but his message was conveyed mentally to me. He said, 'For many eons have I known you, and for many eons will I know you.' The words were in Bengali (*Koto yuga yuga dhore jaani, aar koto yuga yuga dhore jaanbo*) and rang clearly in my mind."

After narrating the dream, I sat quietly and my body was covered with goose bumps. Mother, too, was silent. Then she told me the story of how Lahiri Mahasaya had gone to Ranikhet, high up in the Himalayas, and met his guru, Babaji Maharaj, and been initiated in Kriya Yoga. As she told me the story, I remembered vaguely having heard it before. However, I did not believe that my dream was connected to this vague memory. I did not remember any details of the story until Mother repeated it that morning when I had just returned from Lorne's Ananda Michigan group. I also had no knowledge of Yoganandaji's background that would link Lahiri Mahasaya to the Yogananda group. I kept mulling over the details of my visit to the group until I came to the conclusion that the dream I had was not triggered by any prior knowledge I had regarding Yoganandaji or the gurus. Yet, the dream echoed the story of Lahiri Mahasaya.

"What did the *sadhu* look like?" asked Mother.

"I want to say he looked like Babaji Maharaj, but I think he looked like Balananda Brahmachari (my guru's guru) in his younger days," I replied.

"Well, perhaps you did see our guru's guru because Balanandaji took Kriya initiation from Lahiri Mahasaya," replied Mother.

I did not know about this connection between Balanandaji and Lahiri Mahasaya; moreover, this was the first time I was hearing the words "Kriya Yoga."

We left it at that, and I spent the rest of the day in solitude, quietly wondering how all this had come about.

A year later, when I went to visit my sister, I made sure that I came back to Michigan with the book my mother had been so eager for me to read. It looked like a second-third-or fourth-hand book with its tattered cover and torn flap. On the first page, one of the former owners had inscribed the following words: "To a fellow searcher, from a stumbling, but none-the-less one-minded pilgrim."

The Book that brought me to Yoganandaji. 2004 (Photo courtesy of Kathy Burgess)

219

The inscription inside the book (Photo courtesy of Kathy Burgess)

Chapter 45: Ananda Michigan

A couple of months after my first visit to Ananda Michigan in 2003, I attended one of their kirtans and soon became a regular visitor. Being a disciple of Maharaj, who was a great singer of devotional songs, I was quite naturally attracted to kirtans led by Lorne. He had a powerful voice and was deeply devoted to his guru, Yoganandaji. Most of the songs Lorne sang were composed by Yoganandaji. Some were loosely based on well-known Bengali devotional songs; for example, "Engrossed is the bee of my mind" is based on the Bengali song "Mojlo amar mon bhramara." The kirtans were at least an hour and a half long. As the songs rolled effortlessly off Lorne's tongue, we felt ourselves immersed in the depths of Yoganandaji's deep yearning for God. To newcomers, Lorne explained that the method followed was the call and response method. I was, of course, very familiar with this method of communal singing. We did not have any chant books, nor did we need any. We closed our eyes and listened to Lorne's voice booming with vigor and boundless love for God, and we picked up the chants very quickly. Soon we did not have to wait to hear each line; we were singing along with Lorne. In this way I learned many of the songs composed by Yoganandaji and a few that were composed by his disciple Swami Kriyananda, who was the founder of Ananda.

As my interest in Yoganandaji increased, I read his famous book *Autobiography of a Yogi* and his disciple, Swami Kriyananda's (Donald Walters) autobiography *The Path*. Gradually, I began to learn more about Yoganandaji's work in America and how he had founded the Self-Realization Fellowship and established its headquarters in California. Swami Kriyananda's book described his interesting journey to Yoganandaji, who accepted him as his disciple. Swami Kriyananda spent a few years with his guru and was present when this great sage left the body. Later, Swami Kriyananda left the Self-Realization Fellowship and founded Ananda. The sangha that Lorne had started in Michigan was affiliated with Ananda.

In 2004, my mother visited me for a week and I took her to Lorne's kirtan. She was highly impressed by what she heard and immediately bonded with Lorne. After attending Sunday service the next day at Lorne and Judy's home, we gathered around the dining table to eat breakfast and chat. I had earlier told Lorne that Mother knew Anandamayi Ma, the great saint whom Yoganandaji met when he went back to India in 1936. I had read the chapter in *Autobiography of a Yogi* on her and had told Lorne that I had met her. He was thrilled to hear this and wanted my mother to tell us stories. Mother shyly recounted many of the stories she remembered at the breakfast table as everyone listened in wonder.

Lorne Dekun (Photo courtesy of Carol Kanners)

From then on, whenever she visited me in Michigan, Mother went to Lorne's events. Lorne looked forward to her visits and said she reminded him of Yoganandaji. His fondness for Mother was not based merely on her being a Bengali who lived in Calcutta. He could sense her spiritual nature and felt it was a privilege to have her in his home. When Mother passed away in 2010, Lorne performed a beautiful ceremony for her and honored her in the way people who have passed away are honored according to the Ananda Sangha tradition. At the end of the moving ceremony, we all went to Mother's picture and placed rose petals in front of it.

In 2005, Lorne and his wife Judy had moved to a condominium which was larger than the apartment where I had first met Lorne. There were days when the room was crowded with as many as forty people. Some came from out of town to attend kirtans and retreats. The living and dining room were set up like a temple with the altar at one end of the room to provide space for devotees. In the basement, Judy kept the children busy on Sundays while we attended service. After service, we all gathered around the folding tables and ate a simple breakfast while chatting with each other.

Lorne and Judy Dekun

Among his many gifts, Lorne's ability to make everyone feel comfortable in his presence was quite admirable. Apart from welcoming us to all the events he hosted, he also kept in touch with us personally and was very caring when members of his congregation were sick. He was glad to have me in his sangha, and because I was a Bengali he made good use of whatever meager knowledge I had of Indian languages, history, culture, and philosophy. Often, I would get a call or an email from Lorne asking for help with the pronunciation of Indian words. Sometimes he asked me the meanings of some Bengali songs or Sanskrit *slokas*. In some cases, I did not know the answer but would call my mother and then tell Lorne the answer.

Lorne singing Kirtan (Photo courtesy of Wendy Page-Echols)

The more I got to know Lorne, the more impressed I was by his sincerity. He had an amazing memory and could recite at length verses from Sir Edwin Arnold's *The Song Celestial*. When he sang Yoganandaji's compositions, he included lines that were in Hindi or Bengali or Sanskrit. Sometimes I would wonder why he would pronounce an English word in a manner that was not quite American. Then I would hear a recording of Yoganandaji singing that particular song and realize that Lorne's pronunciation of each word matched Yoganandaji's pronunciation. Such was his devotion that he wanted to sing the songs in the exact manner in which his guru had sung them. Most Americans are not familiar with other languages. Even if they may have taken some courses in school, these are usually courses in European languages. Indian languages are very foreign to them. But Lorne wished to learn chants in Sanskrit, Hindi and Bengali because these were the languages of his guru's country.

One day he sent me a recording of a song sung by Swami Kriyananda. It was a Bengali song and Lorne wished to learn it. One of the first songs I learned at Lorne's was a beautiful composition by Yoganandaji: "Door of my heart, open wide I keep for Thee." Lorne usually started each kirtan with this song. The recording by Swami Kriyananda was the Bengali version of "Door of my heart": "*Jaabe ki hey dina amar biphole choliye.*" I listened and transliterated the song in English. Then Lorne called me and listened to every word and revised my transliteration to make it more accurate. Then he learned the song. At the next kirtan, he provided everyone with copies of the lyrics and tried to teach his congregation the Bengali version of Yoganandaji's famous song "Door of my heart." Incidents such as these, endeared Lorne to me and made us all love him dearly.

The altar at Ananda Michigan at my mother's (extreme left) memorial service. 2010 The Masters from left to right: Lahiri Mahasaya, Babaji Maharaj, Jesus Christ, Swami Yukteswara, Paramhansa Yogananda

Chapter 46: 4 Garpar Road

While attending a retreat in Lansing, Michigan, organized by Lorne Dekun, one of the Ananda ministers leading the retreat asked where I was from and I said, "India."

She then asked, "Where in India?"

I replied, "Calcutta."

Her face lit up and she said, "Then you must have been to 4 Garpar Road?"

A little embarrassed at not having visited the house where Yoganandaji had lived and attained enlightenment, I vowed that I would make this pilgrimage when I went back to India.

In 2010, I had to go to Calcutta (now Kolkata) because my mother was unwell, and I stayed for three months. I told Mother that I wished to visit Yoganandaji's house, and she encouraged me to make arrangements to do so. As we talked, I pulled out the Bengali version of *Autobiography of a Yogi* from my mother's bookshelf in India and asked her if she had read the book. She told me that she had not only read the book but had fond memories of the time she got the book. It was given to her by a friend in 1964 when she was walking through a remote area in the Himalayas while on a pilgrimage to Kedarnath.

Back in those days, one had to walk a long way to reach the temple of Kedarnath, which was situated at a very high altitude in the snow-clad Himalayan mountains. It was a difficult, extremely cold hike through areas that were mostly uninhabited. Much of the time my mother was all alone on the path; on the few occasions when she saw other people, they turned out to be pilgrims. Even though she had initially started walking with some friends, her feet soon developed blisters and she could not walk very fast. Not wishing to delay her friends, she told them to go on and she would catch up with them. Her friends left and making rapid progress were soon out of sight. Mother kept walking slowly and steadily with her strong faith in God supporting her. Finally, she arrived at her destination and was not only able to pay her respects at the shrine of Kedarnath but also met a great sage named Phalahari Baba.

After visiting Kedarnath, her friends departed for Badrinath. My mother was supposed to accompany them, but since her feet were in terrible shape she decided to go back home to Dehradun. As they parted, one of her friends gave her a copy of *Autobiography of a Yogi* and said, "Lily, keep this book with you as you walk back alone." My mother did not know anything about Yoganandaji or the book, but she put the book in her bag and started her long and painful journey down the mountains. Soon she was alone and yet she did not feel alone. She said that she constantly felt someone's presence with her—a benign, protective, gentle presence. Other pilgrims passed her and were surprised to see a woman walking all by herself in those grimly remote areas, but my mother had no fears because she was convinced that she was not alone.

Eventually she came to a section of the road which had collapsed due to a landslide. The road was blocked, and Mother was wondering what to do when a huge shaggy black dog appeared by her side. At first, she was startled to see the dog appear out of nowhere, but soon she realized that he was leading her somewhere. She started following the dog who eventually led her to a rushing stream, and she understood that she would have to cross the stream to get to the section of the road that would take her to her destination. The dog leaped onto a boulder and then went to the next rock and looked back at my mother and waited. Following his cue, she went from boulder to boulder, rock to rock, as the swirling waters of the rushing stream went hurtling through the gorge she was crossing. One missed step and she would be swept away by the current. The dog saw her safely to the other side and then accompanied her for the rest of her journey. Finally, as they approached a slightly populated area, my mother turned around and saw that the dog was gone. Mother was convinced that Yoganandaji had protected her on that perilous journey.

Listening to her story, I became eager to make my pilgrimage as soon as possible. I had heard that the house was still a private residence, and one could not just walk in and see the place. I was looking for a phone number so I could contact the present residents of the house. I could not find a phone number or website for 4 Garpar Road, but I did find a website which listed a couple of phone numbers for Yogoda Math in Dakshineswar. I called the Math (monastery) and spoke with a man working there who gave me the phone number of the contact person at Garpar Road. He told me I had to call and make an appointment so that the house could be opened for me.

I called Garpar Road and made the necessary arrangements to visit Yoganandaji's home. On March 21, 2010, at 5:30 p.m., my uncle, Sankar, and I took a cab and left home. On a regular weekday it would have taken an hour to get from my house in South Kolkata to Garpar Road, which is in North Kolkata. However, it was Sunday and we did not encounter any traffic jams. The day had been hot and humid, but at dusk the evening had become a bit more bearable. Darkness was beginning to settle on the city. The cab seemed to be flying down the streets and the strong breeze whipping through the open windows kept me cool. Enjoying the drive, we found ourselves at the gate of 4 Garpar Road at 6:00 p.m.

4 Garpar Road (Photo courtesy of Wendy Page-Echols)

On the sidewalk, outside the gate that led to the house, some boys were playing cricket in the sweltering heat. Afraid that the ball might hit us (a phenomenon not uncommon on the streets of Kolkata), we decided to open the gate and enter. Thus, we entered the premises but were hesitant to enter the house because we were early. The door was open, and I could see a passage leading to another door through which we would enter the house. I walked over and peeked, then at once beat a hasty retreat. A huge black dog stood on guard, and I was terrified that it would attack us. However, the dog neither chased me nor barked. Gathering courage from the apparent

228

indifference of the dog to strangers, I looked around for a way to announce our arrival. Finally, I saw a doorbell and rang it. The bell rang and again I prayed the dog would not come charging out. A voice from upstairs called out and asked, "Who is it?" and I replied, "It is us." My answer sounded lame, but I could not shout out more details above the din of the city. The person said, "Just a minute" and told us to wait.

We stood and waited outside the entrance to the house for ten to fifteen minutes. The weather was extremely hot and humid. However, I suddenly realized that a deliciously cool breeze seemed to be blowing just where we were. This breeze kept blowing gently all the time we were there, and we felt cool and refreshed. I thought, "Yoganandaji is keeping us cool and comfortable."

Soon we heard someone telling us to enter. Even though I was apprehensive of the dog, I walked in and found that the dog was tied. We walked past the dog and it did not bark at us. We climbed upstairs and met a lady who introduced herself and welcomed us. I apologized for being early, and she said some other devotees were also supposed to come at 6:30 p.m. and she had planned on showing us around together. However, she decided to go ahead and give us the tour instead of making us wait. I thought that was extremely kind of her. She told us that her husband's grandfather was Yoganandaji's younger brother, Sananda Lal Ghosh, who wrote *Mejda*.

The house was old but very well maintained. As is typical of old houses in Kolkata, the stairs were quite steep. My uncle had asthma and was in his late sixties. However, I noticed that he had no problem climbing the stairs and was not gasping for breath. I silently thanked Yoganandaji for yet another kindness. The lady took us to the sage's bedroom which was bare except for the pictures on the wall. Pictures of Babaji Maharaj, Lahiri Mahasaya, Swami Yukteswara, and Yoganandaji were on one wall. The picture of Yoganandaji that hung in this room was the one I had at home; Lorne had given it to me in 2009 and I was happy to see it in Garpar Road. We stood quietly and paid our respects to the great Masters.

The room was small and spotlessly clean. One could feel the vibrations in the air, and I had goose bumps all over me. On the wall behind us were family photographs. One photograph had all four brothers in it: Yoganandaji's eldest brother, Yoganandaji, the third brother who wrote *Mejda*, and the youngest brother. Another picture had all the women of the family, and Yoganandaji's sisters were in this picture. The lady who was showing us around pointed out a figure in one of the pictures and said he was Yoganandaji's tutor. The tutor was supposed to teach his student

Sanskrit; however, apparently, Yoganandaji (then known as Mukunda) kept asking him questions and learned a lot about Kriya Yoga from this tutor. At some point, Mukunda mentioned something to his father, who was amazed at his son's knowledge and asked, "How do you know all this about Kriya Yoga?" Mukunda told his father that he had gathered a great deal of knowledge from his Sanskrit tutor. Yoganandaji's father then discovered that the tutor was a disciple of Lahiri Mahasaya. The lady also pointed at the figure of an elderly lady in a group photograph and said, "She was the aunt (*Pishi*) who took care of the brothers after Yoganandaji's mother passed away."

As we turned to leave the room, the lady said, "This is the room where Babaji, the immortal sage who taught Kriya Yoga to Lahiri Mahasaya, came to Yoganandaji and told him he had to go to the West. Yoganandaji wanted to follow Babaji and go with him, but when he tried he found that his feet were rooted to the ground and he could not move. Babaji left and Yoganandaji went to America to fulfill the mission entrusted to him."

After absorbing the sanctity of Yoganandaji's bedroom, we went upstairs to the attic. No reader of *Autobiography of a Yogi* can forget this room where the sage would retire to meditate. In Bengali, this type of room on the roof of the house is called the *chilekothar ghar*. Houses in Kolkata have flat roofs and people not only sit on their roofs but often sleep there, especially on hot nights. Many roofs have a simple room, often with a tin roof over it, which is used as storage space. It was in such a makeshift "attic" that Yoganandaji meditated, knowing that no one would disturb him.

As I walked up the stairs, I was so overcome with emotion that I felt I was shaking with awe. The room was tiny and very simple, as is typical of such rooms. It had a proper roof and was well maintained. However, one had to almost climb into the room because the threshold was very high. I wasn't sure I'd be able to make it, but when the lady encouraged me to enter I could not resist the temptation. My uncle, too, was a little daunted by the prospect of climbing into the room. However, we both entered and exited the sacred room safely.

Inside was a little shrine with a picture of Yoganandaji as a young yogi sitting in meditation. There was also a tiny picture of him as an adult; a piece of cloth, a lock of his hair, and a flower were pasted on this photo and could be seen through the glass. The lady said the cloth was a piece of a robe worn by him. She said the cloth, the flower, and the lock of hair were sent by Daya Mata from America after the sage passed away. One fourth of the room was filled with a cemented square shelf that rose from the floor, and on top of this shelf were some pictures and tiny statues of deities. We paid our respects to Yoganandaji and climbed out of the room.

I felt I was going to burst into tears of joy and make a fool of myself. The whole place was suffused with strong vibrations, just the kind one would associate with Yoganandaji's strong personality and fearlessness. It is very easy to feel his presence anywhere in the world. One need not be a devotee or disciple of his or even be highly spiritually evolved to feel his presence. Just reading a book by him or even keeping a photo of him in one's room can make one aware of his presence. If one can feel his presence anywhere, then one can well imagine the astounding vibrations of what, for me, turned out to be one of the most sacred places of pilgrimage I had ever visited in my life.

As I stood there on the brink of tears, Yoganandaji saved me from embarrassing myself by ringing the doorbell. Two gentlemen, who were supposed to come and see the house at 6:30 p.m. had arrived and rung the doorbell. I almost jumped out of my skin at the sound of the bell, and the next thing we heard was the dog barking. Perhaps it was because of the special state of spiritual bliss and calm my mind was in that I was really startled by the loud bell and the dog's bark. The lady called out and tried to reassure the guests that the dog was tied, but no one could hear anything above the barking of the dog. We quickly thanked the lady, said goodbye, and made our way downstairs to reassure the frightened visitors. They could not see that the dog was tied and were scared to enter. We went to the door and told them not to be afraid and they went up the stairs as we were leaving 4 Garpar Road.

As we stepped outside the gate, Uncle Sankar said, "Strange! The dog did not bark even once when we entered." In my mind I saw Yoganandaji's beautiful smiling eyes and smiled back. Out on the streets of Kolkata we were hit by the unbearable heat and deafening roar of the noisy tumultuous city. We hailed a cab and climbed in to make our way home. As the cab purred to a start, I took one last look at Yoganandaji's home and bowed silently in gratitude to him for providing me with the wonderful opportunity of visiting 4 Garpar Road.

Chapter 47: Changes

At the end of 2009, a month before my trip to India, Lorne and Judy had moved to Port Huron, which was a two-hour drive from Lansing. Their move was a great loss to the community, and we were devastated. Lorne handed over the East Lansing branch of Ananda Michigan to Drs. Will and Wendy Page-Echols and Mary Thomas, who carried on with Yoganandaji's work. Once a month, Lorne and Judy drove down and held Sunday service. Sometimes, they even held a kirtan session on Saturday night and then stayed over for Sunday service the next day before going back to Port Huron. We were just starting to get used to the changes in the sangha, when, unfortunately, we lost Lorne to cancer in 2013.

Struggling with our loss, Mary, Will and Wendy conducted Sunday service, held meditation sessions, and sang kirtans. I began to attend regularly in an attempt to support the sangha. After every event, I found myself filled with bliss and peace. That is when I realized that my wish to support the group had resulted in Yoganandaji showering me with his blessings. I was getting so much more than I could give.

In 2016, Wendy started a book study group, and we began to read books by Yoganandaji and his disciples. The book study was of immense benefit to all of us as we studied many books by Yoganandaji and the Gita by Swami Kriyananda. *Autobiography of a Yogi* introduced us to the powerful sages of India, *Whispers of Eternity* taught us how to pray, and the trilogy containing Yoganandaji's sermons taught us how to love God. Each time my mind was troubled, I would pick up a book by Yoganandaji and immediately see how the state of my mind would be uplifted by his passionate yearning for God. I would listen to him telling us again and again to not give up meditating until we had communed with God. He would inspire us to stay up all night, as he had done, and to pray to God with all our hearts so we could hear from Him. Yoganandaji taught us not to plead like beggars but to demand our Self-Realization from God because it is our birthright. He assured us, repeatedly, that he would always be there for us. All we had to do was just call.

Through these past two decades, I have noticed how true his words are. When there was a kirtan and I was not sure how to get there, the phone would ring out of the blue and I would be offered a ride. Often, when I showed up at Lorne's for a kirtan, he would look to see who had brought me. Usually, I was followed by a friend who had given me a ride. But on a few occasions, when no one followed me, Lorne would ask, "Aloka, how did you get here?"

I would smile, flap my arms, and answer with a big smile, "On the wings of devotion."

This was a joke between us and we all laughed, but it was also true. Before I asked anyone for a ride, Yoganandaji made all the arrangements for me. Due to such experiences, I am completely convinced that any spiritual wish one makes with a sincere heart will always be fulfilled.

I continue to be associated with the Ananda Michigan Sangha even though the Pandemic of 2020 made us go online. It is nice to be in the company of like-minded people, and there is no doubt that we help each other and learn from each other as we attend the various events of the sangha. Moreover, each time we read Yoganandaji's words, we feel inspired and motivated to continue our journey towards Self-Realization.

Christmas preparations at Ananda Michigan. Will Page-Echols (second from left) and Mary Thomas (first from right). Photo courtesy of Wendy Page-Echols.

Part V: Swami Purnatmanandaji

Chapter 48: Mother and Swamiji

In the fall of 1999, my friend, Manju Saha, invited me to attend a Satyanarayan *puja* at her home in Dearborn, Michigan. She said her guru, Swami Purnatmanandaji, a monk of the Bharat Sevashram Sangha, was visiting and would perform the ceremony. I was familiar with the organization which is renowned for its work among the underprivileged in India. Ralph and I arrived at Manju's and were warmly welcomed by her husband, Partha, and her son, Biltu. I saw a monk in saffron robes sitting quietly on the sofa. Ralph and I went to him and prostrated. He blessed us and asked us our names. Swamiji knows several languages, but he spoke in English because Ralph was present. I felt very comfortable in his presence. As we were exchanging pleasantries, Manju announced that lunch had been served.

After lunch, Swamiji asked me where we lived in Calcutta. When I said our home was in Keyatala, his face brightened with a smile and he said, "That is very close to our headquarters in Ballygunge."

I said, "Yes. When I was a child, monks from your sangha came to our house for donations. I remember that."

He asked, "Who lives there now?"

When I told him that my mother, aunt, and uncle still lived in that house, he brought me his notebook and told me to write down my mother's name, her Calcutta address, and her phone number.

After I had written down the information, I said, "You are welcome to visit our home. I will tell my mother about you. Do drop in."

The rest of the day was spent in preparations for the *puja*. Many people came and Swamiji explained the mantras in English so we could understand the significance of what was being recited in Sanskrit.

After the *puja* was over, we ate dinner and then Ralph and I went home. When I next talked to Mother, who was in India, I told her about Swamiji. I said, "He usually flies to India in the winter and stays at the Ballygunge ashram during the months of January and February. I gave him your phone number. I am telling you about him just in case he calls."

Mother said, "He is a monk. Why should he have to call me? It is I who will call him. Let me know when he arrives."

Manju and I kept in touch regularly. So, when I heard that Swamiji was leaving for Calcutta, I informed my mother. She went to the ashram on the evening of the day he arrived. After spending some time with him, she came home and called me. She said, "You spoke of him as though he were just an ordinary monk. He is a highly spiritually evolved monk and very knowledgeable. I am truly grateful that I will have this opportunity to spend time in his company."

During his stay at the Ballygunge ashram, Mother went to see Swamiji at 7:30 a.m. each day. Thus began a beautiful relationship between my mother and Swamiji. Being extremely knowledgeable about the scriptures, she could ask excellent questions which gave rise to endless Dharma talks by Swamiji. His followers were delighted to listen to these talks. Mother was not his disciple but soon everyone knew her. She was warmly welcomed by his disciples and devotees who looked forward to her questions and their guru's answers. Swamiji recognized in my mother that special spark that was evident to most holy men and women she had met in her life. Each year, she waited eagerly for his return to Calcutta so she could listen to his interpretations of the various scriptures. On each occasion, after meeting him, she would call me and share what she had learned. She would say, "How I wish you could be here when he is in Calcutta!" I told her that was impossible because I had to teach during those months. At that time I did not know that the opportunity to be with Swamiji in Calcutta would come but not in a way that Mother or I had anticipated.

Chapter 49: In Swamiji's Room

In December of 2009, my mother was diagnosed with pancreatic cancer. Reeling with shock at this devastating news, I prepared to go to Kolkata. I arrived at the beginning of February 2010, and the first words she uttered on seeing me were "This is wonderful! Now you can visit Swamiji at his ashram." She was bright and cheerful and seemed to be radiating joy. Knowing my mother, I was certain that she was not in denial. She knew about her illness even though no one had told her about it, and she knew that her end might not be easy since she had seen relatives who had died of pancreatic cancer. But she had detached herself from the body. Swamiji had told her to remember that she was not the body, not the mind; she was the pure, awakened, free Soul. She kept repeating these words to herself silently.

I realized that the disease had entered her body but not our house. Our world revolved around her. But everyone seemed to be functioning normally, and one felt there was no need to worry. I knew that my uncle, Sankar, and her caregivers were convinced that my mother would survive. She never mentioned her illness and neither did she encourage people to visit and talk about disease and death. The house hummed with positive energy. The sadness that had swamped me lifted, and I began to enjoy my stay. Mother never talked about anything but spiritual matters. I sat next to her all day and listened to her as she expounded on the Gita or the Upanishads or the *Chaitanya Charitamrita*. Her brain was sharp and her memory impeccable. Sometimes I urged her to tell me of her own experiences and she complied.

On the very evening of the day I arrived, she sent me to see Swamiji. For a month, until he left for the U.S., I went to visit him regularly, sometimes with Mother and at other times with my uncle. During that month, I realized what my mother saw in Swamiji. Even though I had visited him in Dearborn on more than one occasion, I had heard from Manju and my mother that meeting him in Kolkata was quite a unique experience. What I witnessed that February convinced me that what I had heard was true. Not only was I impressed with Swamiji's presence but the sweet relationship between devotees and their guru, who is their God, took my breath away. He seemed to be a beehive from which the honey of endless love and compassion kept dripping on all of us. As for his devotees, their amazing devotion and love for their guru created a paradise in which I felt I was always floating in bliss. These interactions between Swamiji and his devotees filled the tiny room with radiance and joy and gave me a glimpse of the love that exists between God and those who love him.

Swami Pranavanandaji's picture on the altar
From left to right: Uncle Sankar, Swami Purnatmanandaji, and Mother in Swamiji's room. Kolkata, 2010

The room in which Swamiji resided was on the ground floor of the ashram. It was small and quite ordinary. The entrance to the room was so narrow that if one of the double doors was locked, it was hard to squeeze through the opening. As I entered, I saw him sitting on his bed facing me. The bed was a plain divan, what is known as a *chouki* in Bengali. To my left was a shrine with the picture of Swami Pranavanandaji Maharaj, the founder of the ashram. On my right were shelves and cupboards. Against the wall facing Swamiji was a bench, and in front of it were some chairs on which approximately eight devotees could sit. Most devotees sat on the floor where

239

there was room for another eight devotees. At the most, fifteen to sixteen people could occupy the space in this room at any given time. Nevertheless, disciples and devotees kept flocking to see Swamiji so they could pay their respects to him, find a corner on the floor or bench to sit on and spend some time with this sage.

Swamiji would sit for hours on his bed as endless streams of followers came to meet him. The door to his room was always open, and there seemed to be no restrictions that would hamper the enthusiasm of his devotees to see him. He treated everyone equally irrespective of who they were. Devotee or disciple, newcomer or veteran, rich or poor, young or old, men or women—in his eyes they were all the same as he made them feel at ease in his room. No one hesitated to enter the room, and everyone felt at home.

The devotees felt that Swamiji was their loved one, so they shared with him all their worldly problems. He would laugh and say, "Everyone has problems. Only God has no problems. It is His job to solve the problems." He listened to each devotee's problems with keen attention, and the devotee's burden seemed to lift as his or her heart filled with bliss. I watched with a sense of wonder at the way in which Swamiji unhesitatingly gave himself so completely to his devotees. Surrounded by their joys and sorrows, his empathy knew no bounds; yet he was always equanimous. Waves and waves of devotees seemed to come and go as he remained still, calm, and peaceful like the ocean.

Each devotee clamored for Swamiji's attention, and he tried to satisfy their demands. Even though he was scheduled to be in Kolkata for two months, he had to visit other places in India and was not always available at the Kolkata ashram. During his stay in Kolkata, sometimes his disciples would plead with him to visit their homes for a few hours. At other times he would be in meetings pertaining to the upkeep of the ashram. In addition, he tried to attend the ashram's daily rituals such as the *arati,* gave Dharma talks on auspicious occasions, participated in various festivals held at the ashram, and initiated hundreds of people on a regular basis. Swamiji plunged into these varied tasks with gusto. He was never tired and one wondered when he rested. I had heard that people were often in his room until midnight and sometimes even later. He slept only a couple of hours before waking up each day at 3:00 a.m.

Despite this busy schedule, Swamiji managed to find time for his personal practice. No matter how crowded his room might be, I noticed that Swamiji was always aware of the time at which *arati* was performed at the temple. The minute *arati* would start, he would leave his room and go upstairs to Swami Pranavanandaji's room to participate in this ritual of worship.

He was also very particular about following the rules of the ashram. For instance, Swamiji ate lunch only after the ritual of food offering had been performed in the room of Swami Pranavanandaji, and the sacred food called *bhog* was brought to him. Whatever he did, he did with a perfection that one rarely witnesses these days. Yet he never looked exhausted or drained. Even after initiating fifty or a hundred people, Swamiji's face looked invigorated.

One evening, I asked him, "How can one love God?"

He replied, "True. How can one love God? He is not in the statues or the pictures we have of Him. We cannot see Him. How can I love someone whom I cannot see? Where is He? He is within us. We have to search for Him and find Him within ourselves, and we must establish a relationship with Him. What kind of relationship would this be? Ramakrishna saw God as his mother, Ramprasad saw Him as his daughter, and Meerabai saw Him as her husband. He can be your father, mother, son, and friend. But you will have to establish this relationship."

"So, how should one pray to God?" I continued.

Swamiji said, "Why do you need to pray? Praying usually involves asking for things. We are always asking God to give us this or that. Why should we ask? Instead of asking Him for things, perhaps you can think of what you can give to God. What should I give? I want to give that which I love the most. What do I love most? I love myself more than anything else. Hence, I shall give myself to God. You must think along these lines."

After spending quite a few days in Swamiji's company, I realized that his devotees had established a beautiful relationship with him. Among these devotees, many had known him for a long time. A few families had been in contact with him for four generations. Some of them had met him when they were children, and they had memories of holding the hands of their mothers or grandmothers and coming to the ashram to meet him. Since they had known him all their lives, they were very comfortable in his presence and the relationship was one of closeness and ease. Indeed, several of them used the familiar Bengali word *tumi* instead of the more formal and respectful *apni* while addressing Swamiji, and this was further proof of how close they were to their guru. They seemed to treat him the way they would treat a very dear relative. I watched and thought that this was how one needed to love God. After all, who is closer to us than God? I felt that if one could witness the way these devotees treated their guru, one could learn how to love God.

A variety of people came to visit Swamiji. and he treated them according to their needs. A woman came and said, "Swamiji, my mind is not happy."

Swamiji replied, "Your mind is your greatest friend, and your mind is your greatest enemy. You must tell your mind, 'You do not belong to me. Go where you belong.' This body, this mind—to whom do they belong? They belong to God. So, send your mind to God." We listened to him attentively and were charmed by his reply. He explained to us in a simple and beautiful manner that we must always keep the mind focused on God. As I was mulling over what I had just heard, a few young girls entered the room to bow to Swamiji and he started telling a story.

"One day, Lord Krishna, plying his boat on the river Yamuna, came to the banks of Vrindavan. He told the *gopis* or milkmaids, 'Would you like to go to Mathura? If you sell your ghee, milk, and other dairy products, you will make a lot of money. It is a big city and there are many large markets as well as many people.' The *gopis* were delighted and brought huge pots of ghee, milk, and butter to the banks of the Yamuna to make the trip. Then Krishna said, 'In order to find a seat in my boat, you must be *ek moni*. My boat cannot carry heavy loads. If you are *du moni* or *teen moni*, my boat will not be able to carry you. If you are *ek moni*, you are welcome.'" The Bengali word *mon* can be used as a measure of weight (one maund) and it can also refer to one's mind. The story had a pun on the word *mon*. On the surface, it meant the women needed to be light in weight because the boat would sink if they were heavy. But the deeper meaning was one needed to cultivate one-pointedness of mind (*ek moni*) to be with God. If the mind went in two (*du moni*) or three (*teen moni*) directions and was distracted, one could not be with God.

Having told us this delightful story, Swamiji said, "Now, I would like all of you to go upstairs to the Shiva temple and sit in meditation with one-pointedness."

The young girls left and an elderly lady came and started talking about her son who was ill-treating her. Swamiji listened for some time before interrupting her. He said, "Why do you always think of your son? Think of Him. That is why you are here—to think of Him." With this simple advice, he reminded us that we need to stay focused on God and to contemplate spiritual matters.

Even though we know that our main goal in life is God, we often get pulled away by worldly desires. There is a gap between what we know we should do and what we actually do. Highlighting this gap between theory and practice, Swamiji told us another story.

"One day, a very learned and educated pundit was crossing a river in a boat. During the boat ride, he was chatting with the boatman. Interested in the boatman's education, the pundit asked, 'What have you studied?' The boatman replied, 'Sir, I have never studied anything.' The pundit was shocked and said, 'What? You mean you do not know how to read or write? Have you really never been exposed to geography, history, and other subjects?' The boatman replied, 'No, Sir, I know nothing about such things.' In the meantime, a storm began to brew. The waves grew larger and larger and threatened to sink the boat. The pundit was terrified and asked, 'What will happen if the boat sinks?' The boatman asked, 'Sir, you do know how to swim, right?' The pundit said, 'Oh no! I do not know how to swim!' The boatman said, 'What are you saying? You don't know how to swim? The storm is getting worse and there is a good chance that the boat will sink. I will be able to swim to safety but what will you do?'"

The story highlighted the fact that just reading numerous books on spiritual matters is not enough. One must implement in one's daily life what one has learned. Theoretical knowledge is of no use on the spiritual path if one does not practice. Swamiji said, "As we keep practicing a particular virtue, it becomes a habit. Once it becomes a habit, it becomes part of our character. In this way, we must learn to swim so that we can cross the ocean of this worldly life."

Taking a large container of fried flattened rice, Swamiji poured peanuts, trail mix and other ingredients and shook the container several times with the lid on so that the ingredients would mix evenly. Once he was satisfied that the job had been well done, he said, "See what a devotee has given me: delicious flattened rice fried at home." We all put both palms together and cupped our hands to receive generous helpings of the spicy and tasty mixture. Everyone started happily eating the flattened rice. As I ate, I thought this is how we must receive spiritual advice from the sages. One must receive and understand what they say in order to taste the spiritual bliss that is constantly flowing from them.

As though sensing my thoughts, Swamiji said, "God is always giving, but we have shut our doors and windows to Him. If all the entrances are closed, how will He enter? Whatever He is sending our way is hitting the walls of the house and bouncing off. One must open the doors and windows; one must increase one's receptivity."

Another day, a gentleman entered with an electrician who had come to fix the regulator that controlled the speed of the ceiling fan in the room. Swamiji laughed and said, "While I was away in the U.S., someone thought that this regulator was his and took it with him." We laughed at his humorous way of presenting a theft. Swamiji continued: "There are some, who eat lunch at the ashram and leave wearing someone else's shoes. They think, 'Ah! The monks are so nice. They have arranged for my lunch and also provided me with a nice pair of shoes to wear.'" We all burst out laughing. We all knew what it was to lose our shoes after visiting a temple or ashram. Indians take off their shoes before entering a sacred place. When they come out, they might find their shoes are missing. Sometimes they are stolen, and at other times someone may have mistakenly walked off in the wrong pair of shoes. But we had never heard such a humorous and charming narration of a theft. Swamiji's eyes twinkled merrily, and his words were so sweet that none of us felt any ill will towards the thief. This seemingly ordinary incident gave me insight into his equanimous state of mind. I realized the truth of something I had heard him say: "A monk's mind and heart must always be happy." I saw that he did not just say these words; he practiced what he preached. No matter what the situation might be, he was always equanimous.

A woman, who was sitting on a chair close to him, said, "Swamiji, when I perform my daily rituals at my shrine, if someone interrupts me and asks me something about worldly matters, I do not get upset. But when I sit down to meditate, I get very upset if someone asks me something about household chores."

Swamiji said, "No. You must never get agitated. Gently answer whatever question is being asked. Always keep your mind in a state of calm. Do not be perturbed about anything." I was amazed by the practical nature of his advice. Indeed, if while meditating, one's mind was in turmoil then what was the point of meditating?

As I was reflecting on these words, an elderly lady entered the room and said, "Swamiji, I have brought freshly fried, piping hot *samosas* for you. You must eat them now or else they will get cold. Once they are cold, they won't taste as good." On hearing this demand made by a devotee, Swamiji obliged by eating one of the *samosas* filled with potatoes and peas that she had brought. Referring to knee pain he had been experiencing, the lady asked, "How is the pain in your knees?" Swamiji replied, "The pain is doing its job." Though he had been experiencing some knee pain for a few years as well as some trouble with his eyes, he did not let the mind go to the body. These physical ailments did not bother him. Just as he had made room for all of us in his small room, he had also accommodated his ailments. Such a complete acceptance of whatever life brought his way was not something one could easily find in the world. I knew I was witnessing a rare phenomenon.

As he was eating a *samosa*, a woman said, "Swamiji, I remember seeing you when I was a little girl. You used to visit our home. I recall a day when you performed a magic trick for us. You took a rope and cut it in two. Then you asked us, 'Without tying a knot, can you join these two ropes and make it one?' We said we did not know how to do that. Then you performed a magic trick and joined the two pieces of rope and made them one without tying a knot. When we all asked you to teach us the trick, you said, 'You are young now. When you grow up, I will teach you.'"

Listening to this sweet reminiscence, I felt like saying to Swamiji, "We have now grown up. Please teach us this magic trick. How can we unite ourselves with God? After all, we are manifestations of that *Paramatman* or Oversoul. We were One. But when we were born in these bodies, we became separated like the two ropes. There is just one goal in this human life: to reunite our souls with the Oversoul. Through his words and actions, Swamiji has tried to teach us how to perform this magic trick. Just as two ropes became one when he performed the magic trick, we, too, must aspire to become one with God.

My musings were interrupted by Swamiji's words. Addressing a gentleman in the room, he said, "The goal of this human life is to change oneself. However, we do not like to change ourselves but wish to change everybody else. It is easy to see the faults of others. We see the faults of others and try to change them. But we do not see our faults, and so we do not change. We must change ourselves."

A devotee walked in wearing an orange shirt, and Swamiji looked at him and smilingly said, "Looks like you have become half a monk. Now you must become a full monk." At first, I failed to catch the humor in Swamiji's words. I thought the man was probably a very spiritually evolved devotee. Later, as I heard people laughing, I realized that the reference was to the man's orange-colored shirt. Swamiji was jokingly saying that he had externally become a monk since monks wear saffron-colored robes. Now he must also become a monk in his inner life by coloring his mind and heart with the saffron color. I was taken aback by Swamiji's alert and vigilant nature. His eyes sparkled like diamonds and shone with intelligence. He was always mindful and had an amazing capacity to find profound insights in the most ordinary events and words.

On one occasion, I went with Mother and found that Swamiji was alone in his room. He welcomed us and was very happy to see my mother. We sat down on the chairs as Swamiji, who was eighty-five years old, got off his cot and sat down on the floor with the agility of a teenager. On the floor, there were many green coconuts which devotees had offered to him. The water inside the coconut is cool, refreshing, and nutritious. Swamiji sat with a knife and chopped off the top of each green coconut before drinking the water. It is not easy to cut off the tops of these heavy coconuts, and we watched in amazement at his strength. Mother suggested that we call somebody to cut the coconuts. Swamiji said, "*Apna hath Jagannath*," which meant it was best to be self-sufficient. As he sat cross legged on the cement floor, it was hard to believe that he had so much knee pain. He drank the water from each coconut, disposed the empty shells into a bucket that served as a trash can, cleaned the knife before putting it in its place, and then went back to his sitting posture on his cot. Seeing his actions, I realized the true meaning of the word "independence."

Swamiji does not depend on anyone for any task and is completely independent. However, he is completely dependent on God. Everything he needs to do gets done because he leaves it all to God. To teach us to rely on God, he says, "Stop saying 'I and Mine.' Instead say, 'You and Yours.' Leave everything to God. We board a plane, leave everything in the hands of the pilots, and go to sleep. Who is the pilot? He is just a human being like us. If we can trust him with our lives and depend on him so completely, then how can we forget God who is the greatest Pilot? Why can't you leave everything to Him?"

Gradually, the room began to fill with devotees. Knowing that my mother looked forward to his interpretations of spiritual theories, Swamiji began explaining in beautiful and simple words certain concepts of Hindu philosophy. A stream of nectar seemed to be pouring from his lips. As he expounded the Vedas, the Upanishads, the Gita, the *Mahabharata*, the *Ramayana*, lyrics from songs composed by Tagore full of deep wisdom, we listened to an endless outpouring of the gems hidden in Swamiji's treasure trove. I noted his ability to skillfully analyze profound concepts and to convey them to his audience in a way that made the esoteric simple and accessible. Even an ignorant lay person like me could understand what he was trying to say.

While he was talking, two of his female devotees were massaging his feet. They were chatting among themselves while their guru was giving a Dharma talk. After some time, a smile crept onto Swamiji's face. His eyes twinkled with suppressed laughter as he looked at us and gestured to silently tell us that the women massaging his feet were not listening to his talk. I was impressed by his boundless patience. I thought to myself that if I were a teacher and my students were chatting during my class, I would have scolded them. Swamiji is a great spiritual teacher. Yet these disciples were chatting away while sitting at his feet! But their guru had a benign look on his face. In fact, he was smiling and bubbling over with humor as he watched the actions of his devotees.

As we all fell silent and watched to see what would happen next, an elderly woman entered the room, sat down, and began to tell Swamiji every detail of her spiritual practice: meditation techniques, yogic techniques, *pranayama* or breath control techniques, prayers, recitation of the scriptures, etc. Swamiji gently interrupted her and said, "You should not speak of your practice and your spiritual accomplishments in front of others. These practices should be done privately in secluded spaces and in your heart (*konay konay, bonay bonay, monay monay*)." In a very affectionate manner, he taught his disciple how to proceed on the spiritual path.

This incident was followed by a request from two young girls who wanted Swamiji to read their palms and predict their future. He laughed when he heard their words. At first, it seemed as though he was going to grant the request. But then, using a very gentle tone of voice he said, "You should not show your palms to monks. When you do that, you are wasting their time." The girls were not offended because his manner of speaking was so kind and compassionate that no one could feel hurt.

A middle-aged woman who was sitting beside the young girls turned to Swamiji and began to list her innumerable ailments. Once again, he interrupted the speaker and said, "Talk to your doctor about these matters. He will prescribe medication. When you come to visit a monk, you should not speak of such things. You should ask questions relating to God and spiritual practices." What struck me most was the way in which he spoke. The truth can often be harsh. But he spoke with such love in his heart that his words did not come across as an admonishment. Instead, we all felt that we were learning something valuable which included not only his wise advice but also his compassionate behavior.

The day of Shiva Ratri is a festive day in India and is dedicated to Lord Shiva. Young women often fast on this day and visit a Shiva temple where they pour water on the Shiva Lingam which symbolizes the deity. The belief is that if one can get the blessings of Shiva, one will be married to a good man like Shiva. On the third floor of the ashram building is a Shiva temple. On this auspicious day, I was sitting in Swamiji's room with his devotees when a group of young girls entered. He asked them, "Did you pour water on Lord Shiva's head?" The girls shyly nodded their heads in the affirmative. Swamiji asked, "What did you say to Lord Shiva?" The girls giggled and shyly looked down at their toenails. Swamiji said, "No matter how much water you pour or how many flowers you offer to Shiva, nothing will come of it. You must learn to treat your parents and your elders with respect; you must learn to be honest; you must learn to do things with a pure heart. Only then will your wishes come true. Will you like it if someone were to treat you harshly? No, you won't. Then you, too, must not treat anyone harshly. If someone said pleasing words to you, would you like that? Yes, you would. Then you, too, must use words that make people happy. If you stay on the right track in your daily life, then God's blessings will automatically be showered on you." We listened attentively as he taught us that performing rituals is not enough; one must also be aware of one's actions in one's daily life.

As we were listening to him, a young woman entered the room. On seeing that there was no place to sit because the room was full, she paid her respects to Swamiji and said, "I will go upstairs and bow to Lord Shiva and then return." Swamiji nodded in agreement and the woman left her bag on his bed before exiting the room. In the meantime, a man came and announced that it was time for Swamiji's talk. Due to Shiva Ratri, a special *pandal* or pavilion had been erected where hundreds of people had gathered to listen to talks by the monks and to celebrate the occasion. It was time for Swamiji to move to this venue where a large audience awaited him. As we all began to leave, Swamiji got up and put on his turban. Locking the door to his room, he left. Mother and Uncle Sankar were with me, and we decided to go upstairs to the Shiva temple.

After paying our respects to Lord Shiva and to the great saint Swami Pranavanandaji Maharaj, we came downstairs and were ready to go home when we noticed Swamiji outside his room. Surprised to find him back so soon, I asked, "How did you finish your talk in such a short time?"

Swamiji pointed at a woman and replied, "She left her bag in my room." I recognized the young woman who had left her bag on Swamiji's bed with the intention of returning later when his room was less crowded. But when she had returned, she had found the room locked. So, she had gone to the pavilion in search of Swamiji and found him getting ready to deliver his talk. She told him what had happened. Realizing that she needed her bag to return home, he had walked back with her to his room while his audience waited for him. He opened the door and the devotee retrieved her bag. I smiled as I remembered the age-old saying that God bears the burden of his devotee. It seemed to me that among his many responsibilities, Swamiji had also adopted the responsibility of being accountable for the belongings of his devotees. As this scene was unfolding, most of us were smiling while Swamiji waited patiently. There was not a trace of irritation at having been dragged away from his talk. Nor did the devotee show any signs of remorse. It seemed as though she had dragged her mother to the room and said, "Open the door. I need my bag."

Such is the ease one senses in the relationship between Swamiji and his disciples who are like his children. He has many such children who make various demands on him. They all feel they have a right to make these demands. Like a mother, he gives his devotees what they need. The way a mother treats and loves all her children equally, he also treats and loves all his devotees equally. I watched each day as he gave sweets to one devotee, spicy snacks to another, a sanctified *mala* to a third, and a spiritual book to a fourth. The demands were endless, and Swamiji was untiring in his efforts to fulfill everyone's wishes.

A few of the devotees cooked several dishes for Swamiji each day and offered him the food at lunch. On several occasions, Mother and I were present and he insisted that we stay for lunch. He waited until the ashram's *bhog* or sacred food was brought to him. After eating the *bhog*, he then allowed his disciples to offer their food to him. His disciples first offered the food to Swamiji and then placed generous portions of each delicious item on our plates. I could tell that they were expert cooks. There was a variety of vegetable dishes, and each was extremely tasty. But what I found most enchanting was the sweetness with which Swamiji's disciples fed us. Each time we had the pleasure and privilege to partake of lunch in Swamiji's room, we were charmed by the kindness and generosity of his devotees.

One evening I saw two women complaining to him while massaging his feet. They said, "Swamiji, this year you stayed in Kolkata for a very short time. As a result, we did not get to spend much time with you. Soon after you arrived, you left for Bangladesh. After returning from Bangladesh, you left for Gujarat. Now we are hearing that you are planning a trip to Nabadwip. What about us? When are you going to make time for us? In the past, you used to come to Kolkata in January and leave around the middle of March. This year you are leaving at the beginning of March. We barely got to spend time with you this year."

Swamiji was smiling at the complaints of his devotees and his eyes were twinkling with humor. Then he put on a helpless expression on his face and said, "What can I do? None of you provide me with delicious meals. No one ever cooks a dish or two for me. What incentive do I have to stay in Kolkata? If you offered me some tasty meals, there would be reason for me to prolong my visit. But no one pays me any attention here, and that is why I travel so much."

On hearing this, the women were outraged and retorted, "No, no, no! We will not listen to you. Pray, what is it you eat? All you like is a simple dish made with bitter gourd and plantain. You rarely show any interest in other dishes. You cannot get away with these excuses. Next year, you must stay for a long time."

Swamiji's face beamed with smiles of affection as the rest of us, who were watching, burst into laughter. We all tasted the sweetness of a devotee's love behind the seeming complaints of the women. This mock fight was a "fight" between God and his devotees; hence, it was immersed in the sweetness of love. I had witnessed with my own eyes the love and respect showered on Swamiji by his disciples. Hundreds came from far and wide to pay their respects to him. I had met several women who lived outside Kolkata. They woke up at 4:00 a.m., showered, cooked several vegetarian dishes, and then travelled by train and bus to arrive at the ashram long before food was offered to Swamiji. So, we knew that his "complaints" were meant to tease his devotees. But through this interaction between guru and disciples, we all experienced the sweetness of love and devotion that is an integral part of what is known as God's *lila* or play.

One day Mother was unable to accompany me when I went to see Swamiji. She was extremely devoted and everyone at the ashram loved and respected her. But she was unwell and could not go to see Swamiji as regularly as she had done in the past. On this day, the minute I entered his room, Swamiji asked anxiously, "Where is your mother?" Since I was bowing before him, my response was delayed because I did not wish to reply until I had paid my respects to him. After I had finished, I said, "She is not feeling well and could not come." He kept quiet but looked sad and concerned. I had noticed the manner in which he had looked for my mother when I had entered. His eyes were darting this way and that way in a manner similar to that of a mother's eyes when she is looking for her lost child in a crowd. This incident made me realize the power of a devotee's affection and the strength of the bond that had been forged between Mother and Swamiji. This is how God sits and waits for us, I thought to myself. And when we do not go to Him, He is sad. When I came home and told Mother that Swamiji had expected her to visit him, she said, "I was with you in spirit. I could think of nothing else but being in his room."

Another day, a female disciple said, "Swamiji, during my initiation, I asked you to give me the Krishna mantra. But now I feel I would like to take the Shiva mantra. Can I do that?"

Swamiji laughed and said, "Why not? But what if after a few days you feel you would like to take the Durga mantra? What will you do then?"

The woman said, "No, no. That will not happen. I will be happy with the Shiva Mantra. What do I need to do to be initiated again?" Swamiji told her to come another day and be initiated.

An elderly lady, who was in the room, said, "I was initiated twice by two separate monks, and I have two different mantras. I recite both each day. I hope I am not doing something wrong?"

In a loud voice, Swamiji said, "Carry on (*chaliye jao*)." With these words he burst out laughing and told us a story: "While a play was being enacted, the hero suddenly forgot his lines. The Prompter standing in the poorly lit wings fumbled through the pages of the play to find the right spot. Knowing that the audience was waiting for the hero to say his words, the Prompter whispered to Sanjay, the actor, 'Sanjay, carry on.' With these words the Prompter was trying to convey the message that the actor needed to improvise until the Prompter had found the right page."

We all laughed on hearing the story. I understood that Swamiji was saying that whether it is a Shiva mantra or a Krishna mantra, whether one is reciting one or two mantras, what is most important is to keep reciting God's name. He said, "Success lies in the recitation of God's name. One can attain everything by doing this." The words "carry on" found a place in my heart, as I realized that no matter what, we must keep on with our practice.

On another occasion, Mother, Uncle Sankar and I went to see Swamiji and surprisingly enough found him alone in the room. He said he had just finished initiating fifty people. On his bed lay a variety of things: saffron-colored robes, stainless steel plates, fruits, vegetables, rice, etc. People who had taken initiation had made these offerings. Within half-an-hour, Swamiji organized all these items and prepared the room for his devotees who would soon arrive to see him. We were speechless as we looked on and took note of his amazing skills. All the fruits, vegetables, and rice were sent to the ashram's kitchen. The robes were sent to the storage so they could be distributed among the monks according to their needs. Other items, such as the plates, were stored to be distributed among the needy. Within minutes the room was clean. Not a grain of rice lay on the floor, not a petal lay on the bed. It seemed as if the monumental task was done in the blink of an eye. Swamiji did all the work while nonchalantly chatting with us. There was not a trace of fatigue on his face. He did everything with a smile, and the energy was so calm that we were barely aware that so much was being accomplished as we watched.

Swamiji said, "You all (meaning householders) have to keep a small house clean. We have to take care of a huge house (meaning the ashram)."

I thought of how efficient and diligent one needed to be to manage such a large ashram. Not only do the monks take care of the various ashrams of Bharat Sevashram all over India and in many parts of the world, but they also work tirelessly for the welfare of the marginalized sections of society. This is a well-known fact that is much appreciated by Indians.

Swamiji said, "We do not earn an income by holding a job as you do. We depend solely on God for everything. Just look at all the things He provides for us! He gives so much that at times we have more than we can use. After all, how much do we monks need? Our needs are few, so most of these things will be donated to lay people who need them."

Swamiji's complete dependence on God is best revealed in the story of his journey to the United States. The first time he landed in New York, he found that no one had come to meet him at the airport. The Indian devotee who was supposed to come had been held up due to some unavoidable circumstance. This was long before cell phones were available, and all Swamiji could do was sit and wait. Sitting quietly, he began to recite God's name because he had firm faith in the belief that God's name is the only support one has in life. After some time had passed, an American man approached Swamiji and asked, "Are you an Indian?"

Swamiji replied, "Yes. I am an Indian." While telling us this story Swamiji explained to us that "a person who wants to know his or her True Self is a True Indian." The American man heard Swamiji's story and took him to his apartment in New York. His wife arranged for Swamiji's accommodation and food. She bought new pots and pans, listened to Swamiji's instructions and cooked *khichuri* with rice and lentils. Even today Swamiji is in touch with this family. Whenever I think of this story, I realize that everything is possible if one completely surrenders to God.

One day, we were in Swamiji's room when his phone rang. The caller asked if Swamiji was feeling good (*Bhalo achen?*). Swamiji replied, "We are monks. We must never feel bad (*Sadhuder kharap thakte nei*). Yes, I am well." I remembered a story Mother had told me earlier. One day, she had called and asked, "Is your room empty? (*Ghor khali?*)" Mother meant to ask if he was free so she could visit him. Swamiji replied, "A monk's room should never be empty. A thief could enter such a room (*Sadhuder ghor khali rakhte nei. Chor dhuke jabe.*).” Mother said he was trying to teach us that our minds should always be focused on God or else our senses will distract us from our goal in life. The room represented the Mind. Distractions are like thieves who enter an empty mind, but a mind that is filled with thoughts of God has no room for anything else.

In this context, Swamiji told us an interesting story one day. A king was performing some austere practices when suddenly, a genie appeared before him. The genie said, “My lord, I will serve you for free and do whatever you command me to do. But there is one condition. You must constantly supply me with work. If you cannot give me work, I will break your neck.” The king was delighted at first, but soon a problem arose. Whatever he asked the genie to do was accomplished within minutes. The king knew that it was just a matter of time before he would run out of jobs for the genie. Afraid of losing his life, the king ran to his guru and begged to be saved from the clutches of the genie.

The guru laughed and said, “There is a bamboo grove behind your castle. Tell the genie to go up and down a bamboo stalk. That will be his job when you run out of work to give him. Again, when you need him, just call him and tell him what you need done. When he has done the job and asks for more work, tell him to go up and down the bamboo stalk. In this way, the genie will always have something to do.” The king followed his guru’s advice and thus managed to escape from having his neck broken.

In the story, the genie is our Mind. If we do not keep our mind occupied, it will cause us suffering. Climbing up and down the bamboo stalk represents inhalation and exhalation used in a method of meditation called *pranayama* which focuses on breath control. When we are done with all our worldly chores, we should meditate. As we inhale and exhale, we focus on our in-breath and out-breath. Gradually the mind stills and becomes concentrated.

In this manner, Swamiji would tell us many stories to encourage us on the spiritual path. One of my favorite stories was that of an occasion when he went to a factory where biscuits or cookies were made. The company had offered to donate cookies to the ashram. Swamiji, who was quite young at that time, was given the task of fetching the cookies. On his way back from the factory, he was accosted by a group of young men who were standing around chatting and making fun of the passersby. Seeing a monk in saffron-colored robes, the men thought they had found an easy prey.

“Hello, Swamiji,” they said. “We see a big package of cookies in your hands. Do you eat cookies?”

Swamiji replied, “Yes. Sometimes I do.”

One of the men asked, "Are you married?" This was obviously a taunt because most Indians know that monks are celibate.

But Swamiji replied, "Yes."

The men laughed and asked, "What is your wife's name?"

Swamiji said, "Sadhana Devi."

At that time, everyone knew that Sadhana Devi was the name of a famous Bengali film star. The men thought Swamiji was just being witty. They said, "You are married to a film star? Wonderful! Perhaps you can arrange for some free passes for us so we can watch her movies. Anyway, since you are married, you probably have children?"

Swamiji nodded and said, "Yes."

The men were now a little embarrassed and were wondering how to back out of this conversation. But unable to quit, they asked, "What are their names?"

Swamiji calmly replied, "My son's name is Gyandeva and my daughter's name is Bhaktirani."

On hearing this, the men fell at Swamiji's feet and begged forgiveness for their impertinence and irreverence. *Sadhana* means spiritual practice, *gyan* means knowledge, and *bhakti* means devotion. The men realized that Swamiji was telling them that he followed the paths of Knowledge and Devotion and had dedicated his life to his spiritual practice. Ashamed of their behavior, the men wanted to do something to make amends for their transgression. They asked Swamiji to command them to do something. He told them to come to the ashram that evening.

The men kept their word and went to the ashram that evening. Preparations were being made to attend to the pilgrims at the great festival of Ganga Sagar, where thousands would gather in a few days. Swamiji asked the men to go as volunteers to the festival and help the monks to take care of the pilgrims. The men were grateful for this opportunity and left with the monks for Ganga Sagar.

As I listened to this story, I felt that in Swamiji's little room I could clearly see the "family" he had mentioned to the young men. Swamiji's knowledge knows no bounds, his devotion is unshakeable, and the results of his austere and diligent practice are apparent to anyone who spends time with him.

Once we entered that room, none of us really wanted to leave. Even when the room was full, Swamiji never asked anyone to leave. At times, devotees would stand in the doorway and see that the room was full. Swamiji would gently tell them to go upstairs to Swami Pranavanandaji's room so they could pay their respects to the founder of the organization. I don't know how we all managed to spend so much time with Swamiji in that room. Even when we spent very little time with him, usually due to our busy schedules, we went away feeling happy and fulfilled. As children, we had all heard the story of Madhusudan Dada's little pot of yogurt which never emptied. No matter how much yogurt the characters in the story scooped out of the little pot, it was always full. Swamiji's room reminded me of that story because it always seemed to have a festive air about it. Whether he was expounding on the scriptures or giving practical advice to elderly women on how to live harmoniously with their daughters-in-law, the room was always filled with happiness. It felt as though we were attending a festival of joy. People came and went, but the festival was unending.

Even after we left the ashram, we could feel our beings wrapped in that divine happiness. I would come home and feel I could see Swamiji's radiant face before my very eyes. Thoughts that usually distract the mind, and make it run in different directions, did not arise. The mind was still and calm, like the vast ocean. A mellow happiness bubbled gently in my being. This happiness was indescribable. It could not be likened to the jubilant happiness one experiences when one succeeds in the material world. It was a silent deep happiness that reflected the priceless gem of our inner divinity. This is something we all possess, but it is hidden within us. However, when we are in the presence of great sages, we taste this hidden happiness. This is an experience that cannot be described because it is beyond words. As the sages say, such experiences cannot be shared. They must remain in the secret cave of our hearts.

I will always remain indebted to Swamiji and his devotees for all the happiness I experienced in the month of February in 2010. Without his blessings, I would not have been able to observe and participate in the endless festival of joy I found in his room. I also know that without his devotees I would not have witnessed Swamiji's boundless affection for humanity. Each devotee seemed to open a door through which I glimpsed a particular aspect of Swamiji's multi-faceted personality. Through the love of each devotee, I saw the various roles Swamiji played to teach us God's love, sweetness, and compassion. One cannot understand this without seeing the interaction between God and his devotees. To see how devotees can trap God with their love, one must go and spend some time in Swamiji's little room.

Chapter 50: My Mother's Passing

In March of 2010, after showering Mother with his blessings, Swamiji left for the United States. I stayed for three months and left in May knowing that I was never going to see my mother again. It was at her behest that I was leaving. She said, "Go and get back to teaching. If you stay here, I feel I need to hurry up and die." Leaving her in my uncle's care, I reluctantly came back to Michigan and started teaching during the summer. In June, Manju Saha called and said Swamiji was going to visit her in Dearborn, Michigan, and stay for a few days. When I called Mother to tell her this, she was overjoyed and told me to go and stay at Manju's house during Swamiji's visit. I hesitated and said I would go and see him and then come back to my home, but Mother insisted that I stay in Dearborn.

On June 10, I went to Manju's house and Swamiji was happy to see me. Naturally, he asked about Mother and told me that she was very spiritually evolved. The next day, June 11, my mother called and talked for a long time with Swamiji. When I went to the phone, she sounded very happy and energetic. She said, "Don't waste your time on the phone. Go and sit with Swamiji." That evening many people came and Swamiji gave a wonderful talk.

On the morning of June 12, I was sitting at Swamiji's feet when his cell phone rang. I listened to him talking to someone and realized that the person at the other end of the line was ill. Swamiji said, "Just keep reciting God's name." And then I heard him say my name as he asked, "Would you like to talk to Aloka?" My heart was in my mouth as I realized that the person whom he had been talking to was my mother! He gave me the phone and I said, "Hello." But she had already handed the receiver to my uncle. After a few words with me, Uncle Sankar hung up. Within a few minutes, Manju invited Swamiji to the dining table for lunch. We all went and stood around him as he ate. He had just finished his lunch when the phone rang again. My uncle told me that my mother had just passed away.

As I got ready to leave and come back to my home with Ralph, Swamiji calmly reminded me that I would need to perform a ceremony for my mother on the fourth day after she had passed. I had a voice recorder on which I had taped Swamiji's talk on the evening of June 11. He told me to eat lunch. While I tried to swallow some food and stop my body from shaking, Swamiji recorded the mantras I would have to recite while performing the ceremony.

He also told me what ingredients I would need and what rituals I would have to perform. Even these details were recorded in a calm voice. Gradually I began to feel calm, and I knew that Swamiji was playing a major role here in controlling my grief and filling me with the strength I would need to get through the next few days. Armed with his powerful energy and generous blessings, I left to take care of the multiple tasks I needed to accomplish apart from comforting my sister and Uncle Sankar and many others who had all broken down and needed support.

Soon after I left, Swamiji left for Canada and my friend, Manju, was alone at home. Late that evening, she had dozed off when suddenly something woke her up. She saw my mother standing in her living room.

A stunned and bewildered Manju stuttered, "Aunty, you here?"

Mother asked, "Where is Swamiji?"

Manju said, "He left for Canada."

Mother disappeared.

Even today when I tell this story of Mother's passing, people are shocked to hear that during her last call she chose to talk to Swamiji instead of me. But knowing my mother, I see how she made a wise decision. She had witnessed many deaths and knew that her time had come. At the very end, she was finding it hard to breathe. While my uncle was trying to arrange for oxygen, Mother had asked him to call Swamiji. My uncle could not understand why at this moment, when she was gasping for breath, she wished to speak to Swamiji. My guess is Mother knew she was taking her last few remaining breaths. She spoke to Swamiji and he told her to stay focused on God. She did not speak to me because a mother's attachment to her child is probably one of the strongest forces in the world. She wanted her mind to stay focused on God and not lapse into worldly attachments. I had always known that Mother was a very special person, and her last act provided ample evidence of that. So, when I heard Manju's story, I was not surprised that soon after her death Mother had come in search of Swamiji.

I am strongly convinced that I met Manju so that my mother could meet Swamiji. Our guru, Maharaj, had passed, and Mother was aging. She could no longer go to the Himalayas in search of sages as she had done when she was young. So God sent a sage to her doorstep. The ashram in Kolkata is so close to our home that one can walk to it. Each year Swamiji visited Kolkata, and Mother spent as much time as possible nurturing her spiritual practice by visiting him regularly and listening to his interpretations of and commentaries on the wisdom that has been handed down to us through the centuries by the great sages of India. At home, her bed was strewn with copies of the Gita and the Upanishads. Toward the end of her life, she discouraged all worldly conversation, focused only on spiritual matters, and encouraged her caregivers to take refuge in God.

Swami Purnatmanandaji on the steps of the Bharat Sevashram Sangha. Chicago, 2007.

Part VI: The Hugging Saint

Chapter 51: Amma

In 2006, Judy Dekun lent me Lisa Hallstrom's book *Mother of Bliss*. Judy was Lorne Dekun's wife, and I knew her from the Ananda Michigan group I used to visit quite regularly. Paramhansa Yogananda in his *Autobiography of a Yogi* had written a chapter on his meeting with Anandamayi Ma in India, so it was natural for followers of Yoganandaji to be interested in Anandamayi Ma. Knowing that I had met Ma when I was a child, Judy lent me Lisa Hallstrom's book after she had read it. I brought the book home, started reading it and could not put it down. After finishing the book, I wanted to tell the writer how much I had enjoyed it. So, I contacted the publisher and they gave me her phone number. I called and the author answered the phone. I told her about my childhood visits to Anandamayi Ma and showered her with effusive praise for writing such an excellent book even though she had not met Ma in the flesh.

As we conversed, Lisa asked me if I had met Amma, known as the Hugging Saint. Even though I had not met Amma, I had heard of her from my mother who had seen her at a gathering in Kolkata. Lisa looked up Amma's schedule and told me that I was very fortunate because Amma was going to visit Detroit during the Thanksgiving week, which was just a month away. Providing me with the necessary information, she told me to go and see Amma. She also said that she planned on being in Detroit at that time and this would be a lovely opportunity for us to meet. I did not wish to commit because that is a busy time in the semester for teachers, but I promised that I would try and see if I could meet both Amma and Lisa during Thanksgiving.

As the Thanksgiving week neared, I told Ralph about my wish to visit Amma and meet Lisa. I checked the schedule and found that the only day we could go was a Sunday evening. On Monday morning both Ralph and I had early morning classes to teach. Furthermore, Judy, who had visited Amma the year before, warned us that we could be there all night if we wanted a hug from Amma. I did not receive any signs of encouragement from Ralph and wondered whether it would be possible for me to keep my word.

On Saturday, one day before Amma would arrive in Detroit, Ralph and I came down with influenza. In a way, it was a relief because I felt I had an excuse not to go. After eating lunch on Sunday, I took a nap. Around 3:00

p.m., Ralph woke me up and said, "Get ready. Let's go." Both of us were still sick and running a temperature, but I got dressed and we left. It took us more than an hour to get to the hotel where the event was taking place, but we were standing in line by 5:00 p.m. The volunteers asked us if we were going to see Amma for the first time and we told them we were. Newcomers are given preference and we were placed ahead of those who had already seen her. We were given tokens with numbers on them, and when the huge conference room opened we entered and sat down on the chairs that had been placed in neat rows.

Amma arrived at 7:00 p.m. and her smile lit up the room. Representatives of the city gave speeches to welcome Amma and then Amma gave a talk which was followed by devotional chants. At 9:00 p.m. the volunteers announced that all who wished to be hugged by Amma should line up in accord with their token numbers. I saw that there were two flashing boards on which the token numbers were being displayed. Still feeling quite sick and knowing that it would be impossible to find Lisa in this huge crowd of thousands of people, I turned to Ralph and said, "We can go home now. All I promised was I would see Amma. I have seen her and we can go." Since Ralph had been so reluctant to commit to this trip, I naturally was surprised when he said, "Let's wait a bit and see what's happening."

We sat and watched Amma as she began to hug all who had come. Each hug was full of unconditional love. It was not as though she were going through some ritual. She was completely present as she hugged each and every one irrespective of whether she knew them or not. There were people who were her devotees and disciples and people who were seeing her for the first time. Even though I could see many Indian faces, there were people of various ethnic backgrounds and nationalities. Some went up to Amma reluctantly, submitted to her hug with skepticism ruling their minds, but came away beaming. Others, who had waited the whole year for her hug, flung themselves into her open arms and could not have enough of her. There were elderly people who were being helped by volunteers as well as fidgety children in the clutches of their mothers. Some poured out all their problems to Amma and she listened attentively while others just sobbed and sobbed as she held them tight in her arms trying to console them. At times the volunteers needed her attention and talked to her while she was hugging. In such a case, the person who was being hugged remained in Amma's arms while she listened to the volunteer and even gave instructions for what needed to be done. Only after she had brought back her attention to the person in her arms and completed her hug did she let go of the person. I watched and thought of how lucky the person was to get such a long hug from Amma.

Suddenly Ralph told me to get in line and soon our numbers showed up on the boards. As we approached closer to Amma, a volunteer asked me what language I spoke. I said, "Bengali." Within seconds I was engulfed in Amma's arms. I cannot find the words to describe my experience. I remember seeing her brilliant smile just before I was in the folds of her hug. The hug was as strong as that of a tigress and yet soft. I sensed tremendous power that was much more than just physical strength. It was the power of love. Dazzled by the brilliance of her smile, the whiteness of her sari, and the strength of her love, I felt the world disappear for a few seconds and my mind went blank. I heard her whispering something in my ears: "*Shonar meye, shonar meye, shonar meye.*" Our mothers and grandmothers often use these terms of endearment when they address us. Literally it translates as "golden girl," but "my darling child" or "my precious child" are perhaps more apt translations. When I emerged from the hug, there was Amma's radiant face and smile looking at me with unconditional love. She pressed something in the palm of my hand, and I later found a tiny chocolate (a Hershey's Kiss).

Both Ralph and I walked away in a daze and drove home without saying a word. Much later, I realized that we were both well and had no fever. The influenza had left our bodies. We went home, slept, and went to teach the next morning. After my class, I came home and wrote to Lisa Hallstrom. She wrote back and said she was delighted to hear that I had visited Amma. Unfortunately, Lisa had not been able to come to Detroit and had cancelled her trip. I was stunned when I read her email. I had gone so I could meet Lisa. I had gone out of a sense of politeness. I had gone because I like to keep my word. But once I was there, I had forgotten my original purpose for being there. All I could think of was Amma. If I had not read Lisa's book, if I had not called her, if she had not told me about Amma, if Ralph had not insisted on taking me, I would have never seen the woman who is known all over the world as the Hugging Saint. Moreover, what were the chances of Amma coming to Detroit? Here she was, practically at my doorstep, and all the arrangements were made for me to see her. How could I not see this as an example of Amma's blessings?

The next year, I went to see Amma with my friend Anna Fisher. After looking at our work schedules, we found that the only day we could go was the last evening of Amma's stay in Detroit. This evening was special and it was called *Devi Bhava,* which meant the followers would dress Amma as a goddess (Divine Mother) and worship her before the hugging began. This evening usually attracts the most people and sometimes Amma keeps hugging people through the night. We were aware that we might not be able to hug her, but we still decided to give it a try.

Michigan weather is famous for being unpredictable and Amma comes at the end of November when winter is fast approaching. So it was not a surprise to find that not only was there snow, but we had a winter weather warning with blizzard like conditions and freezing rain. Most people would stay home but Anna is a fearless driver and showed up to pick me up. We drove for two hours in a blizzard, unable to see even the hood of our car. Nevertheless, we arrived at Amma's hotel and went in. We were among the last ones to enter. As we walked into the spacious conference room, we saw thousands of people seated on the floor. Managing to squeeze in, we sat and waited for Amma. She always wears white, but on this special occasion she was dressed in a red silk sari with golden embroidery and on her head was a gold crown. She was the epitome of Divine Mother and love seemed to be pouring out of her. On the floor, seated far from her, I could feel the vibrations of her love. For a couple of hours her devotees worshipped her, sang kirtan, and one of the monks gave a talk. Then came the announcement for people to queue up for their hugs.

Anna and I had tokens, but our numbers would not come up until later and so we decided to go get some food. Dinner was being served in the dining area of the hotel, and we went and stood in line while volunteers ladled food onto our plates. With our plates piled high, we looked around for a place to sit. There were round tables with chairs around them, but most were occupied. However, as we passed by one table, an Indian woman gestured to us and made two seats available for us. We sat down and began eating. The people at our table were all chatting with each other. They talked about their experiences with Amma, the places they had visited to see her, how many times they had visited her and so on. I was very hungry and was focused on the delicious food and not engaging in the conversation, but Anna soon started talking with these followers of Amma. Most were Caucasian; only the woman sitting next to me, who had made room for us, and I were of Indian origin.

At some point in the conversation, someone asked Anna what had made her come to see Amma. Anna pointed at me, and I told them the whole story of how the journey to Amma had started with Lisa Hallstrom's book. The Indian woman sitting next to me jumped up and said she was good friends with Lisa Hallstrom. She was excited to hear my story and got Lisa on her cell phone and handed the phone to me. I talked to Lisa who was very happy to hear that I was not only there to see Amma again but had also met someone she knew. Somehow this connection made the whole group of veteran Amma followers adopt us as one of their own. They asked if we were staying at the hotel and were horrified when we told them we had driven in a blizzard. They insisted that we stay in the hotel until morning and not go back while it was dark. I did not tell them that the forecast was for freezing rain after midnight.

Anna and I finished dinner, thanked all the wonderful people we had met, said goodbye to them, and went and joined the queue to hug Amma. We both had work the next day and knew we would have to drive back after hugging Amma. After midnight, we hugged Amma and it was as blissful an experience as it had been the year before. We walked away with our Hershey's Kisses and looked at each other, wondering if we should attempt the perilous drive back home. Anna said, "Let's give it a shot," and I agreed even though freezing rain is extremely dangerous. As we came out of the hotel, we sensed something was wrong. We were still immersed in Amma-Bliss and slightly disoriented, so we could not put our finger on the problem at once. We stood in the parking lot and looked around feeling slightly befuddled. And then it hit us! Gone was the snow, gone was the blizzard, gone was the freezing rain! The air was soft as velvet. It was the night air of a Michigan summer. Without a word we got into the car and drove home safely.

Through the years, I have never missed an opportunity to visit Amma. Each experience has been as fulfilling as the first one. People fly from all over the U.S. to see her in Detroit. When she comes to the U.S., she stops in three or four places. It still amazes me to think that she comes to Detroit. People hear about her from me and want to see her. But her visit often clashes with their Thanksgiving plans and they cannot make it. As for me, the minute someone offers me a ride, I jump up and go. Amma's presence is so strong that the whole hotel vibrates with her loving energy. Sometimes I can feel her vibrations reaching out to me in the parking lot of the hotel accommodating Amma and her devotees. Even as I write this chapter on her, I am amazed at the fact that living here in a small university town in Michigan I have had the opportunity to see Amma so many times.

Part VII: Spiritual Support

Chapter 52: Sri Ramakrishna

In 1984, I left my home in Calcutta and went to teach in Midnapore, India. There I met three extraordinary women who were my Aunt Dolly's friends: Professors Bharati Ghosh, Rekha Sarkar, and Tapati Sinha. All three were devotees and disciples of Sri Ramakrishna and had been initiated by monks of the Ramakrishna Mission. The day I arrived with my aunt to check out my surroundings, I was told that her three friends had started a charitable trust called Sarada Kalyan Bhandar to help the needy students of Midnapore. I taught in Midnapore for six years and became very close to these women. Naturally, I became involved with Sarada Kalyan Bhandar and helped during my spare time with the work that needed to be done. On certain occasions, nuns from various branches of Sarada Math (which is the sister branch of Ramakrishna Mission) would come and there would be kirtan, *puja*, and Dharma talks. I felt a deep bond with Sri Ramakrishna and enjoyed this spiritual friendship with his followers. Even though I left Midnapore in 1990 to come to the United States, I stayed in touch with my friends in Midnapore.

From left to right: Tapati Sinha, Rekha Sarkar, Bharati Ghosh. Midnapore, 2000

Ralph and I moved to Michigan in August of 1997. Once we had settled down, I expressed my wish to go home and spend some time in India. Ralph was busy teaching, and I booked my ticket for early October. Michigan State University, where Ralph was teaching, had a good library and I went and checked out *The Gospel of Sri Ramakrishna* by M (translated into English by Swami Nikhilananda). As I started reading, I was spellbound. Before leaving for Calcutta, I told Ralph to read this book whenever he felt stressed. Within a few months, Ralph had finished the whole book. He wanted to read more books written by monks of the Ramakrishna Order, and when I came back in 1998 my suitcases were full of books for Ralph. By June of 1998, Ralph was ready for initiation and was initiated by my guru.

We were still new in Lansing, Michigan, when I came back from Calcutta in February of 1998 and we did not know anybody. One snowy morning, Ralph was scraping the snow off his windshield when the gentleman who owned the car parked next to Ralph's began to talk to him. It turned out that he was a Bengali and his name was Partha Saha. Mr. Saha began to visit us often, and one day he told us something that we found hard to believe. We knew that there was a Vivekananda Vedanta Society of Chicago, but that was a four-hour drive from where we lived. However, Mr. Saha told us that an hour-and-a-half away from us was a place called Ganges, Michigan, where there was a retreat center that belonged to the Vivekananda Society of Chicago. I could not believe that in the Midwest there could be a place called Ganges. We could not wait to visit this center, and that very weekend Ralph and I headed out. It was truly in the midst of nowhere, but we soon found ourselves on the driveway of the Vivekananda Retreat Center in Ganges, Michigan.

It was a stunningly beautiful building with a huge shrine room, a bookshop, a dining hall and kitchen, a museum, and a library. On the grounds were cottages for retreatants, trails for walks, and a small pond. As I walked into the shrine room and saw Sri Ramakrishna's face, I felt as though I were meeting a dear old friend. Ralph and I began to go there often. We would meditate in the shrine room and browse in the bookshop. We went on weekdays when no one was around. The place was full of peace and love, and the presence of the sages was palpable. Every time I go, I feel He (Thakur or Sri Ramakrishna) has been sitting there waiting for me. There is no judgment, no scolding for not having visited more often, just a warm welcome that melts my heart and makes me know that I am home.

My close relationship with the great teachers of this Order continues through books and occasional trips to Ganges. Due to technology, we now

have monks of the Ramakrishna Order teaching in our living rooms. I listen
to Swami Chetanananda of St. Louis who has devoted his life to preserving

The altar at the Vivekananda Retreat Center in Ganges. Michigan, 2019
From left to right: Jesus Christ, Swami Vivekananda, Sri Ramakrishna, Sri Sarada Devi,
and the Buddha. The Om symbol is above Sri Ramakrishna's photo.

the stories of monastics and lay people associated with this Order. These
stories would have been lost if he had not painstakingly collected them and
published them in his books. In recent years, Swami Sarvapriyananda, who
lives in New York City, has become very popular and I listen to him, too.
One day the thought crossed my mind that it would be nice to see Swami
Sarvapriyananda. The very next day, I found out that he was going to give a
talk at our university. Sri Ramakrishna had fulfilled my wish.

In this way, and in many other ways, Sri Ramakrishna and His children
have blessed me with their spiritual teachings, and I am grateful to them for
all I have received from them through the years.

Chapter 53: Balananda Brahmachari

Sri Balananda Brahmachari was my guru's guru. Whenever Maharaj came to our house, I noticed that his guru's picture was placed on the wall behind the sofa on which Maharaj sat in our living room to receive his devotees and to sing kirtan. I also noticed a large locket with Balanandaji's picture on it that hung from my guru's neck. From time to time, when my guru's disciples visited our home and talked about their varied experiences with our guru, some of them mentioned Balanandaji and shared stories of him as well as stories he would tell. Whenever we visited Deoghar, we went to Balanandaji's ashram (which was our ashram) and saw beautiful statues of this great sage and the cottage where he had lived.

In August of 1997, while waiting to go to India, I found a book on my shelf that I began reading. It was *Splendour in the Cave* by Shyamananda Banerjee, and it was a biography of Balananda Brahmachari. The death of my grandmother in March 1997 in Calcutta had changed my life. Unfortunately, I could not leave the U.S. because I was in the process of getting my Green Card. Thus mourning in isolation had exacerbated my grief. However, this book brought about a transformation in me and marked a turning point in my spiritual life. I received my Green Card just as I finished reading this beautifully written biography. With nothing to prevent me from going to India, I left Michigan and went to Calcutta for four months.

When I was ready to return to the U.S. in February of 1998, Uncle Debkumar Ray, a close friend of our family who was also a disciple of my guru, gave me a book just as I was leaving Calcutta to come back to the U.S. The book was written in the Bengali script and the title was *Katha Prasanga* (Spiritual Discourses). It was written by Saralabala Mitra and contained the Dharma talks given by Balanandaji at his ashram in Deoghar. I was excited to receive the book because I had already read the biography of this sage before leaving Michigan.

Back in the U.S., I had just started reading the book in June of 1998 when my father passed away. I was inconsolable and cried all the time. However, each day I read a few pages of this book and realized that while I was reading I felt no grief. It was almost as though the book soaked up my grief. Seeing me praise the book, Ralph suggested that I translate it so he could read it. I was not teaching at that time and so each day I translated a page. Ralph came home after teaching and read what I had translated. In this way, before I knew it, I had translated the first volume.

In August of 1998, my mother came to stay with me for two months. She was familiar with the book and was very excited to read my translation. She asked me to give her a photocopy of a couple of chapters. When she went back to India, she showed my translations to a family friend, Dr. Govinda Gopal Mukhopadhyay. He was not only an erudite scholar of the Hindu scriptures but also a disciple of Balanandaji. Govinda *babu* was thrilled to see his guru's talks translated into English. He spoke to me on the phone and told me I needed to publish the book. I told him I did not know Sanskrit, and I did not know how to use diacritical marks. There were many verses from the Gita and other scriptures that Balanandaji had quoted in the book, and I felt one needed to be a scholar to translate such a book. It was one thing translating the book for Ralph but quite another to publish it. The script was in Bengali, and I had had no formal education in Bengali because we had lived outside of Bengal and I had studied Hindi in school. Balanadaji spoke in Hindi, so I could easily understand what he was saying. But I had no qualification at all to publish this book. Govinda *babu* told me to send him the manuscript and said he would edit and proofread it.

Having grown up in a culture where one can never deny a request made by an elder, I did as I was told. Once the manuscript was ready, I contacted several publishers, but they were not ready to publish a book on spiritual discourses. As the years went by, I began to fret that I would not be able to give Govinda *babu* a published copy. He was in his nineties, and we were running out of time. So, in 2006, I went to a local printer and ordered twenty copies of the book to be printed by them. When the job was done, I sent a few copies to my mother in Calcutta, and she presented Govinda *babu* with his copy. I heaved a sigh of relief and felt that my work was done. The relief lasted for a few days and then Govinda *babu* called and told me to translate the remaining two volumes. He said I needed to hurry because he did not have much time and would like to edit and proofread the remaining volumes. I was ready to faint. This was a huge task.

I began to spend every spare minute I could find translating the remaining volumes. I had started teaching in 2004 and had many responsibilities and obligations. But somehow each chapter got done. My mother visited me in 2007 and we went over the translation of the second volume before mailing it to Govinda *babu*. He was extremely pleased and made the necessary corrections. By now I had picked up some knowledge of diacritical marks and was making fewer mistakes. Finally, I went to Calcutta in 2008 with the manuscript of the third volume and Govinda *babu* finished editing it just before passing away in 2009. I was grateful to have fulfilled his wishes and knew that the translation had made him very happy.

Govinda *babu* had wanted the spiritual discourses of his guru translated into English so they would be accessible to many people. People who could read Bengali would not understand it if they did not also know Hindi, while people who understood Hindi would not be able to read the book because they did not know the Bengali script. However, most educated Indians could read English. In 2013, I self-published the book through Amazon under the title *Of Ascetics and Emperors: Teachings of an Indian Sage* with all three volumes contained in one book.

Saralabala Mitra's *Katha Prasanga* translated into English. 2013

I had spent fifteen years on this invaluable book and learned so much. Govinda *babu* had said this book contained everything one needed to know about Hinduism. Through beautiful parables and stories, the sage had

271

explained many of the essential concepts of Hinduism. Later, when I began to read the Hindu scriptures or listened to Dharma talks, I found that I was familiar with these concepts because of the time I had spent translating the book. Only then did I realize the truth of Govinda *babu's* words. Moreover, I felt the presence of the great sage each time I sat with the book. All sages tell us to visit saints and to listen to Dharma talks. Translating the works of great sages is an excellent way to enjoy the company of the sages. Translation requires intense concentration, and I could see how the state of my mind was uplifted every time I finished translating a page or proofread a chapter or edited the stories. Finally, I noticed how peaceful it was to do any work when the ego is not involved. I never thought of the book as my book; it was always Saralabala Mitra's book. This great woman probably never thought of it as her book; for her it was her guru's book because it contained his talks. I also did not worry about whether anyone would read the book or if it would sell. Translating was truly a labor of love and all I received in return was joy and knowledge.

In 2016 I came back to Michigan after spending a year in Calcutta selling my grandmother's home and began to attend the Ananda Michigan group again. Later in the year, the group started a book study in which we were going to read books by Yoganandaji and his disciples. Several people joined this book study, and I became close friends with a woman named Lynda Group who loved to read. She had already bought the book on Balanandaji that I had translated and had read some sections of the book. Another woman I became close to was Kathy Burgess, who was also interested in Balanandaji's teachings. Over the years, whenever we were about to finish a book and were looking for suggestions for the next book, Lynda, Kathy, and a few other members of the group suggested reading Balanandaji's teachings. However, we always ended up choosing a book by Yogananda or his disciples. I did not have a problem with this and enjoyed every book we read.

Then in 2020, before Covid struck, Lynda asked me if she and I could do a one-on-one book study of *Of Ascetics and Emperors* over the phone. I agreed and we studied the book I had translated and held wonderful discussions on the phone each Sunday. I had not touched the book since 2013 and was surprised to find how much I was enjoying it again. In the Ananda study group, we were getting ready to finish a book that contained the stellar sermons of Yogananda. What was my surprise when Wendy, who leads the book study, suggested that we read *Of Ascetics and Emperors*! We started the book in March of 2021 and finished reading and discussing it in October.

Lynda and I continued our one-on-one study on Sundays, but Lynda also attended the Tuesday sessions with the group.

This was a wonderful experience for me to see how my lack of ego with respect to this translation had been richly rewarded through not one but two book studies. Moreover, the members of the group were not Indians who would have been familiar with some of the concepts. They were all Americans, and this was foreign material to them. It was very fulfilling for me to see how much they enjoyed the teachings and the stories. Finally, I understood the meaning of the verse in the Gita that tells us to do our work but not attach to the outcome. This was one work I had done with no attachments, and I had reaped the benefits of such an attitude. I learned a lot about Hindu philosophy, I enjoyed the presence of Balanandaji, and I was able to share the Dharma with like-minded people.

I with my nephew in my lap, Aunt Dolly, and Uncle Debkumar Ray. Calcutta, 1997

Chapter 54: A Devotee of Gopal

From 1984 to 1990, I taught English Literature at Midnapore College. During my stay in the town of Midnapore, India, I became good friends with Basanti Chatterjee who was a schoolteacher. She had been a student of Aunt Dolly's friends, and they had introduced me to her. She and her husband were a very caring and affectionate couple who all but adopted me. They did not have any children. He was a government officer and a kind and gentle person.

Basantidi (as I called her because she was older than me) was a great devotee of Gopal (baby Krishna) and had a beautiful statue of him. Many homes in India have statues of various deities and Gopal is commonly found in Bengali homes. In our home in Calcutta, we also had several statues of Gopal. A devotee who has a Gopal statue bathes the statue, clothes it, offers some lumps of sugar called *nakuldana*, places flowers before the statue and moves on to his or her tasks each day. At night, Gopal is undressed and put to bed.

In Basantidi I found a true lover of Gopal. She treated him as though he were truly a living child who was at an age when he could crawl. She bathed him and dressed him in beautiful clothes stitched by her. She fed him a variety of foods at different times of the day. She talked to him, scolded him, coaxed him to help others, tried to teach him the Bengali alphabet, complained that he was always "sleeping, eating, playing, gossiping, and not studying," and took him with her wherever she went. I was moved by her devotion. I had heard of and read about women who worshipped Gopal in this manner, but now I was witnessing this kind of worship with my own eyes.

One week, Aunt Dolly visited me and stayed with me at my residence in Midnapore for a few days. She was deeply spiritual and when she met Basantidi's Gopal, she had an interesting experience. My aunt was very shy and did not like to share her experiences, but she said to me, "Basanti's Gopal is alive (*bhishon jagroto*)." When I asked her why she had felt that way, she told me that when she had lifted her head after bowing to him she clearly saw him blinking his eyes.

In 1990, a few months before I was leaving for the U.S., I had two interesting dreams. One night, I came home after visiting Basantidi, ate dinner, and graded some papers before going to sleep . That night I dreamt

Gopal was sleeping in a little cot under my bed, the cot that Basantidi used to put him to bed every night at her house. The next day, I told Basantidi about my dream and she said, "Oh dear! I think he went with you last night and slept in your house."

Basantidi's Gopal (Photo courtesy of Basanti Chatterjee)

Basantidi loved me dearly and she wanted to buy me a dress (a set of *salwar* and *kameez*) before I left for the U.S. "I am going to go this weekend and buy the cloth so you can give it to the tailor and get it made," she said each week, but somehow she never got around to ordering my clothes. One night I dreamt that Gopal was sitting under my bed, and he looked very angry. He had taken all his clothes and was stitching a garment for me. When I shared the dream with Basantidi, she said, "Oh my goodness! I am going this weekend with you. Gopal is angry!"

We did go to Calcutta that weekend and went and looked at bolts of cloth in a store near Gol Park. Every bolt of cloth looked fine to me, but Basantidi kept rejecting what the salesman was offering. It seemed as though she was looking for something particular. Finally, her eyes lit up and she chose a beautiful brick-colored cloth. I asked her later what was special about it. She pointed at the pattern. There were tiny peacock feathers in the design, and Krishna wears a peacock feather on his crown. She said, "Gopal is giving you this outfit." We went to a tailor and ordered the *salwar* and *kameez*. The day I boarded the plane for the U.S., I was wearing that outfit.

Through the years, I have stayed in touch with Basantidi. Her husband passed away in 2000, and ever since then she focuses solely on Gopal. Only by associating very closely with such a person can one really tell the depths of his or her devotion. I listen to her stories of Gopal and notice that the stories never change. They are stories that some may call miracles and others may call a coincidence. For more than four decades now, she has treated Gopal like her child. By watching her and listening to her, I have witnessed what it is to truly love God.

Basantidi with her Gopal and Jagannath (Photo courtesy of Basanti Chatterjee)

Chapter 55: Sister Shivani

In 2009, Lorne Dekun, the founder of Ananda Michigan, emailed me and told me that an Indian woman had come to see him and he had told her to contact me. Soon I received an email from Monica Bhargava who said she wished to meet me. I agreed to meet her, and we set up an appointment. When I first met Monica, we both thought that I was going to help her by sharing spiritual advice. However, life is full of surprises and there was one in store for me. As we began to talk on the phone, I tried to find some common ground on which we could meet so Monica could relate to what I was trying to share with her. This proved to be difficult. She was younger than I was and very respectful towards me, but whatever I was sharing just did not seem to be the right fit.

One day she told me that she had listened to a talk on YouTube by a woman called Sister Shivani. Monica wondered if I would like to listen to her and I agreed. We began to meet at Monica's home where we would listen to a talk by Sister Shivani, discuss what we had just heard, and then eat a delicious lunch prepared by Monica. I did not know anything about Sister but had gone with an open mind. My goal was to encourage Monica in her spiritual practice. However, soon I was listening to Sister's talks almost every day. I shared her talks with my friends and they began to listen, too. When I told my mother about it, she said that Sister Shivani belonged to a group called the Brahma Kumaris and they were well known in India.

Monica was busy raising her children and helping her husband with his business, so it was not always possible to get together and listen. But we both listened separately in our respective homes and discussed what we had heard with each other on the phone. What attracted me to these talks was their practical down-to-earth advice on how to live our daily lives. Most of what I heard was already familiar to me from my years of practicing meditation, studying Buddhism, and observing life. But listening to a skilled practitioner and a brilliant teacher made a deep impression on my mind.

Almost every teaching of Sister Shivani, which I listened to with close attention, came in handy in 2015 when, after all my loved ones had passed away, I went to Kolkata to sell our home. I was all alone and quite sick. It took me a year to complete my job and come back to the U.S. This was a long year of dealing with bureaucrats, lawyers, courts, and all the red tape one faces when getting anything done in India. I was surrounded by greedy people who saw in me a helpless woman they could take advantage of. Obnoxious developers, dishonest potential buyers, and obstreperous bankers tried to make my life miserable. The heat, the crowds, the traffic jams, the unanswered letters and calls, the rude refusals, the veiled threats were enough to make my health grow worse. I turned on my laptop and listened to Sister Shivani each time the mind was agitated.

Sister Shivani and Monica Bhargava. Delhi (Photo courtesy of Monica Bhargava)

Sister has a voice that can calm one instantly. I sat and listened while waiting and waiting for the probate to come through, for the house to be sold, and for money to be sent back to the U.S. after all taxes had been paid. When I was about to lose my temper, Sister taught me patience. When I was furious at the incompetence of a bank official or the arrogance of a government officer, Sister taught me forgiveness. Everything I had learned from Maharaj's angelic behavior while I was in his presence, everything I had learned from the Buddha's teachings on the Brahma Viharas (loving-

278

kindness, compassion, sympathetic joy, and equanimity), and everything I had learned from Sister Shivani was put to test during that year. No matter how challenging the situation, I was able to face it with courage and equanimity. As I watched myself, I saw how I was benefitting from my spiritual practices. By responding to each situation with calm, and by not harboring anger and resentment within me, I was able to get everything done.

After I came back to Michigan in 2016, I continued to listen to Sister. Monica had met her in Delhi during one of her trips to India, and I wished I could meet her, too. Once again, the wish was granted when Sister Shivani visited Dearborn, Michigan, in 2017 and gave a talk. Monica and I went and listened to this wise and pure woman whose voice is full of compassion, whose glance brims over with kindness, and who practices what she teaches.

Even today, when I look back at my first meeting with Monica, I am struck with wonder at the thought of how things turned out. I was supposed to help her; instead, it was Monica who was coming to me with this wonderful gift. She would introduce me to Sister Shivani who would have a significant impact on my life.

Part VIII: Wish Fulfillment

Chapter 56: Krishna

People are impressed when they hear stories of miracles, but I find that miracles happen all around us all the time. It is just that we do not notice them. When we do notice them, we usually find some rational explanation for the event or just label it a coincidence. However, my experiences have taught me to believe in spiritual miracles as God speaks to us in many ways.

In 1997, after we had moved to Michigan, I told Ralph I needed a break from constantly studying and teaching. My grandmother's death had brought about a change in me. I felt a strong wish to turn away from worldly aspirations and focus on my spiritual life. Taking time off from work, I went home to Calcutta and spent four months with my family.

When I arrived in Calcutta, Mother sensed the change in me. I immersed myself in spiritual books and actively participated in the discussions that took place between Mother and Aunt Dolly. Every evening, Uncle Debkumar Ray, a family friend and disciple of my guru would come and join in the conversations. He only spoke of spiritual matters, and we felt privileged to be in such good company as we listened to stories of Balananda Brahmachari and Maharaj. He visited us each evening while I was there in 1997.

While most of my evenings were spent listening to stories of sages, during the day I spent hours meditating and reading spiritual books. Even though it took me time to read Bengali, I started reading a book in six volumes on the life of Sri Chaitanya Mahaprabhu, the great devotional singer of the Bhakti movement in India. This book was *Sri Amiyo Nimai Charit* by Shishir Kumar Ghosh. It was written in simple Bengali that I found very accessible, and it was full of the nectar of devotion. I was mesmerized.

Amidst this environment of love and devotion, I regularly had a strange experience. Each time I closed my eyes to meditate, I seemed to see a beautiful picture of Krishna in my mind's eye. He was standing and looking at me sideways. It was not a vision or a dream. It was just a picture that would show up each time I closed my eyes to meditate.

One evening, Uncle Debkumar came to visit us and we were chatting over cups of tea. Somehow the conversation moved to his sister, Aunty Reba, whom he missed a lot. She and her husband had lived in a beautiful house, and I had visited them several times before leaving for the U.S. Both had passed and the house now belonged to their son. Suddenly, I remembered a painting of Krishna that hung on the wall facing the landing of the second floor. Out of curiosity I asked about the picture and was told that it still hung in its old place, but no one much cared about it. I asked if

the new owner of the house, Aunty Reba's son, would give it to me and was told that he probably would.

After reminding Uncle Debkumar almost every day to ask his nephew about the painting, one day he showed up with the painting. I was delighted. It was this Krishna I had been seeing in my mind's eye. I brought it back with me to Michigan and it hangs on my living room wall to this day.

However, the story did not end there. Within a year, the owner of the house passed away and the house was sold, demolished, and replaced by a high rise. I was stunned when I heard this and wondered what would have happened to my Krishna if he had not made his escape from a home that was soon to be razed to the ground.

Uncle Debkumar had once told us a story of how he had found a large picture of Paramhansa Yogananda on a pile of trash outside an old house that was being demolished. Shocked to see the portrait of a great sage discarded in this manner, Uncle Debkumar had rescued the portrait and brought it home. Perhaps, with other things, my Krishna too would have ended up in a dumpster. Whenever I look at the painting, I feel so grateful that Krishna had chosen to come and live in our humble abode in Michigan.

Chapter 57: The Christmas Nativity Ornament

December is a happy month for me as people all over the world prepare for Christmas regardless of whether or not they are Christian. There is joy in the air as folks bustle around, shopping for presents that will delight their loved ones. Packages start arriving at the door, Christmas cards have to be written, and pretty paper needs to be bought to wrap the gifts. The Christmas tree goes up in the living room and is decorated with ornaments and tinsel, CDs of joyous Christmas carols and deeply spiritual hymns are played, and the house is fragrant with the aroma of cookies baking in the oven.

A couple of weeks before Christmas in 2016, I was driving home with a friend after enjoying a Christmas party and found myself ruminating aloud about how I feel during this season. "There is something in the air," I said. "Something deeply spiritual. Perhaps it is the energy of devout Christians all over the world who are preparing for the season. I don't know why I feel so drawn to the spiritual aspect of Christmas. Even when I was a child, I remember being fascinated by the Nativity Scene at a time in my life when I am not sure I even knew what it meant."

As the words left my lips, a long-forgotten memory made its way through the winding dusty cobwebby tunnels of half a century. In 1965, Father's regiment was posted in a town called Jhansi and I was in the second grade (Class II). I cannot remember the name of the school, but it was a Christian school and my class teacher was an Anglo-Indian woman.

One day, someone came to our school to sell some pretty knickknacks and I was drawn to a Christmas decoration: a tiny hut with a woman, a man, a baby, two lambs, and a tree. I was mesmerized by the piece and thought it was the most beautiful thing I had ever seen. I went home and told Mother about it, and she gave me the money to buy it. The next day I came home with our one and only Nativity Scene.

Through the years, we moved from place to place as is typical of those in military life. Mother always took care of this tiny fragile decoration, and wherever we set up our home the Nativity Scene found a place on the mantel over the fireplace. Finally, after father retired, we settled in Calcutta, and I still remember seeing the decoration in our drawing room.

The Nativity Scene

Time flew by, my sister and I grew up and left for foreign shores, the elders aged and passed away one by one, and finally I was faced with the task of selling the ancestral home and clearing out sixty years of accumulation. While going through one of Mother's cupboards, I saw a tiny piece that looked familiar. It was Joseph. The pieces must have come apart and the hut must have crumbled, but somehow Joseph had survived. I did not know what to do with him. Without a home and his family, he was as lost as I was.

Reluctantly, I abandoned him . . . until December 2016 when the Holy Family came back into my life through this casual conversation with a friend.

A couple of days after the conversation, something made me turn to technology on a cold snowy morning in Michigan. I googled "tiny nativity scene" and at once was bombarded by innumerable images. I am not a shopper, and it wearies me to go through too many items to find what I need. But right there on the screen facing me was my Nativity Scene. I could not believe my eyes. I clicked on it and found, to my disappointment, that it had been sold. Now that I had seen it, none of the other Nativity Scenes attracted me. I turned away from the computer and let go of my nostalgia.

The brain works in strange ways. Two days later, I went back to the same image and read the information posted next to it: "1960s. Plastic. Made in Hong Kong." I took this information and googled it adding the words "miniature Nativity Scene." Voila! There it was. Only one was available. With a couple of clicks I bought it and waited with bated breath for its arrival. It was going to travel all the way from Canada to Michigan. Fifty years ago, it had traveled from Hong Kong to a tiny town in India.

Finally a small package arrived and as I unwrapped the object wrapped in old tissue paper, I saw it was an exact replica of what I had bought fifty-one years ago. I had been worried that as an adult I may find it not so beautiful. Indeed, it may seem tacky since the word "plastic" is a bit of a wet blanket. But it was every bit as beautiful to my eyes as it was when I was a child.

Of course, I took pictures and shared them with the friends with whom I had shared my memory. Suffice it to say they did not react as they may have if I had purchased the *Mona Lisa*.

Perhaps it is just a tacky plasticky little thing, but to me it provides a magic carpet ride to a past of loving parents who did not tell their little Hindu child that she could not buy a Nativity Scene. They not only helped me buy this decoration but also welcomed its presence in our home and took care of it through the years. Many of us who grew up in the India of my time are very open to all religions and cultures. I think we owe this openness to our parents and their actions. I was never told to respect all religions. I did not have to be told. My parents' actions taught me to find a place in my heart for all beings.

Chapter 58: *Madonnina* or *Madonna of the Streets* by Roberto Ferruzzi

In 1968, when my family lived in Roorkee, we were good friends with Father Charles, the Italian priest of the Roman Catholic Church in Roorkee. He had given us two pictures: one was a picture of Jesus with a prayer blessing our home, and the other was a picture of the Virgin Mary with baby Jesus. Mother treasured these gifts and kept them safe as we moved from place to place and finally settled in Calcutta. Both pictures hung on the walls of our dining room in our house in Calcutta. I was fascinated by the second picture and never tired of looking at the beautiful Madonna and Child.

In 2016 when I was emptying the Kolkata house of all its belongings, I did not find either of the pictures given to us by our kind Italian friend. There was no one alive to tell me what had happened to the pictures. I missed the one that had fascinated me and knew that I would have taken it back to the U.S. if it had still been on the wall.

Two years later, in October of 2018, I was attending a Sunday service at Ananda Michigan when I started talking to Mary Thomas, who is one of the ministers. Although she was very busy making arrangements for an annual retreat that is held each year, she was planning on staying after service and decorating the altar with some new fabric she had bought. Some of us stayed back to help her. After she had finished decorating the altar, she brought a painting of the Virgin Mary and placed it next to the altar. I froze as I saw the painting. It was the same painting that Father Charles had given us of the Madonna and Child. I asked Mary where I could buy this painting. She did not remember where or when she had bought it but mentioned a couple of websites where I might find it.

I came home and googled "Madonna and Child" on my computer and the painting I was looking for was the third one on my screen. I did not know that this painting called *Madonnina* was commonly known as *Madonna of the Streets* and had been painted by a painter named Roberto Ferruzzi. Once I had this information, it was easy to find a seller online and order a print. The painting arrived, beautifully placed in a golden frame, and I placed it on the mantel in my living room where it stands today.

Madonnina by Roberto Ferruzzi

Chapter 59: Kirtan

Having grown up listening to Maharaj's mellifluous voice, my heart always longed for kirtan. Perhaps it was this wish to listen to devotional chants that took me to Lorne Dekun's kirtan in 2003. Anyone who has tasted the nectar of kirtan sung by Maharaj will testify that it would be hard to listen to devotional songs sung by anyone else. Hence, it was with some trepidation that I first went to listen to Lorne. But within minutes, I was captivated by the power of Yoganandaji's chants.

Lorne arranged for a kirtan once a month and I made sure that I arranged my schedule in such a manner that I never had to miss his kirtans. Unfortunately, after Lorne passed away in 2013, there was a period of time when we did not hold regular kirtans at Ananda Michigan. I used to yearn for them and my friend, Anna Fisher, took me several times to listen to a group called the Ann Arbor Kirtan, which had some powerful singers who fulfilled my longing for devotional singing. However, Ann Arbor is an hour's drive from where I live, and it was not possible to go on a regular basis, so I kept missing kirtan.

The room set for kirtan at Kathy Burgess' house (Photo courtesy of Kathy Burgess)

When I came back to Michigan in 2016, after being in India for a year, I found a few new members at Ananda Michigan. One of them was Kathy Burgess who soon became a dear friend of mine. She had read about Anandamayi Ma and was very devoted to her. When Kathy found out that I had met Ma as a child, she wanted to know more and this became the foundation of our friendship. Moreover, Kathy was a gifted musician and was very interested in learning to play the harmonium. Within a couple of years, Kathy began to offer kirtans at her home and at a public venue near my home. Suddenly I found that there were some weeks when I was attending three of Kathy's kirtans and one hosted by Ananda Michigan! I still cannot understand how this happened. I had been yearning for kirtan with such intensity that my wish had been granted. I no longer had to go to distant places to listen to the chanting of Sanskrit verses or the singing of devotional songs; I had kirtan at my doorstep.

In March of 2020, Covid temporarily put a stop to all events, and I began to rely on the tapes I had of Maharaj's songs. Even though the world soon began to communicate via various online apps, I decided to use this time to focus on my own practice. Maharaj's kirtans played an important role in my spiritual practice as I listened to his singing for an hour each morning.

In July of 2020, a disciple of Maharaj contacted me and asked if I had any pictures of her and her family with Maharaj. Her name was Jayati Sanyal and she lived in Kolkata. I remembered that she had been close to my Aunt Dolly. She, her husband, and her son had visited us when Maharaj was visiting my uncle's house in Malda. At first, my mind drew a blank. I had no memory of any pictures taken in Malda and felt bad that I would have to disappoint her. Thinking about what to do, I suddenly remembered that when I had sold our home in Calcutta I had brought home only two things: pictures and letters. I went down to the basement of our home in Michigan and looked at a box labelled "Photos and albums from Kolkata." I opened the box and saw that it contained several albums. I took out the first album and opened the first page. Right there, on that very first page, was a picture of Jayati and her family!

I took pictures of the photo with my cell phone and sent them to her. I told her that I was in awe of her devotion. What a great devotee she must be for this miracle to happen. I truly had no idea that such a picture existed, and I felt Maharaj led me by the hand and took me straight to it. We became friends and she told me stories of how she had spent time with Maharaj when she was a little girl. From time to time, she would send me a video clip of

Maharaj singing kirtan. These were short clips that had been posted on YouTube. As I listened, I realized I should share my tapes with her. Gradually, it dawned on me that I would have to upload these kirtans to YouTube so I could share them with her.

During the Christmas break of 2020, at my request, Ralph learned how to upload the kirtans and Maharaj's pictures on YouTube. At first we worked on it together, but soon I knew what to do. It was a lot of work but in a couple of months I had twelve volumes of Maharaj's kirtans, each ranging from 70 to 75 minutes, on YouTube. I had taken on this task with Jayati in mind, but soon hundreds of followers of Maharaj began to listen and comment. It had not struck me that this simple act would benefit so many people. It was truly a joy to share what I had with Maharaj's followers. I just wish I had done it earlier. But things happen as and when they are supposed to happen. I still look back at all the connections and am amazed at how Maharaj continues to work through each of us. By January of 2021, all the kirtans I had recorded of Maharaj singing in our house at Burnpur had been uploaded to YouTube and were accessible to the public.

Some of the listeners began to communicate with me on YouTube expressing their gratitude, and after several decades I felt connected to Maharaj's disciples and devotees who were members of our sangha.

Part IX: Some Afterthoughts

Chapter 60: Turning Inwards

Covid brought a stop to my spiritual activities out in the world when Michigan went into lockdown in mid-March of 2020. I could no longer go to Kathy's kirtans or the Sunday service at Ananda or meditation at Quan Am Temple. However, I have always enjoyed being at home and I found a sense of peace when my activities came to a stop. No matter how many spiritual events I had attended since 1999, I had never neglected my personal practice. I continued to meditate as I had for the past forty-nine years and found my days flying by as I spent time listening to Dharma talks on YouTube and Maharaj's kirtans on my computer.

It took the sanghas some time to start online activities via Zoom, but I did not feel compelled to join every event. I remembered something that I had heard Govinda Gopal Mukhopadhyay say in 1997 when he had come to our house in Calcutta for lunch one day. After lunch, he spent some time telling us stories of many great Indian sages and sharing their wisdom with us. As he was speaking, he said, "Now is the time to decrease the number of friends you have (*Ekhon gondi choto korar shomay*)."

These words came back to me in 2020 and I told myself that I had spent two decades with various sanghas in Michigan and it was time now to turn inwards. I was extremely grateful for all the support I had received from my Dharma friends, but I was curious to see if I could practice on my own for a few months. Not much changed because I still had kirtan and meditation in my life. However, one aspect of my practice did evolve during the Covid years.

I have never been much interested in performing rituals. While growing up in India, we did have a *puja* room where there were images of gods and goddesses and pictures of sages. Sometimes, when the elders were unable to perform the daily rituals, I was asked to do what was considered necessary. I would perform the rituals, such as bathing the statue of Gopal (baby Krishna), dressing him, offering him some sweets and water to nourish him, and putting him to bed at night. An elder would supervise and tell me what to do. I also had some training in the household rituals that are commonly performed in the shrine rooms of most Hindu homes such as lighting incense sticks and placing flowers on the shrine. I performed these rituals mechanically before dashing off to school or college.

In 2015 when I went to Kolkata to sell my grandmother's house, I became the self-appointed "priest" of the *puja* room. Each morning, after bathing, I would perform all the rituals that had been performed for decades by my ancestors. One daily morning ritual was that of bathing, dressing, and feeding Gopal. I returned after dusk and cleared the shrine table of the wilted flowers, lit an incense stick and walked with it through the house paying respect to all sages, gods, goddesses, and ancestors in every room, and then put Gopal to bed. Soon I noticed that I really enjoyed this different way of interacting with God. There was a sense of peace and calm as I dipped the flowers in sandalwood paste before offering them to the deities, poured water on the Shiva Lingam, and lit the wick of the tall brass oil lamp.

Perhaps repeated acts have a way of calming the mind, but there was more to it than just that. As the March sun blazed forth in all its glory, I found the heat overwhelming and moved to my grandmother's room which was the only room that was air conditioned. One day, as I was leaving the shrine room, I thought of how little Gopal would sit all day in the heat. I remembered that Uncle Sankar used to take Gopal into his room where the fan kept my uncle cool. I wanted to do the same and took Gopal each day to my air-conditioned room. This act of mine took me by surprise. Without my knowing it, Gopal had crept into my heart.

Aunt Dolly's Shrine Room. Calcutta, 1998

I spent a lot of time that year finding suitable homes for the various pictures and images in the shrine room, but Bonie asked me to bring back the statues of Radha, Krishna, and Gopal which had been worshipped by Aunt Dolly. So, when I came back to the U.S. in 2016, Radha, Krishna, and Gopal were in one of my suitcases. I landed in Boston, where I was to spend a few days with my sister and her family before going home to Michigan. When I opened the suitcases, I handed over the statues to Bonie. She placed them on the mantel above the fireplace in her living room. After my stay was over, I was sitting in Bonie's living room with my luggage and was about to leave when my eyes were drawn to Gopal on the mantel. I felt a strong urge to take him with me. I asked Bonie if I could and she said, "Of course!" I grabbed him quickly and brought him home with me.

Aunt Dolly's Gopal

I was quite astonished by my desire to care for Gopal. Why this need for a statue at my age? When we are initiated, the guru usually asks which god

296

or goddess we like, and when I was initiated, I had said I liked Krishna. I was twelve and naturally a child will be attracted to the Gopal image of Krishna, which is that of a little baby crawling on his knees, holding a sweet in one hand. Maharaj had told me to focus on the image of Krishna while meditating, but no matter how hard I had tried to focus on Krishna, I always found myself focusing on Maharaj. He was someone I had seen with my own eyes. The concept of God was distant.

However, in 2015 Aunt Dolly's Gopal had decided to come home with me. In my hurry to leave, I did not bring his clothes. He just had one dress. I told my friends in Kolkata to send clothes. Many dresses arrived but the best were the ones handmade by Basantidi, a lover of Gopal. She also sent many warm clothes when she heard how cold it was in Michigan. I learned to knit and crochet so I could make him some clothes.

Each morning, I woke up Gopal, bathed and dressed him, and offered him some candy and water. These were the rituals I had seen Aunt Dolly perform and I did not wish to add to them. After a couple of months, however, it seemed to me that Gopal was all alone in the shrine room (which was my bedroom) while I spent my day and evening in the living room. So I made a small cushion which I placed on top of my bookshelf in the living room and placed Gopal on it each day after the morning rituals. When it was time to go to bed, I took Gopal back to the shrine room and put him to bed.

After Gopal had arrived at our home in Michigan, my friend, Manju Saha, invited us to visit her and have dinner at her house. When we go to Manju's, it is a whole day affair and I suddenly found myself wondering how I could leave Gopal all alone at home. I asked Manju if I could bring him along and she enthusiastically told me that she would be delighted to have him visit her home. Since then, whenever we go to Manju's, Gopal goes with us. Manju has a little table and chair for him and spoils him with lots of goodies.

With the spread of Covid in 2020, we all became home bound and I spent more time with Gopal. I began to play Maharaj's kirtans while performing in the shrine room the simple rituals taught by my elders. Typically, devotees of Gopal cook lavish dishes for him and sing beautiful devotional songs to him. I am not a very good cook and cannot sing. But I do what I can to please Gopal, and I have found that he is easily satisfied. It took several decades, but eventually Maharaj found a way to make me bond with my chosen deity.

Chapter 61: Spiritual Friends

The spiritual path is challenging and littered with obstacles. I always see it as a game of Chutes and Ladders. One second you climb up the ladder and feel you are one step away from enlightenment, and the next second you slide down the chute and go back to square one. However, there is never any loss on this path. Every effort accrues over lifetimes and will be helpful at some time or the other. Even when I feel I have slipped up or stagnated, I have faith that my guru, Maharaj, is keeping my practice safe. He is always holding my hand and leading me on. Sages say that to succeed on this path, one needs three things: God's grace, the guru's blessings, and one's own desire for liberation. God's grace is showered on us and comes to us through many channels. Even when we are faced with difficulties and sorrows, we learn from them and grow. But one channel through which I have always experienced God's blessings is the *kalyanamitta*—the spiritual friend who helps me proceed towards my goal of liberation.

One hears of students in ancient India going and living with their teacher or guru who was there to guide them at every step of their journey on the spiritual path. Most of us do not have that today, but if we look around we will find that God and Guru send us the same help through other means. This is where our spiritual friends play a significant role, and I have been blessed to have many such friends in my life.

During the first thirty-one years of my life, I lived in India where Maharaj, my family, disciples and devotees of our guru who visited our home, Aunt Dolly's friends in Midnapore (who were followers of the Ramakrishna Mission), and my friend Basanti Chatterjee (in Midnapore) made sure that my practice was protected and nourished. Moreover, India is known for its spirituality and one can find spiritual encouragement in every nook and cranny of this country.

However, when I left for the U.S. in 1990, there was a good chance of my practice dwindling or stagnating or even disappearing. Instead, the very opposite happened. Leaving home had been so hard for me that I felt displaced and rootless. Work is what keeps people going in America, and graduate school provided me with a lot of work. There was not much time for practice even though I never missed meditating twice a day, as I had always done. And then I met Ralph Pyle whose first words to me were "Life is *dukkha*." Ralph was in the Sociology department and his special field of interest was religion. Having lived a happy life, I did not quite understand why Ralph thought that life was *dukkha* (suffering). It took many of life's challenges and the death of several loved ones for me to realize the significance of Ralph's words. Much later, I realized that Ralph had been talking about the Buddha's First Noble Truth. After we met in 1990, our friendship grew. In 1996, once we had both graduated with our doctoral degrees from Purdue University, we were married. The Hindu sages like to initiate both wife and husband together so that they help each other in their spiritual practice. Both Ralph and I were initiated by Maharaj in 1998, and Ralph has helped me significantly in continuing and deepening my spiritual practice. He has been a true *kalyanamitta*.

When we moved to Michigan in 1997, I met many people who helped me continue to stay on this path. In 1999, we met Ajahn Khemasanto and he played a very important role in kindling an interest in Buddhism in us. As his sangha grew, we became friends with American, Thai, Taiwanese, and Chinese Buddhists. Together we listened to Dharma talks, studied Buddhism, and meditated. Some of these friends are still a part of my life even though twenty-three years have gone by.

Within two months of having met Ajahn Khemasanto, Ralph and I met Sister Medhanandi on the beaches of Florida. She introduced us to Ajahn Sumedho by giving us a tape and a book with his talks. Ralph and I immediately took to his teachings, and he became the most important influence in our practice of Buddhism. Then while we were attending Ajahn Khemasanto's sangha, we became good friends with Bill Rittenberg who had been practicing Buddhism for many years. It was through him that we met Richard Smith who was a follower of Ajahn Sumedho. Ever since I first listened to Ajahn Sumedho's talks, I had wanted to meet him, and in 2010, my wish was fulfilled when he visited Richard in Michigan. This was truly a dream come true and I can never thank Richard enough for all the Dhamma he has brought to Michigan. I have a large collection of Dhamma books given to me by Richard which I cherish. During the Covid years, he has kept in touch by sending us information of online Dhamma events which we can all attend.

In 2000, while attending a ceremony at Ajahn Khemasanto's temple, I met Maureen Bodenbach and gradually got to know her well. She had been a novice and spent two years at Ajahn Sumedho's monastery in England. Maureen and I met often to discuss the Dhamma. Through her, I met Sister Dipankara and Sister Susila. They were her teachers and visited Michigan where they held retreats organized by Maureen and members of LBA. Our friendship, centered on our love of the Dhamma, has lasted more than two decades now.

In 2002, I met Anna Fisher and we became good friends. Anna had been practicing Buddhism for a decade before we met and together we went to sanghas, attended Dharma events, meditated, and discussed Buddhism. I do not drive and Anna took me everywhere. We called her Honda Civic Hybrid our Dharma Vehicle because it took us to so many places where we participated in Dharma events. Among many wonderful events we attended was a two-day retreat with His Holiness, the Dalai Lama, which took place at the Crisler Arena in Ann Arbor, Michigan. Anna was also responsible for introducing me to Lorne Dekun and the Ananda Michigan group. Her interest in kirtan made her attend Lorne's kirtans and she always gave me a ride. After Lorne passed away, Anna took me to listen to the Ann Arbor Kirtan group on several occasions. Due to Anna, I was able to visit Amma more than once when she came to Detroit. In 2004, Anna not only helped the members of the Quan Am Temple establish their temple but also requested Thay to start the Thursday Evening Meditation Group for Americans, who did not understand Vietnamese. She took me to the group each Thursday so we could meditate with Thay and listen to his talks. Later, in 2010, after Thay left, Anna led the group. I continued to support her until Covid stopped us from continuing the group.

From 2003, when I first went to see Lorne Dekun, until the present I have been involved in the activities of the Ananda Michigan sangha. I am grateful to Lorne Dekun for bringing Yoganandaji into my life. This great sage, through his writings and songs, has been a significant source of spiritual nourishment and enrichment in my life. I always feel very close to him and find him extremely accessible. After Lorne and his wife, Judy, moved away in 2009, and Lorne passed away in 2013, the sangha continued due to the efforts of Mary Thomas and Drs. Will and Wendy Page-Echols. Attending kirtans, Sunday service, meditation, and book study kept me busy and kept my mind on the spiritual teachings of Yoganandaji. Two friends I met at Ananda turned out to be *kalyanamittas*, too: Kathy Burgess and Lynda Group. Both gave me many rides to Ananda Michigan and I am grateful for that. But what was most precious was that Kathy began to offer kirtans close to my home, and Lynda shared my love of reading, which led to many Dharma discussions.

Manju Saha, whom I met in 1998, became a source of inspiration for me in my spiritual world. It was through her that I met her guru, Swami Purnatmananda, and I am grateful to him for bringing so much joy to my mother in her last years. Manju was very supportive when I was translating the book which contained Balanandaji's talks. I would translate each chapter and email it to Manju. She read what I sent with great enthusiasm and encouraged me to keep translating. Moreover, the two of us spent many happy hours listening to online Dharma talks by monks of the Ramakrishna Order; discussing what we heard and sharing new talks became a habit with us.

The same can be said of Monica Bhargava who introduced me to Sister Shivani. I met Monica in 2009 and we have remained friends because our conversations focus mainly on the Dharma as we share what we read and listen to. She tells me stories she has heard while listening to Dharma talks, and I tell her stories that are similar to hers which I found while translating Balanandaji's talks. Sometimes she asks me a question that I have to mull over before I can suggest what could be an answer. For years I have told her to meditate and she just couldn't. But during the Covid years, she has become a serious meditator and has managed to astonish me by her sincere efforts at making spiritual progress.

I have had friends who were not interested in being a member of a sangha or in meditation but had a strong belief in God. Such a friend is Zeynep Altinsel who has shown me through her invincible faith in God that one can be spiritual without being part of institutionalized religion. Always respectful of my beliefs, she is openminded enough to buy a Christmas gift for Gopal even though she did not grow up in a culture of ritualistic worship.

During the Covid years, I stayed at home and the Dharma came to me via Zoom: Ajahn Viradhammo's talks, book study with Wendy Page-Echols, and a Buddhist study group with the members of the Lansing Buddhist Association kept me busy. I had not been in touch with any of my guru's disciples ever since my relatives had passed, but during the Covid years a few of them contacted me. They write to me from time to time, and it is very nice to share memories of Maharaj with people who knew him well. Papri Mitra, whom I knew when we were both teenagers, found me on Facebook and we spoke of the times we had spent in the Deoghar ashram with Maharaj. Joytee Dutt, who had been a member of the group that visited Munnar, helped bring back memories of the trip by sharing photos and stories. Ratna Sinha, who had visited Maharaj in our Burnpur home in the 1970s, renewed our acquaintance after listening to the kirtans I had posted on YouTube. She has been a major motivating force in encouraging me to publish this book.

Finally, I do not have the words to express my gratitude to my greatest well-wisher, Maharaj, my guru, for taking me under his wing. He has been my constant companion from the time he initiated me at the age of twelve. I talk to him all the time and share my joys and sorrows with this sage whose unconditional love for all his disciples is palpable. I feel he has always looked out for me. I am grateful to him for the wonderful family he gave me because they were deeply spiritual and were responsible for bringing him into my life. I am grateful that he found the perfect husband for me who would help me with my spiritual practice. I am grateful that after Maharaj left the body, he continued to teach me through all these different channels. It did not matter to me whether a sangha followed the Buddha's teachings or Yoganandaji's teachings because wherever I went I felt my guru's presence. In everyone, I found his compassionate blessings; in every teaching, I heard what I had already heard in his kirtans. In the past, when I was a girl in India, whenever I visited Maharaj, I felt at home. This is how I have felt in the last two decades. Wherever I have gone, whether it be a Buddhist temple or a Yogananda sangha or a Sufi gathering or a visit to see Amma, I have always felt at home. Maharaj has been, and will continue to be, my God, my Guru, and my *Kalyanamitta.*

My family: Mother with me in her lap (extreme left), Grandmother with little Bonie in her lap, Aunt Dolly (next to Grandmother), Father (extreme right), and Uncle Sankar with glasses. We all have black dots on our foreheads, which means we have come home after a visit to Maharaj. Calcutta, 1966

Standing (left to right): Anna Fisher, Zeynep Altinsel, Maureen Bodenbach
Seated: Ralph Pyle. Michigan, 2015

Manju Saha

Lynda Group and I (Photo courtesy of Mary Thomas)

Will and Wendy Page-Echols (Photo courtesy of Wendy Page-Echols)

Kathy Burgess (Photo courtesy of Kathy Burgess)

Anna Fisher and I (Photo courtesy of Wendy Page-Echols)

Maharaj. Calcutta 1997

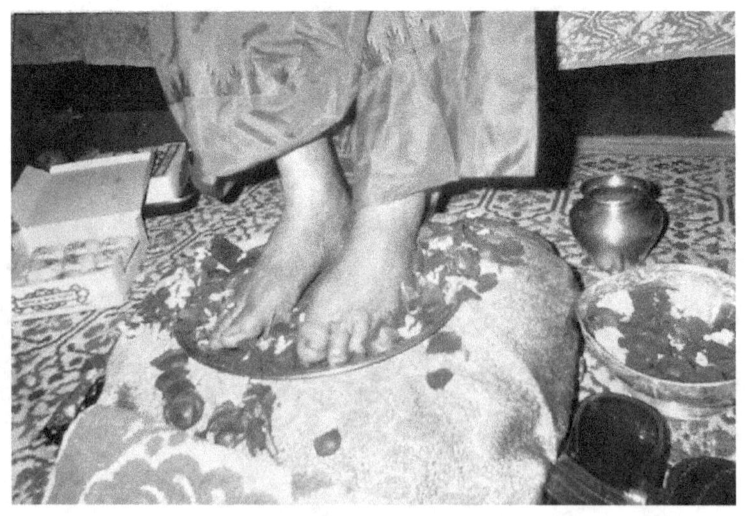

Maharaj's Lotus Feet

www.ingramcontent.com/pod-product-compliance
Lightning Source LLC
Chambersburg PA
CBHW071358150726
48000CB00001B/72